S0-DZE-981

THE ELITE

The Special Forces of the World

Editor-in-Chief Dr John Pimlott

Editorial Board
Brigadier-General James L. Collins Jr (Retd)
Ian V. Hogg
Brigadier-General Edwin H. Simmons (USMC)

Managing Editor Ashley Brown

MARSHALL CAVENDISH
New York   London   Toronto

CONTENTS

THE ELITE

The Special Forces
of the World

VOLUME
7

Reference Edition Published 1987

Published by Marshall Cavendish Corporation
147 West Merrick Road
Freeport, Long Island
N.Y. 11520

Printed and bound in Italy by L.E.G.O. S.p.a. Vicenza.

Library of Congress Cataloging in Publication Data
The Elite:
Special forces of the world
    Includes index
    1. Military history, Modern-20th Century
1. Marshall Cavendish Corporation
U42. E45   1987 356'.167 87-88
ISBN 0-86307-788-9 (set)
     0-86307-795-1 vol. 7

EDITORIAL STAFF

Editor-in-Chief	Dr John Pimlott
Managing Editor	Ashley Brown
Editor	Jonathan Reed
Deputy Editor	Adrian Gilbert
Sub Editors	Alastair Gourlay
	Francis Ritter
	Barry Smith
	Paul Szuszkiewicz
	Ian Westwell
	David Williams
Picture Editors	Stasz Gnych
	David Moncur
	Andrea Stern
Art Editor	Richard Burgess
Designers	Paul Ashby
	Henry Nolan

REFERENCE EDITION STAFF

Editor	Mark Dartford
Designer	Graham Beehag
Consultant	Robert Paulley
Indexer	Pat Coward
Creation	DPM Services Ltd.

INDEX

Entries in bold refer to main articles.
Entries in italics refer to illustrations.

A comprehensive set index appears in Volume 8.

In 1979 a column of Rhodesian SAS men infiltrated into Zambia to strike at the nerve centre of ZIPRA – Joshua Nkomo's personal command post in the heart of Lusaka

SAS
STORMING THE BASTILLE

THEY CALLED Operation Bastille Rhodesia's own Entebbe; so dramatic and unbelievable was the mission, that when the SAS commander, Major Dave Dodson, briefed his men, one trooper stood up, uttered a soldier's well-known expletive, and asked the officer if he was totally mad. As the bold plan unfolded, the SAS realised that their commander was not joking and that they were indeed going into the heart of the Zambian capital, Lusaka, to the home of Joshua Nkomo, leader of the Zambia-based Rhodesian nationalist group ZIPRA (Zimbabwe People's Revolutionary Army). If all went well, they would assassinate Nkomo and reduce his personal command post to rubble.

The situation in Rhodesia by the Easter of 1979 was critical. The war had escalated considerably since the signing of a political agreement by Ian Smith (the Rhodesian prime minister) and three internal black leaders, and although black majority rule was about to become a reality, both Joshua Nkomo's ZIPRA and Robert Mugabe's rival ZANLA (Zimbabwe African National Liberation Army) had refused to take part in the elections and had threatened to disrupt them by force.

Then, fresh intelligence warned of a far more serious threat. Joshua Nkomo, who had always held the majority of his men back in Zambia, had put his army on a conventional footing and was now poised to mount an invasion. Eight of ZIPRA's regular battalions were said to have regrouped northeast of Lusaka and another was reported to be near the Rhodesian border. To counter this apparent threat, the government forces were immediately deployed along the border to monitor crossing points and defend the countryside. Within Rhodesia itself, some 60,000 men were called up to protect voters as they went to the polling booths. Despite these precautions, the Rhodesians considered it imperative

Below: The Rhodesian SAS at war. Below left: Heavily laden with weapons and kit, a group of SAS men pose for the camera after the completion of an operation in the bush.

RHODESIA'S ELITE

In the early 1950s Major Mike Calvert arrived in Rhodesia to recruit men for his Malayan Scouts; some 100 Rhodesians, 90 civilians and 10 regulars, were selected for the Far East Volunteer Unit. The volunteers were to be known as C Squadron Malayan Scouts (SAS) and would wear Rhodesian shoulder flashes.

Two men, Peter Walls and his second-in-command, Lieutenant Ron Campbell-Morrison, were ordered to knock the squadron into shape, and once in Malaya a British-trained major would take command of the men. In the event, no-one could be found to take charge of the squadron so Peter Walls himself led the force in Malaya.

The Rhodesian commitment in Malaya lasted two years and the squadron returned home, with most men returning to civilian life. However, several men including Walls stayed in the army, using their recent experience to train units in counter-insurgency methods.

The early 1960s saw the Rhodesian armed forces undergoing expansion and a small team of men from the original squadron was ordered to select and train recruits after taking part in a refresher course with the British SAS. Returning home, it was decided to form six Sabre (combat) Troops with a total strength of 184 men. After Rhodesia's unilateral declaration of independence from Britain in late 1965, the Rhodesian SAS began to carry out operations against black nationalist groups. For most of the war, the SAS carried out hit-and-run raids into neighbouring Mozambique, Zambia and Botswana. Never more than 200 strong, units attacked the enemy with an audacity that produced results out of all proportion to their size. In 1978, the unit was retitled 1 Special Air Service Regiment (Rhodesia). However, majority black rule and the political success of Robert Mugabe, led to the disbandment of the regiment in late 1980; many members moved to South Africa, some taking up arms in the South African Defence Force.

that the threat of invasion be removed by decisive, pre-emptive action: the very heart of the ZIPRA organisation would have to be attacked.

Yet the odds against carrying out a successful attack in the centre of the Zambian capital were formidable. Nkomo lived in a well-to-do suburb just two kilometres from the Zambian Army barracks; there were armed guards at the Zambian president's official residence, a stone's throw from Nkomo's sprawling bungalow, and guards at the target itself. The SAS team might also have to deal with the Zambian police and air force. The unknown factor facing the SAS was the Zambian reaction to an attack in the capital. This imponderable meant that the strike force would have to be flexible, have a lot of firepower and be completely mobile.

There was only one solution to the question of mobility: they would have to drive to Lusaka in their own transport, and do so at night. It was decided to use Sabre Land Rovers, the SAS's redundant pre-bush war specialist vehicles. By giving them a dark-green colour scheme with yellow paint splodges, it was hoped that they would resemble Zambian security force vehicles. A commercial ferry, the *Sea Lion*, would take the Sabres across Lake Kariba to the Zambian shore and from there the strike force would follow a rough track and a dirt road until they reached the main Lusaka road for the drive into the Zambian capital. The biggest hurdle facing the SAS would come long before they reached Lusaka, however. They would have to cross a river bridge at Kafue that was reportedly guarded by a strong detachment of the Zambian Army, supported by several heavy weapons. If the SAS men had to fight their way across this bridge the extent of their casualties would decide whether they aborted the

mission or not. After the initial briefing, the assault teams were put through exhaustive rehearsals for the operation, with everything being worked out down to the finest detail. The Sabres were made serviceable for the 200km trek to Lusaka, and then driven to the ferry. There were seven vehicles in the convoy which was to carry 42 men. As well as the hit on Nkomo, two other targets, a Liberation Centre housing several southern African nationalist groups, and an arms store, would also be attacked.

Eventually, the strike force was ready. All they needed now was the word. An externally-based undercover agent was to alert them when Joshua Nkomo was home and 'all go' was eventually flashed to the SAS waiting on the ferry on 12 April. There was still a bit of daylight left and the commander, Major Dave Dodson, decided to risk landing in Zambia as soon as possible. The ferry nosed into a deserted

landing spot and a protection party went ahead to secure the beach-head. It was just after 1800 hours; the attack was scheduled for 0200 hours on the 13th. The strike force drove off and set course for Lusaka. Their vehicle lights were on and the bright moon helped the drivers to negotiate the dirt track. Most of the men were apprehensive, but acknowledged that they were so well-armed that they would be able to deal with almost every problem – except, perhaps, the Zambian detachment at the Kafue bridge.

For the first 10km they made good time, but then the track deteriorated and, at times, faded away completely. It was necessary to use a lot of four-wheel drive and fuel, but the commander had anticipated most of the problems and each vehicle carried three times the fuel it needed. By this stage the men's initial excitement had faded and there was very little talk. Everyone settled down to a long, hard slog on the poor track. The drivers bounced their vehicles through the mud and, where the track was washed away, they felt more like sailors than soldiers, as the passengers put their weight on one side, then the other, to stop the listing vehicles sinking into the morass. Then, one vehicle broke down completely, and Major Dave Dodson had no option but to order the six passengers to stay behind. It meant that their task, an attack on the arms store, would have to be abandoned. Leaving six very unhappy men behind, the remaining vehicles moved off into the gloom of the night. They were now running very late, but the commander decided he was ready to continue and risk being caught in Lusaka at first light.

As they approached Kafue bridge, the machine guns were placed on their mountings and the men took the safety catches off their rifles.

Then came the biggest surprise of the entire operation. There was nothing and no-one to hinder their progress: no Zambian troops, no heavy weapons, and no barriers. The SAS sped across the bridge hardly daring to believe their good luck. They headed for Lusaka. There was far more traffic than they had been expecting and the men deliberately kept their faces averted to avoid their features being recognised in the glare of the on-coming lights. When a vehicle pulled up behind them, Captain Martin Pearse stood up and waved the driver on. The man obeyed and pulled out, hit the accelerator and disappeared without suspecting a thing. Soon, an orange glow ahead warned that they were approaching Lusaka. Traffic rolled on its way and, off in the distance, the SAS could make out the blink of traffic lights. As the 36 Rhodesians drove into Lusaka under the full glare of the city lights, their watches showed 0240 hours. Lieutenant Rich Stannard, who was to lead the attack on the Liberation Centre, was at the back of the convoy and turned off with two vehicles to his target, leaving the others to continue to Nkomo's home.

Driving through Lusaka was an eerie experience, as Major Dave Dodson remembers:

Top: Joshua Nkomo, leader of the Zambian-based ZIPRA and target of Operation Bastille. Centre: Nkomo's residence and command post in Lusaka after the SAS raid. Bunker bombs and machine-gun fire reduced the building to ruins but a tip-off from a well-placed ZIPRA spy warned the African leader of the impending attack and his life was saved. Far left: For the clandestine raid into Zambia, the SAS painted their Sabre Land Rovers to resemble Zambian security force vehicles. Centre left: SAS troopers check their kit aboard the ferry Sea Lion during the trip across Lake Kariba. Left: The Rhodesian SAS column moves northwards through the bush.

'There we were, fairly well gunned-up – two machine guns and an RPG-7 per vehicle – each gun having 1500 rounds in it; troops in the back, helmets on and blackened-up. The traffic lights were working and, to keep the convoy together and delay any suspicions of the locals drifting around, we stopped at the lights. A bloke pulled up next to us; we half waved at him and he half waved at us.'

The lights changed to green, the drivers slowly let out their clutches, and the blackened-up Rhodesians were on their way again. Soon, the SAS were closing in on Joshua Nkomo's home which was screened from view by a wire security fence covered with hessian. The convoy stopped briefly, while Dave Dodson gave his last command. Then the vehicles

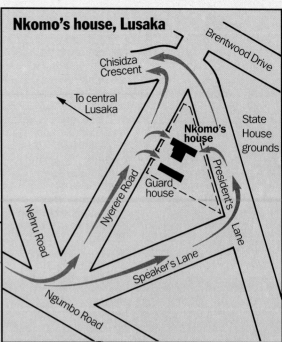

Below right: Lieutenant Rich Stannard, leader of an attack on one of the secondary targets in Lusaka – the Liberation Centre. After knocking out the operations room Stannard's men rigged the centre with explosives and the building was totally destroyed. Bottom: The SAS column makes a brief stop during the journey through the bush.

Nkomo's house, Lusaka

Brentwood Drive

Chisidza Crescent

To central Lusaka

Nehru Road

Nyerere Road

Nkomo's house

Guard house

State House grounds

President's Lane

Speaker's Lane

Ngumbo Road

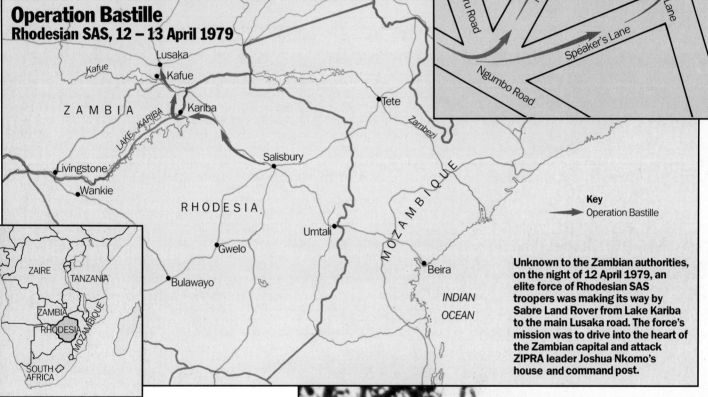

Operation Bastille
Rhodesian SAS, 12 – 13 April 1979

Kafue

Lusaka

Kafue

LAKE KARIBA

Kariba

Tete

Zambezi

Z A M B I A

Livingstone

Wankie

Salisbury

R H O D E S I A

Umtali

M O Z A M B I Q U E

Gwelo

Bulawayo

Beira

INDIAN OCEAN

Key
→ Operation Bastille

ZAIRE

TANZANIA

ZAMBIA

MOZAMBIQUE

RHODESIA

SOUTH AFRICA

Unknown to the Zambian authorities, on the night of 12 April 1979, an elite force of Rhodesian SAS troopers was making its way by Sabre Land Rover from Lake Kariba to the main Lusaka road. The force's mission was to drive into the heart of the Zambian capital and attack ZIPRA leader Joshua Nkomo's house and command post.

roared off at speed, two in one direction and the third in another. It was 0255 hours. The plan was for Martin Pearse to breach the security wall, then lead a team into the house to assassinate Nkomo. Dave Dodson and a sergeant-major were to breach the two main gates, then bunker bomb and rocket their side of the bungalow, leaving Pearse to get on with the house-fighting. Six men would be in a reserve vehicle on Dodson's side to watch for outside interference.

Martin Pearse's vehicle came screeching up, but, even before it stopped, a guard behind the security fence began firing. Pearse's rear gunner opened up in response, letting rip at a cluster of security huts and emptying his first belt in record time. Pearse leapt from his Sabre and raced to the fence to attach an explosive charge to blast an entrance. However, there was a problem with the attachment, and so he whipped out his wire-cutters to force an entrance big enough to take a man with webbing. The twinkle of lights could be seen from Nkomo's house, and once the enemy fire was neutralised near his entrance, Pearse led two other men into the garden.

On the opposite side of the target, the two front gates had been breached and the SAS were machine-gunning the house, the vehicles and anyone they saw moving. There was some return fire, but the SAS quickly suppressed all opposition from the 30 or so guards. Fifteen bodies lay sprawled around the grounds and the remainder of the guards wisely kept a low profile. Then, everyone on the commander's side of the house began rocketing and bunker bombing the bungalow. Dave Dodson lobbed a bunker bomb into the main building and the lounge burst into flames. Masonry and timber were sent crashing to the floor, and the lights were blown out. Fire quickly took hold, and smoke, dust and flames rose over the residence. The noise from the exploding bunker bombs, machine guns, rockets and smallarms was fantastic. It was a spectacular sight; the machine guns had one tracer in three rounds, so the SAS could see the red sheets of tracers hitting the target.

At the nearby Zambian president's palace, the presidential guard began firing, their red and green

tracer criss-crossing and ricocheting across the night sky. But it was merely a token show; nothing and no-one came near the raiders. Elsewhere in the capital, Zambians ran into the streets in their night-clothes, alarmed at all the commotion.

Martin Pearse was by now racing to Nkomo's bedroom, but his original plan to throw in a bunker bomb was frustrated as the window was barred. He doubled around to the back door, blew the lock off and hurried inside with his team. Faced with a two-sided passageway and four doors, they set about clearing the choking smoke and dust-filled house with chilling precision. They had 15 minutes to do the job. Aided by a torch strapped to the underside of his AK rifle, Pearse fired into every likely hiding place in Nkomo's bedroom. But there was no sign of their man. The bathroom and storeroom were cleared but, again, there was no sign of life.

Pearse and the corporal then returned to the room and killed the two enemy soldiers

As the SAS burst into the last remaining room, a guard opened up on them from under a bed and another man shot at them from inside a cupboard. Pearse and his corporal grenaded the room, and the third team member fired a very long burst from his cut-down RPD machine gun. Pearse and the corporal then returned to the room and killed the two enemy soldiers. Pearse called the overall commander on his radio to report that he had finished. The Bastille had fallen, but the SAS reluctantly came to the conclusion that Nkomo had not even been in the house. Although the Zambian-based undercover agent had seen him go into the house, he had not seen Nkomo leave.

Martin Pearse had done an excellent job, and had Nkomo been there that night, there is no doubt what the outcome would have been. Later, Joshua Nkomo's claim that he had escaped by climbing through a toilet window was met with hilarity by the Rhodesians. The truth, however, was not so funny. Nkomo survived, not through bad luck on the SAS's part, but because he had been tipped off by a well-placed spy. It was the closest the Rhodesians were to come to assassinating Nkomo, for the operation was the last attempt on his life. The entire operation had been pulled off in 25 minutes and all the detailed planning had made it unnecessary to give orders during the raid as everyone knew what to do at each stage.

The first Zambian reactions to the attack had been picked up by the SAS radioman as the assault team hurried from the ruins to their waiting vehicles, meeting up around the corner to reorganise. In quick time, they were on their way again, passing several military vehicles heading towards Nkomo's suburb. However, the Sabres were on the other side of the carriageway, and the Zambians showed no interest in the convoy as it observed the speed limit and made its way out of town to rendezvous with Lieutenant Rich Stannard and his team who were attacking the Liberation Centre. By now, the city lights were doused and air-raid sirens whined across the capital as the Zambians thought that the Rhodesians were about to carry out an air strike.

Rich Stannard and his demolition teams had already hit the enemy operations room, and were rigging up their charges and lighting their safety fuzes. The ops room was still blazing furiously as they roared off at high speed, well away from the forthcoming fireworks. At the rendezvous point, the men

RAID ON BEIRA

Operating mainly in the border areas during Rhodesia's long bush war, the Special Air Service (SAS) was called upon for clandestine missions. As the conflict escalated, the SAS was used in Zambia, Botswana and Mozambique, from where nationalist guerrilla groups were operating.

Their single largest economic target was Beira, a well-defended city on the coast of Mozambique. The destruction of Beira's giant oil-storage depot would deal a crippling blow to the country's already faltering economy.

Aerial reconnaissance by Captain Bob McKenna, the strike-force commander, showed a well-illuminated target, and the attack was planned for 23 March 1979. After silently making their way through the back streets of the city, McKenna divided his force into three groups. Captain Colin Willis, after laying a suitcase bomb on a large oil pipeline, took charge of the first group and set up a position on the far side of the depot. The second group,

under Lieutenant Peter Cole, peeled off to lay explosives against an electricity pylon, before rejoining McKenna's main attack force next to the fuel tanks.

At 0015 hours, having waited anxiously for Willis to get into position, McKenna initiated the attack using an RPG-7 rocket launcher. Moments later, Willis's raiding party followed suit. Under a relentless cross-fire of rockets and armour-piercing bullets, the fuel tanks erupted, pouring smoke and flames into the night sky. The depot's anti-aircraft gunners and guards, convinced that they were under air attack, fired into the night sky. Their mistake allowed the raiders to make good their escape.

Confident that the attack had succeeded, Captain McKenna gave the order to pull out. Suffering only two casualties, the raiders disappeared silently into the night, the suitcase bomb exploding behind them. Within a few hours, the charges on the electricity pylon would detonate, cutting off the city's power supply. Mission accomplished.

who had attacked Joshua Nkomo's home heard the sudden rumble of heavy vehicles. Was the Zambian Army reacting? Would Rich Stannard's escape route be blocked? But they saw no sign of the Zambians and within minutes Stannard and party had joined them. Seconds later, a massive orange mushroom billowed into the sky, followed by an enormous thunderclap as the Liberation Centre went up.

Frightened civilians came streaming out of their homes heading for the safety of the bush, their suitcases and chattels stacked high on their heads. It was also time for the SAS to take their leave. It was 0400 hours, and light enough for them to be seen. However, on the long journey south there was no-one to stop them. They crossed the Kafue bridge without incident, picked up the six men left behind with the broken-down vehicle, drove to the ferry and then set sail for home. It was 18 hours since the ferry had

Top left: The officers who led the three assault groups at Beira. From left to right are Captain Colin Willis, Lieutenant Pete Cole and the commander of the op, Captain Bob McKenna. Top right: Willis (left) goes over the details of the suitcase bomb that was used to blow the pipeline; with him are Cole and Les Clark. Above right: Captain Martin Pearse, the officer who led the house fighting on Operation Bastille.

delivered the SAS to the Zambian shore and now the prospect of a couple of hours well-earned sleep lay ahead.

One of the most dramatic operations of the war was over. Later the Rhodesian elections went ahead without too much disruption and Nkomo did not begin developing his invasion strategy until seven months later. But it was his old foes, the SAS, who finally put paid to his plans in a series of further slick pre-emptive strikes into Zambia that repeated the successes of the earlier raids.

THE AUTHOR Barbara Cole is married to a former Rhodesian SAS officer and has written a book entitled *The Elite: the Story of the Rhodesian SAS*. It has been hailed as a classic in counter-insurgency writing and Cole is currently working on a pictorial edition.

NYE'S
ANNIHILATORS

322ND BOMBARDMENT GROUP

The 322nd (Medium) Bombardment Group was activated at McDill Field, Florida, on 19 June 1942 and comprised the 449th, 450th, 451st and 452nd Squadrons. Training began immediately on the B-26 Marauder. The group was then ordered to Britain, but a shortage of aircraft delayed the arrival of the first air squadron at Bury St Edmunds until March 1943.

The 3rd Bomb Wing, to which the 322nd had been assigned, had adopted a strategy of 'zero' altitude bombing, in order to avoid German flak and maximise the number of missions possible under low cloud cover. Targets within a radius of 400 miles were to be attacked by forces of no more than 12 aircraft, flying below radar range to achieve surprise.

The 322nd's first mission, on 14 May 1943, also marked the first bombing sortie of a UK-based Marauder. Three days later, the group lost an entire strike force on a low-level attack, forcing a fundamental change in USAAF thinking. Then on 31 July the 322nd flew its first medium altitude operation, attacking Triqueville airfield. An Fw190 was shot down by a waist gunner, and the raid signalled a change of fortune for the group.

In October, by which time the 322nd had completed 34 missions, the proposed invasion of Europe necessitated the formation of a new tactical air force to support ground operations, and on 16 October 1943 the group was assigned to the Ninth Air Force (whose shoulder sleeve insignia is shown above).

Following the cessation of hostilities, the group returned to the USA and was deactivated. In 1954 it re-emerged flying F-86s and F-100s, but it survived only a few years.

The 322nd Bombardment Group's early operations were dogged by disaster but the group soon became the scourge of German airfields

THE DUTY FLYING control officer in the Bury St Edmunds watch-tower glanced at the wall clock as the minute hand moved to 1330 hours. It was two and a half hours since the bombers had set out from the airfield and his worst fears were now realised; all 10 aircraft were missing in action. Their estimated time of arrival (ETA) at Bury was 1250, and when they failed to appear the hope had been that the force had landed at another English airfield on the east coast to refuel. But no USAAF or RAF base had any such news, increasing the apprehension felt by the senior officers waiting in the Bury tower. The next hint of disaster was an RAF intercept of Luftwaffe radio messages which mentioned the shooting down of enemy aircraft. Now, 40 minutes past the ETA, there was no hope of the aircraft still being airborne as fuel would be exhausted.

The officers left the tower. Little was said, but each one knew that the Eighth Air Force's attempts at conducting low-level bombing operations with medium bombers had proved disastrous. Moreover, this débâcle threw serious doubt on the combat future of the aircraft involved, the Martin B-26 Marauder. Indeed, 17 May 1943 was the blackest episode in the extraordinary story of the Marauder. It was also the darkest day in the history of the 322nd Bombardment Group, the unit involved in this, the only total loss of a strike force, albeit small, suffered by American air forces in Europe during World War II.

When the prototype Martin B-26 Marauder first flew in November 1940 it was hailed as the most advanced medium bomber in the world. So far, however, its record had left a great deal to be desired. Since its introduction into service in the summer of 1941 there had been a spate of accidents. Pilots had experienced great difficulty adjusting to

Page 967: Never an aircraft to suffer from a lack of armament, the B-26 Marauder eventually carried almost as many guns as the heavy American bombers. Later variants of the B-26 had a pair of 0.5in Colt-Browning machine guns mounted in individual blisters on each side of the forward fuselage. Left: Colonel Stillman briefs crews of the 322nd before their first low-level operation. Below left: B-26 'Mister Period Twice', so named because it missed the group's first two raids due to mechanical problems. Below: One B-26 was severely damaged by flak on the first raid and crash-landed at Bury St Edmunds, killing the pilot. Bottom: A formation of Marauders warms up on the runway.

the aircraft, especially to the unfamiliar necessity of landing at high speed, and mechanics could not quickly grasp the complex electrical and hydraulic systems. As the rate of accidents rose, the plane had become notorious as the 'Widowmaker' and the 'Martin Murderer'.

Although the Marauder had performed badly in service in the Pacific and then in North Africa, high hopes were held for operations from England, where airfield facilities were good and many enemy targets in occupied Europe were within range. The first Marauder group sent to Europe flew its aircraft across the North Atlantic via Greenland and Iceland during the autumn of 1942, and in December the ground echelon of the 322nd Bomb Group arrived, the first squadrons of the air echelon being delayed until the early spring of 1943 by a shortage of new aircraft. The 322nd immediately began training for low-level attack, hedge-hopping over the East Anglian countryside, for their operational plan was to come in low to escape the enemy's radar detection screen and, with the advantage of surprise, strike the targets and escape before defences could be brought into action.

The 322nd Bomb Group set out on its inaugural mission on 14 May 1943, when a dozen Marauders attempted to bomb an electrical power station at Ijmuiden in western Holland. The force was met with heavy ground fire and several aircraft were dam-

aged, one so badly that the pilot lost control when the aircraft was in the landing circuit at Bury St Edmunds, resulting in a fatal crash. The cost of this accident, and of the hot reception at the target, was accepted in the belief that the target had been badly damaged, but two days later Colonel Stillman, the Group CO, was summoned to 3rd Wing, the controlling headquarters. He was informed that reconnaissance photographs showed that the target was untouched and, in consequence, the group was to be sent back to try again. Stillman objected, opining that the enemy would be expecting a return, and without the advantage of surprise the B-26s would suffer heavily. His objections overruled, Stillman decided to lead the next raid himself. Only 11 B-26s were available

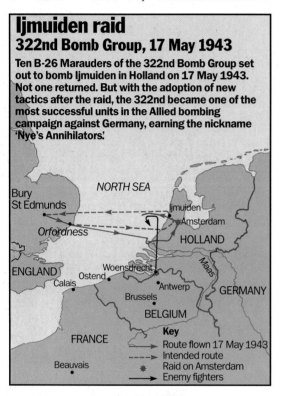

Ijmuiden raid
322nd Bomb Group, 17 May 1943

Ten B-26 Marauders of the 322nd Bomb Group set out to bomb Ijmuiden in Holland on 17 May 1943. Not one returned. But with the adoption of new tactics after the raid, the 322nd became one of the most successful units in the Allied bombing campaign against Germany, earning the nickname 'Nye's Annihilators.'

NORTH SEA

Bury St Edmunds

Orfordness

Ijmuiden

Amsterdam

HOLLAND

ENGLAND

Woensdrecht

Ostend

Maas

Calais

Antwerp

GERMANY

Brussels

BELGIUM

FRANCE

Key

Beauvais

— Route flown 17 May 1943
---- Intended route
* Raid on Amsterdam
→ Enemy fighters

for the mission and they took off at 1100 hours on the next morning, 17 May. One aircraft turned back over the North Sea when a generator failed; the others continued on course for the enemy coast, never to return.

Two days later, a British destroyer picked up two crewmen from a life raft, survivors from a Marauder which had been shot down by an enemy fighter. These men were able to provide some information on what had happened, but the full picture did not emerge until after the cessation of hostilities. It appears that after leaving Orfordness on the Suffolk coast, the 322nd formation had gradually veered south in a brisk cross wind, eventually making landfall on the Dutch coast some 30 miles from the briefed entry point. Moreover, landfall was made near the Maas estuary, one of the most heavily defended points in the Low Countries. The Marauders were met with a hail of ground fire and the lead aircraft, commanded by Stillman, was hit and crashed inverted on a sand dune. Stillman and two airmen were extracted from the wreck alive but badly injured. Another bomber also fell to the coastal barrage while the rest found themselves hopelessly lost. Two collided and went down, and another had to crash-land after being struck by wreckage. After unsuccessfully trying to locate their briefed target the remaining five aircraft had bombed a gasometer near Amsterdam and then turned west. Crossing the coast, misfortune again took a turn for they flew over another defensive stronghold and four were brought down by ground fire. The remaining aircraft escaped out to sea only to fall to the guns of a Messerschmitt Bf 109 that had been despatched to intercept.

Further B-26 operations were suspended while the USAAF reviewed the situation. Three more B-26 groups were in the process of moving to the United Kingdom, but the Eighth Air Force had come to regard the aircraft as a liability. As a result, pending a decision on their future use, all the B-26s in Britain were moved from Bomber Command to Air Support Command, which was non-operational, and all further movement of B-26 groups from the US was called to a halt.

A staff officer from 3rd Wing Headquarters, Lieutenant-Colonel Glenn Nye, was given command of the demoralised 322nd Group. Nye was one of a small band of US officers in England who had been

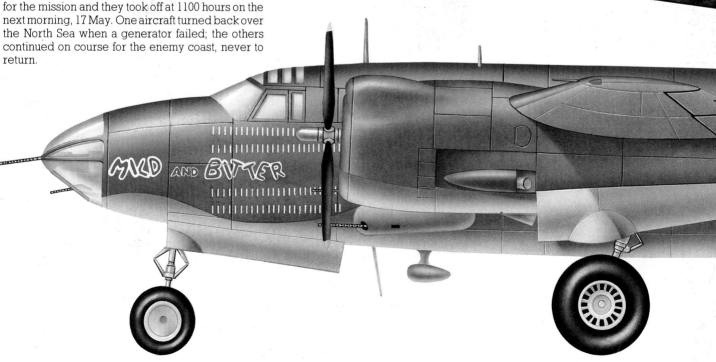

THE MARAUDER

The Martin B-26 Marauder was designed to provide the USAAF with a fast, heavily armed medium bomber, and so impressed was the Air Corps with its characteristics that 200 aircraft were ordered 'straight off the drawing board'.

The B-26 introduced many innovations in aircraft construction, including high strength clear plastic mouldings, large alloy castings and advanced electrical and hydraulics systems. It featured a streamlined, cigar-shaped fuselage, circular in cross-section, and its top speed of 315mph equalled that of many single-engined fighters of its day. The bomb bay was larger than that of the B-17 Flying Fortress and it could carry an equivalent weight of bombs, 4000lb, for half the distance of the heavy bomber. It was powered by twin 1850hp Pratt & Whitney R-2800-5 Double Wasp radial engines, and in addition to nose, ventral and tail-cone guns there were two 0.5in Browning machine guns housed in an electrically-operated Martin 250CE dorsal turret, the first powered turret to be installed in an American bomber.

However, one design feature of the B-26 was to help create the plane's early reputation as a killer. To gain maximum speed, the wing span and area had been cut to a minimum, and low-speed handling proved hazardous. The aircraft also required a long take-off run, and its fast landing speed of 100mph was well beyond most USAAF pilots' experience at the time. With the introduction of design improvements and better training, however, the Marauder went on to record the lowest losses in action of any US bomber type over Europe.

Above: Marauders arriving straight from the production line were named by their first commanders. 'Pappy's Pram', for instance, was Captain 'Pappy' Pursel's aircraft. 'Mild and Bitter', the first B-26 to complete 100 missions, went on tour in the US covered with the autographs of 322nd Bomb Group personnel. 'Flak Bait' completed 200 missions, the only US bomber to do so.

involved with the B-26 since its introduction into service and he had analysed the problems. Nye knew that the Marauder's bad name was primarily due to weaknesses in the original crew-training programme. In the hands of good pilots and competent mechanics, he believed it to be as reliable as any other combat aircraft in the USAAF inventory. He further believed that the operational failures of the B-26 were due to its method of employment. As CO of the 322nd, his first priority was to build confidence in the aircraft, but this was to prove a difficult task, particularly after the tail broke off a B-26 flying low in the vicinity of the airfield. The aircrews inevitably saw this event as yet further proof that the Marauder was not fit to fly, let alone fight. However, investigation of the wreckage revealed that securing bolts had failed, and to prove that the mishap was peculiar to that particular aircraft, Nye took up an identical B-26 and performed a series of manoeuvres to prove that the tail unit was robust. Through such incidents, the men of the 322nd gradually warmed to their new boss.

Going back to war again in the B-26 was another matter. A series of top-level meetings had brought a decision to operate the B-26s at medium altitude, as they had been forced to do while operating from North Africa. The bombers were to adopt the large, tight formations that the B-17 heavy bombers were using so successfully over Europe, and arrangements were made with the RAF to furnish strong Spitfire escorts. The first operation of this type was flown by a new bombardment group in late July 1943, and was conducted without loss. Following three more successful raids, the 322nd forsook its low-level training and joined the operations being flown at between 9000 and 14,000 feet, altitudes beyond the range of German light flak. From a new base at Great Saling in Essex the 322nd led three other groups in a sustained campaign of bombing enemy airfields during the following three months; sometimes two

missions were flown in one day. The bomb group became the scourge of German air bases within its range, at the same time sustaining very low losses.

Having found a role for the Marauder where it could contribute to the Allied aerial onslaught on Europe with telling effect, the USAAF ordered four B-26 groups still retained in the USA to Europe. A tactical air force, the Ninth, was formed in Britain during the autumn of 1943 with the object of supporting the cross-Channel invasion planned for the following spring, and to this the Marauder units were transferred to form the basis of IX Bomber Command. Under the new command, target priorities were initially unchanged, with enemy airfields at the top of the list. Late in 1943, however, the Marauders were given a new objective, the destruction of the V-1 flying-bomb sites that were being rapidly constructed in the Pas de Calais region. The 322nd Group opened the campaign on 5 November, and found that the flak defences in the target area were vicious. Many Marauders were to fall to the guns of the Pas de Calais during the next few months.

Like the heavy bombers of the Eighth Air Force, the Ninth's B-26s were frequently prevented from

Right: The 322nd's 'Lil' Pork Chop' banks away as trains of bombs pound the dispersal area of a Luftwaffe airfield at St Andre de l'Eure in France. Below right: Groundcrew use a trolley jack to arm a Marauder with 500lb M43 bombs. Background: A Marauder strike force led by 'Mild and Bitter' heads for Schipol in Holland on a diversionary raid.

Bombardier, Medium Bombardment Group, USAAF, 1944

First Lieutenant Benjamin McCartney is wearing light uniform of the US Army Air Force. Under the life vest, a light khaki shirt (with one silver bar on the collar to denote rank) is worn with khaki dress trousers, russet shoes, and the standard officer's peaked cap.

bombing their targets by cloud cover. Following the lead of the strategic air force, the Ninth turned to the British for help in the form of radar blind-bombing devices. Such special equipment was in short supply, but a few sets of 'Oboe II', an American-made version of a British system, were at last obtained. Major Robert Porter, a survivor of the 322nd's first Ijmuiden raid, was selected to head an experimental unit at Great Saling. The airborne Oboe set allowed the operator to receive signals from two transmitting stations in England and enabled him to pin-point his aircraft's exact position to within 200yds. Apart from its accuracy, Oboe had the advantage that its signals were almost impossible for the enemy to jam. Porter's little unit was formed into a provisional squadron at the 322nd's base in February 1944, providing Oboe pathfinders for all the other B-26 groups in IX Bomber Command.

On 26 March 1944, the 322nd Bomb Group, now known as 'Nye's Annihilators', was given its long-awaited opportunity to avenge the 10 Marauders destroyed on the disastrous second raid on Ijmuiden in 1943. An enormous force of 380 aircraft from several bomb groups was despatched, with veterans from the 322nd's inaugural mission of 14 May 1943 aboard the leading Marauders. This time their objective was Ijmuiden harbour and installations · used by E-boat strike forces in the North Sea. The formation of bombers flew into a maelstrom of flak over the port, but this time their loads of high explosive found their mark. All but one of the bombers returned to England, many of them bearing scars from the hail of steel fragments they had endured.

Following the Allied cross-Channel invasion in June 1944, the Marauders flew most of their missions against tactical targets whose destruction would aid the advancing ground forces. Particular success was obtained against bridges and other communications targets, and the Annihilators were usually in the forefront of these attacks. In September the Ninth Air Force began moving its bombers into Europe to extend their range, the 322nd moving to Beauvais/ Tille in France, and from there to Le Culot in Belgium in the following March. After more than a year in command of the group, Glenn Nye was assigned to higher headquarters and replaced by Colonel John Samuel, who continued in command until after the end of hostilities. For the intensely active period of Nye's command, the 322nd received the coveted Distinguished Unit Citation.

When the war in Europe came to a close in May 1945, Nye's Annihilators and their brother bombardment groups had fully vindicated the much-maligned Marauder, proving it more durable than any other American bomber in Europe. The first Marauder to complete 100 sorties from Britain had been the 322nd Group's 'Mild and Bitter', which had achieved this feat as early as 8 May 1944. Many Marauders from numerous bombardment groups survived 150 sorties over Europe, but the supreme champion was the Annihilators' 'Flak Bait', which on 18 April 1945 completed its 200th mission, the only Allied medium or heavy bomber of the war in Europe to amass such a record. Holed some 900 times by enemy flak in 21 months of combat flying, that battered aircraft has come to symbolise the 322nd's determination to contribute towards Allied victory.

THE AUTHOR Simon Clay is a leading authority on the history of the US Army Air Force in World War II and has written numerous books on the subject.

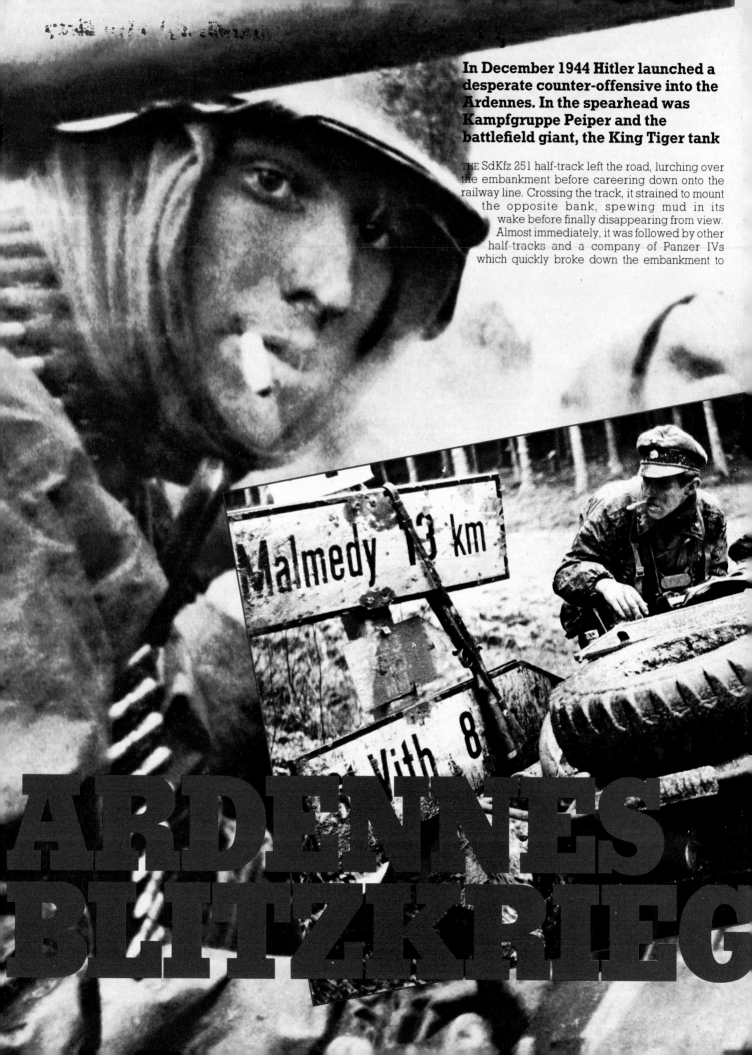

In December 1944 Hitler launched a desperate counter-offensive into the Ardennes. In the spearhead was Kampfgruppe Peiper and the battlefield giant, the King Tiger tank

THE SdKfz 251 half-track left the road, lurching over the embankment before careering down onto the railway line. Crossing the track, it strained to mount the opposite bank, spewing mud in its wake before finally disappearing from view. Almost immediately, it was followed by other half-tracks and a company of Panzer IVs which quickly broke down the embankment to

ARDENNES BLITZKRIEG

In mid-December 1944, the sorely pressed Germans unleashed their final Blitzkrieg in the west and some 25 divisions descended on the thinly held Ardennes sector of the front. Kampfgruppe Peiper, a powerful all-arms force, was ordered to grab vital bridges across the Meuse in preparation for an advance on Antwerp. Left: Short of every necessity, the Kampfgruppe survived on captured supplies. Here, a weary member of Peiper's command searches a knocked-out US armoured car for food. Below: Driving a mud-covered Schwimmwagen, a reconnaissance team, often identified as being led by Peiper (left), searches for a way through the enemy's lines.

make a rudimentary roadway. It was late afternoon on Saturday 16 December 1944 and Kampfgruppe (Task Force) Peiper, spearhead of the 1st SS Panzer Division 'Leibstandarte Adolf Hitler', was about to enter the Ardennes battle.

Led by SS-Obersturmbannführer (Lieutenant-Colonel) Joachim (Jochen) Peiper, a 29-year-old veteran of campaigns in Poland, France, the Balkans and Russia, the force was a formidable all-arms group. Its task was to follow a precise route through the Losheim gap in the northern sector of the Ardennes, pushing aside the thin American defensive screen and advancing along the Amblève valley to Stavelot and Trois Ponts. This would open the way to the Meuse river, where bridgeheads were to be seized for other panzer divisions to break out towards Antwerp, the main objective of an overall German plan, code-named 'Wacht am Rhein'. Peiper's role was an ambitious one, dependent for success upon the speed and impact of an armoured Blitzkrieg that would spread confusion in the enemy rear before the Allies could respond.

The Kampfgruppe left its staging area around Blankenheim, to the east of the Belgian-German border, at 0200 hours on 16 December, led by the half-tracks of No. 10 Company of the 3rd SS Panzer-grenadier Regiment and the Panzer IVs of No. 6 Company, 1st SS Panzer Battalion. At first all went well; at 0530 the sky to the west was suddenly set ablaze by the short, sharp artillery bombardment which opened the Wacht am Rhein assault and, as dawn broke on a cold, misty winter's day, sounds of firing could be heard as infantry of the 12th Volksgrenadier Division pushed forward to isolate American outposts and probe for lines of least resistance. But a few hours later, as Peiper's column approached Losheim, the first of a series of problems occurred, the results of which were to

delay the armoured breakthrough and make the build-up of momentum extremely difficult. A bridge over the railway line to the east of Losheim, destroyed by retreating Germans two months earlier, had not been repaired and the road was a solid mass of supply trucks and horse-drawn wagons belonging to the Volksgrenadiers. Peiper forced a way through in his Schwimmwagen command car, calling for field engineers to follow, but little could be achieved. In desperation, he ordered the tanks to clear the road, pushing the trucks into the ditches and fields on either side, while he led the way down the railway embankment to bypass the broken bridge. He was already 10 hours behind schedule.

Emerging onto the Losheim road, it soon became obvious that Peiper's problems were only just beginning, for the Volksgrenadiers had failed to make much headway, pinned down by small pockets of American defenders around the Losheimergraben crossroads less than a mile further on. In a fuel-consuming diversion, therefore, the Kampfgruppe left its prescribed route, moving across country towards the village of Lanzerath, where elements of the 3rd Parachute Division were apparently making

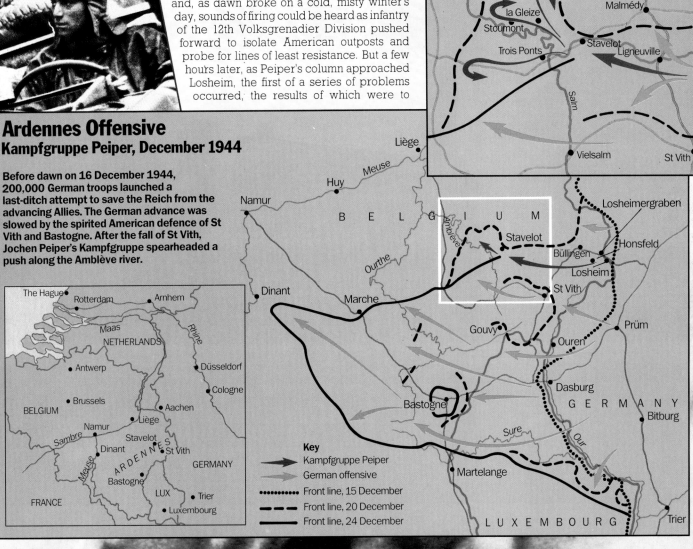

Ardennes Offensive
Kampfgruppe Peiper, December 1944

Before dawn on 16 December 1944, 200,000 German troops launched a last-ditch attempt to save the Reich from the advancing Allies. The German advance was slowed by the spirited American defence of St Vith and Bastogne. After the fall of St Vith, Jochen Peiper's Kampfgruppe spearheaded a push along the Amblève river.

The Amblève valley

Key
→ Kampfgruppe Peiper
→ German offensive
•••••• Front line, 15 December
- - - Front line, 20 December
—— Front line, 24 December

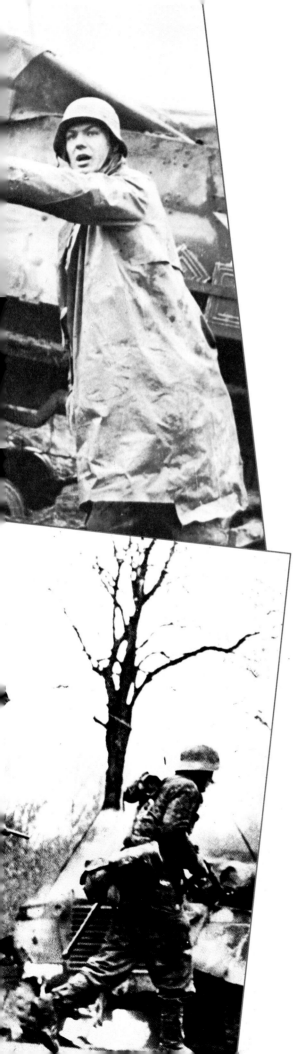

better progress. The Panzer IVs of No. 6 Company set out in gathering darkness along unknown tracks, only to encounter a minefield left uncleared by the paras. Despite the loss of three tanks and five half-tracks, Peiper urged his men on, but when he entered the village at 2300 hours, to be greeted by a para colonel who was convinced that American troops were waiting in ambush in woods between Lanzerath and Honsfeld, he decided to halt for the night.

The situation did not seem to improve as the advance was resumed at 0500 on 17 December, for although the para colonel's fears proved unfounded, Peiper had to waste more time and fuel flushing out Americans from defended positions around Buchholz station. Nevertheless, evidence of enemy confusion was beginning to emerge – at 0700 the panzers entered Honsfeld by the simple expedient of joining a column of retreating American trucks – and Peiper could congratulate himself on finally having broken through the initial defensive crust. This should have enabled him to push forward at speed, but yet another problem delayed his advance. The diversions and skirmishes of the previous 24 hours had drained the fuel tanks of the Kampfgruppe, making it essential to capture enemy stockpiles of petrol.

An American fuel dump was known to be at Büllingen, a few miles to the north of Honsfeld, and although this was some way beyond his route, Peiper had no choice but to order another diversion, particularly when he received reports that some of his King Tigers, bringing up the rear of the column, had already run dry. Shrugging aside an attempted ambush by US tank destroyers, the panzers moved forward to capture an airstrip at Morschheck and then the precious fuel. By 0900, American prisoners of war were pouring petrol into thirsty tanks and half-tracks, while reconnaissance units probed north and west to prevent enemy interference. But it was midday, before the Kampfgruppe could resume its advance and even then it took time to get back onto the original route.

Peiper may have gained flexibility and endurance, but he still had to create momentum. A combination of unexpectedly effective defence by small, isolated groups of Americans and the need to make diversions to search for lines of advance or fuel had denied him the chance to build up a Blitzkrieg-style assault and, as he began to realise this, signs of frustration emerged. Already at Honsfeld and Büllingen, American prisoners had been shot out of hand. During the next phase of operations, the Kampfgruppe was to reach new depths of atrocity just to the south of the Belgian town of Malmédy.

Once refuelled, Peiper led his column south to Moderscheid and then west towards his next key objective: the town of Ligneuville, at the head of the Amblève valley. His reconnaissance unit went ahead, opening up a reasonable route through Ondenval to Thirimont, but the most direct approach thereafter was little more than a muddy track. Peiper, therefore, turned north, aiming to join the main road to Ligneuville at Baugnez, a couple of miles outside Malmédy, after which he would turn south towards his objective. Such a move meant that for a

Left: Scenes from the Battle of the Bulge. Enjoying local superiority, the Kampfgruppe scythed a bloody path through the defences with the burnt-out wreckage of US vehicles marking the line of advance. However, the strain of fighting in sub-zero temperatures and the tenacity of the Allied resistance quickly took their toll.

SPEARHEADING THE OFFENSIVE

By early December 1944 the Germans had secretly massed 24 divisions along the Ardennes sector of the western front in preparation for their final offensive against the US and British forces. The high command planned to split the Allies in two by driving north to the Belgian port of Antwerp and south through Luxembourg. Kampfgruppe Peiper was the linch pin of the northern push. This well-balanced column was to lead the race to Antwerp and seize vital bridges over the river Meuse near Liège. The importance attached to their mission can be judged by the calibre of the troops under Peiper's command and the quality of their equipment. Consisting of 70 tanks of the 1st SS Panzer Battalion, 30 King Tigers of the 501st Heavy Tank Battalion, and the 2nd Battalion, 3rd Panzergrenadier Regiment, the Kampfgruppe contained the cream of Hitler's armed forces. Their leader, Joachim Peiper, a veteran of the bloody battles around Kharkov on the Eastern Front, was widely recognised as a cunning fighter, able to respond to any adversity with great daring and tenacity. Despite the undoubted quality of the Kampfgruppe, its fighting abilities were severely undermined by fuel shortages that forced Peiper to waste valuable time searching for US petrol dumps and allowed the Allies to organise a devastating response.

Below: Smiling paras hitch a lift on a King Tiger during the early phase of the onslaught. Bottom left: German infantry loot winter equipment from dead GIs. Bottom right: Vast stockpiles of petrol were destroyed by US troops to slow the Kampfgruppe down. Far right: Inspecting a 'tamed' Tiger. Starved of vital fuel, these leviathans failed to maintain the momentum of the advance.

short distance he was travelling parallel to the main road, less than 1000yds to his left, and it was as the lead tanks probed north from Thirimont at about 1330 hours, that they saw an American column moving away from them along the road to Ligneuville. Opening fire, they destroyed the leading truck and, as panzer grenadiers dismounted to clear the road, American troops began to surrender. They were in no position to offer resistance, lacking heavy weapons and suffering the full effects of surprise.

As the panzers wound round the Baugnez crossroads, panzer grenadiers gathered in about 120 prisoners and herded them into a nearby field. Leaving two Panzer IVs to stand guard, Peiper lost no

time in pushing on towards Ligneuville, particularly as he now had reports that an American headquarters was stationed there. As the column disappeared down the road, the prisoners were suddenly subjected to machine-gun fire and 85 men of Battery B, 285th Field Artillery Observation Battalion were killed. It was the single worst atrocity against POWs in northwest Europe during the campaign of 1944-45 and, as the bodies were discovered soon afterwards by American troops advancing out of Malmédy, it ensured a hardening of Allied resolve that was to prove crucial in the following days.

Peiper, unaware of this development, entered Ligneuville at 1430. A small group of Shermans crippled the leading Panther outside the Hôtel des Ardennes, but was quickly forced to withdraw. Nevertheless, a bridge over the Amblève river was seized intact and Peiper, by now under considerable pressure from his divisional commander, SS-Oberführer (Brigadier) Wilhelm Mohnke, lost no time in pressing forward to Stavelot. At first, the way seemed clear, and the column passed through the villages of Pont and Lodomez without incident; but it was beginning to get dark and snow was falling heavily. This part of the advance was a gamble, for Peiper had no way of knowing if Stavelot was defended, yet he needed to capture the town and its bridge across the Amblève if he was to reach the road to Trois Ponts and more American fuel dumps.

In fact, Stavelot was protected by nothing more than a group of 13 men from Company C, 291st Combat Engineer Battalion, but their actions late on 17 December were perhaps the most important factor in stalling Kampfgruppe Peiper. Led by Sergeant Hensel, the engineers set up an ambush position to the east of the town, where the road skirted a cliff with a steep drop on the other side, and when the first of Peiper's tanks approached, it was destroyed by a single bazooka shot. In total darkness, Peiper called a halt for the night, enabling the Americans to send forward more troops to bolster local defences.

When the Kampfgruppe resumed its advance at 0800 hours on 18 December, it had to fight to gain control of Stavelot, and although the Americans were overwhelmed before they could destroy the vital bridge, yet more delays had been imposed. Peiper was forced to push through towards Trois Ponts as quickly as he could, ignoring the existence of a fuel dump just a few miles to the north at Francorchamps.

TIGER II

It was a major miscalculation, made worse by the fact that by now the Americans were beginning to discern the pattern of the German advance. As Peiper left Stavelot to be guarded by a small detachment of panzers, the first elements of the US 30th Infantry Division were moving towards the town from the north, intent upon containing the threat.

Trois Ponts proved to be the turning point in the battle, however, for it was essential for Peiper to capture its bridges across the Amblève and Salm rivers if he was to reach open country on the road to the Meuse. By midday on 18 December, he should have been carving out his bridgeheads somewhere between Huy and Liège, so speed was vital, but once again the advance was stalled by hastily-prepared American defences. In this case, men of Company C 51st Combat Engineer Battalion were responsible,

priming the bridges for demolition and deploying a single 57mm anti-tank gun to cover the Stavelot road where it narrowed to pass beneath a railway viaduct. At 1045 the leading Panther nosed forward towards the viaduct, only to be destroyed by a lucky shot and, although the gallant gun-crew was wiped out, the road was blocked. Thirty minutes later, the Amblève bridge was blown and, as Peiper heard the explosion, a crucial decision was made. Instead of continuing into Trois Ponts, the Kampfgruppe turned right towards La Gleize, hoping to find an alternative crossing further up the river. The panzers were by now desperate for petrol – one of the King Tigers, its fuel tanks dry, had to be abandoned just outside Trois Ponts – and Peiper was being channelled onto minor roads where the chances of capturing American stockpiles were minimal. The destruction of the Salm bridge at Trois Ponts at 1300 reinforced the point.

The leading Panthers followed the Amblève, moving through La Gleize to the southwest. They were lucky: in mid-afternoon a bridge was found intact at Cheneux and the tanks began to cross. But their luck did not hold. Suddenly there was a break in the weather, an Allied spotter plane flew over and, despite frantic orders from Peiper to scatter the panzers under cover, fighter-bombers swept down to hit tanks and half-tracks in a devastating attack. One of the King Tigers slewed across the bridge, blocking it for over two hours, and although Peiper did not give up – he sent surviving panzers to seize yet another bridge, across the steep-sided Lienne river at Habiemont, in a final attempt to break clear – it was obvious that time had run out. US combat engineers reached Habiemont first and, as the Panthers approached, they blew the bridge. At 1630, with the light of a third frustrating day beginning to fade, Peiper accepted the success of the American

When the mighty Tiger II (King Tiger) entered service with the German Army in late 1944, it was the most potent main battle tank in existence, able to out-fight any Allied opposition.

Like the Tiger I, the King Tiger had an all-welded hull, but its armour was thicker, up to 185mm, and sloped to deflect anti-tank rounds. The Tiger II packed a fearsome punch: the long-barrelled 88mm gun and two 7.92mm MG34 machine guns.

Although the King Tiger was a first-rate piece of engineering, its sheer weight and size undermined its battlefield performance. The tank's maximum speed, 38km/h, was often cut by half over difficult terrain, and even with full fuel tanks its range was just over 100km. The high-velocity gun was a cause of complaint; wearing out quickly, it had to be changed frequently.

Despite these shortcomings, the arrival of the King Tiger came as a nasty shock to the Allies. Even when deployed in penny packets, it was able to take on and beat much larger forces.

By the end of the war some 500 models had been produced. Despite heavy Allied bombing, Henschel, the manufacturers, were taking only two weeks to complete a single unit; only shortages of fuel ended the King Tiger's reign of terror.

blocking moves and fell back to La Gleize.

By now, the Americans were intent on destroying Peiper's force, sending elements of two divisions to surround La Gleize and interdict the vulnerable supply line at Stavelot. By nightfall on 18 December, a battalion was preparing to attack Stavelot from the north, while an equivalent force entered Stoumont, to the west of La Gleize, inflicting a significant defeat on Peiper's reconnaissance unit. Peiper pulled his perimeter tight, concentrating his remaining force, about 2000 men and 200 vehicles, into a pocket which included La Gleize, Cheneux and the eastern outskirts of Stoumont. It was just as well that he did, for early on 19 December Stavelot was attacked. The battle for the town was to take another 48 hours to resolve in favour of the Americans, but to all intents and purposes Peiper was cut off.

He refused to give in, however. At 0700 on 19 December, a counter-attack was mounted towards the Amblève bridge at Targnon, a few miles beyond Stoumont and, despite initial problems, some progress was made. But as news of the Stavelot battle filtered through and American defences hardened around Stoumont station, Peiper was forced to pull back, sending the remains of his reconnaissance unit to reinforce the threatened supply link. They failed to make much headway, weakening the Kampfgruppe at a time when American units were rapidly closing in. Deploying the remnants of 1st SS Panzer Battalion at Stoumont, the King Tigers at La Gleize and anti-aircraft units around Cheneux, Peiper waited for the inevitable attack.

The American plan was for the 82nd Airborne Division, supported by tanks, to secure a line from Stavelot to La Gleize while two regiments of the 30th Infantry Division continued to squeeze in from the flanks. A co-ordinated assault began at 1830 hours on 20 December, when men of one regiment seized the sanatorium at Stoumont, initiating a savage hand-to-hand battle which extended well into the night. Peiper's panzer grenadiers held on, but it did them

On 19 December, elements of Peiper's column carried out one of the worst atrocities seen during the campaign in northwest Europe. On the outskirts of the Belgian town of Malmédy, 85 US prisoners of war were murdered in cold blood. Below: Pictorial evidence of the killings. News of Malmédy did much to stiffen the resolve of the American units battling for survival in the Ardennes and signalled the end of the Kampfgruppe. As the scattered pockets of resistance slowed the German attack, Allied commanders plotted a devastating counter-stroke. The US 82nd Airborne Division pounced on La Gleize and Stavelot, interdicting Peiper's line of retreat. Below left: Paras bring in a young SS trooper for interrogation. After suffering heavy losses, Peiper ordered his men to make their own way back to friendly lines.

little good. During the night US patrols began to infiltrate the German perimeter, and attempts by other elements of 1st SS Panzer Division to break through at Stavelot failed. Peiper was by no means finished, however, and at dawn on 21 December he pre-empted an American attack at Stoumont, inflicting heavy casualties on one unit; but time was running out. As the American pressure increased and air strikes became more frequent, Peiper was forced to pull in his perimeter even more. Stoumont and Cheneux fell on 23 December; at 0100 on the 24th, the remains of the Kampfgruppe, less than 800 men, were given permission to make their own way to safety. Very few succeeded.

Indeed, by 24 December the tide had begun to turn throughout the Ardennes sector, as Allied forces closed in to counter the German thrusts. Kampfgruppe Peiper had been destroyed, worn down by blocking moves, ground and air attacks and supply deficiencies. Peiper's failure to build up the momentum so essential to an armoured thrust, guaranteed his ultimate defeat.

THE AUTHOR John Pimlott is senior lecturer in War Studies and International Affairs at the Royal Military Academy, Sandhurst. He has written *Strategy and Tactics of War* and edited *Vietnam: the History and Tactics.*

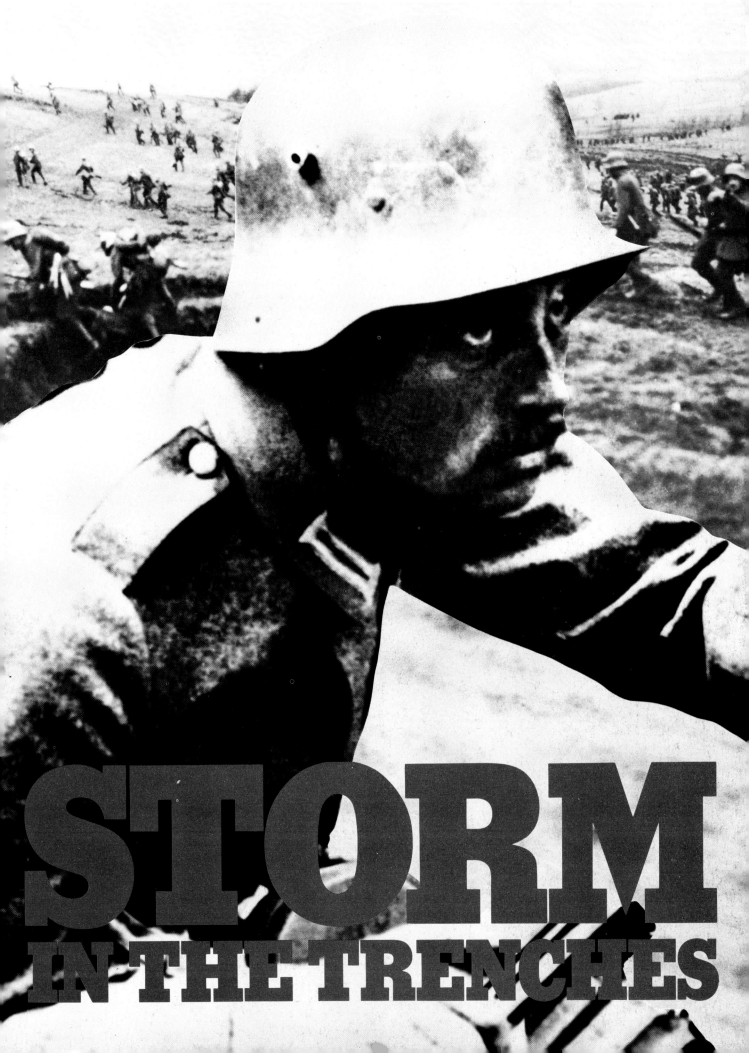

VANGUARD OF VICTORY

By early 1915, after several months of fruitless slaughter on the Western Front, German military leaders began to look for a means of ending the deadlock. It was decided that instead of launching attacks with large bodies of men in the hope of achieving pre-arranged objectives, spearhead units, known as Sturmtruppen, would lead the assault and seek out weaknesses in the enemy's defences that the follow-up forces could exploit to the full.

Although the first experiments proved unsuccessful, an officer of the Garde Schützen Bataillon, Hauptmann Eric Rohr, set about perfecting the idea, and developing the weapons and equipment for his new force. His unit, Sturm-Bataillon Rohr, was first used successfully in late December 1915.

The men to form more new battalions were drawn from frontline units and then sent on specialised training courses. Expansion was rapid and by the end of 1916 some 13 battalions were attached to divisions throughout the army. Each battalion consisted of four assault companies, a 3.7cm gun battery, light mortar and flame-thrower detachments, and a machine-gun company. In action the men carried little kit and concentrated on firepower. By the close of 1916, Rohr's early experiments had proved so successful that many divisions established their own storm companies – 120-strong units were attached to each regiment. Despite the high quality of the storm units and their undoubted value in the Michael Offensive, they remained only a relatively small part of the German Army in World War I. Above: The badge of a flame-thrower detachment.

Western Front, 1918: deafened by the thunder of heavy artillery shells, German stormtroopers charged into a mêlée of hand-to-hand combat as the Michael Offensive got underway

JUST BEFORE 0940 hours on 21 March 1918, the men of the German Army's 73rd Hanoverian Fusilier Regiment scrambled out of their frontline trenches into no-man's land, in preparation for the critical dash over the 800m that separated them from the British positions. This move was undertaken during the last few minutes of a five-hour preliminary artillery bombardment. Leutnant (Second Lieutenant) Ernst Jünger, commanding the 7th Company of the regiment's 2nd Battalion, led his men forward wearing a cloak, with a revolver in his right hand and a bamboo riding cane in his left. He was boiling with fury and had been filled with an overpowering desire to kill after half his company had been lost to a stray shell. His company pushed through some battered wire and jumped over the abandoned first-line British trench before coming under machine-gun fire from the second line. The Michael Offensive was under way.

The German strategy was to break through the British lines between Flesquières and St. Quentin in northeast France, and then swing north towards Arras. By forcing the British Army to retreat to the Channel, it was hoped to divide it from the French Army to the south. Preparations for the attack had taken several months, and the Germans planned to use 76 divisions to assault the 29 divisions forming the British Third and Fifth Armies. A high proportion of the German divisions were classified as *Stoss-divisionen* (attack divisions). Included in these special units was the 111th Division, part of the German Seventeenth Army, and one of its regiments was the 73rd Hanoverian Fusiliers. The Germans intended to cut through the British lines in a surprise attack, using sophisticated artillery techniques, and with refined assault tactics developed from battle experience and realistic training. Much would depend upon the offensive spirit of assault regiments such as the 73rd Hanoverian Fusiliers.

The regiment had served continuously on the Western Front from 1914 and had fought against both the French and the British, the latter during the Somme battles of 1916. By March 1918, the regiment consisted of three battalions, each with about 600 men. Leutnant Jünger's 7th Company consisted of about 150 fusiliers. After nearly four years of action, there were few pre-war soldiers left, and the majority of the fusiliers were 17-year-old youths or 35-year-old married men.

Their commander, Leutnant Ernst Jünger, was a wartime soldier. A restless, rather bohemian youth, he had volunteered for the army in 1914 and had served as a fusilier with the regiment before being commissioned in 1915. A romantic, but also a ruthless trench fighter, he revelled in the excitement of battle, and by 1918 had been wounded five times, awarded the Iron Cross second and first class, and had won the Knight's Cross with Swords of the House of Hohenzollern. In September 1918, he was to be awarded the Pour le Merité, one of only 14 junior infantry officers to receive this Prussian award for bravery. Jünger had two officers in his company, and most of the platoons were commanded by experienced NCOs who were given limited status and the authority of officers. His fusiliers were armed with 7.92mm Mauser (Model 1898) rifles, Maxim 08/15 light machine guns, grenades, and a variety of coshes and clubs for trench fighting. By 1918, although well armed, the German soldier was a shabby creature, who, in Jünger's words, had existed for four years 'in torn coats and worse fed than a Chinese coolie.'

The 73rd Hanoverian Fusiliers formed part of the first assault wave in the Michael Offensive and, along with specially trained and equipped storm battalions, were to follow closely behind the creeping artillery barrage and infiltrate the British trench

Page 981: Despite intensive training (above), few of the stormtroopers were prepared for the full horror of the Michael Offensive in early 1918 (inset).
Above and below: Over the top, assault troops head for the British lines. Below right: Bruchmüller, the German artillery strategist.

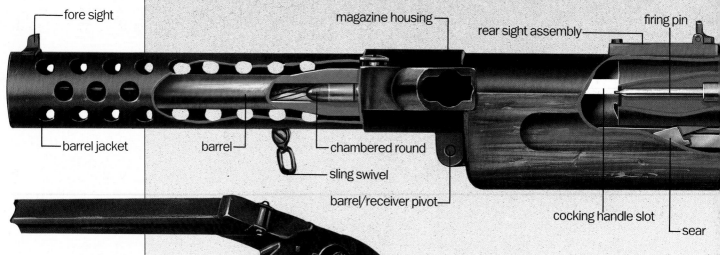

fore sight

barrel jacket

barrel

chambered round

magazine housing

sling swivel

barrel/receiver pivot

rear sight assembly

firing pin

cocking handle slot

sear

32-round 'snail' magazine

THE BERGMANN MP 18.I

In 1916, by which time the opposing forces in northern Europe were trapped in a savage war of attrition, the German High Command called for an effective new close-quarters weapon. Hugo Schmeisser, a designer at the Theodor Bergmann armaments works at Suhl, set to work on a gun which incorporated the stock of a rifle and the capacity to fire bursts from a magazine. His design, which went into limited production in 1918, is now seen as the true prototype of the modern sub-machine gun. Named the Maschinen Pistole 1918, and better known (after one modification) as the Bergmann MP 18.1, the gun (shown above) was a blowback weapon firing from an open breech. Its cyclic rate of fire was 400rpm and the rounds, 9mm Parabellum pistol cartridges, were fed into the left side by a 32-round 'snail' helical magazine, a feature which was already in service on the long-barrelled Luger.

The Bergmann was formidable at close quarters but had little stopping power beyond 200m. It was issued to stormtroopers and NCOs during the last months of World War I, and the German intention was to arm six men in each company with a Bergmann, each of whom would have an assistant to carry ammunition. The war was fast drawing to a close, however, and the 35,000 manufactured did not seriously affect the course of the war.

system before pushing into the open country beyond. The ranks of the storm battalions were filled with highly trained soldiers with their own special weapons and equipment, but they were too few to undertake all the tasks planned for the assault. However, the 73rd Hanoverian Fusiliers was effectively a storm battalion, and Jünger had trained the

2nd Battalion's storm company in 1917. In the months preceding the offensive, the regiment had practised over and over again the assault tactics to be used, with Jünger demanding absolute realism. His wartime diary records: 'Sometimes I made practice attacks with the company on complicated trench systems, with live bombs, in order to turn to account the lessons of the Cambrai battle [of November 1917].' This involved taking casualties and inflicting them as well. Jünger recounts, 'a machine-gunner of my company shot the CO of another unit off his horse while he was reviewing his own troops.'

On 17 March Jünger's company marched forward to the German front line. The regiment's task was to thrust between the villages of Ecoust-St Mein and Noreuil, across ground cut up by sunken roads, railway embankments and quarries. This area of the British line was held by the 2/6th Battalion North Staffords, part of the Third Army's 59th Division. The soldiers of this battalion were second-line territorials.

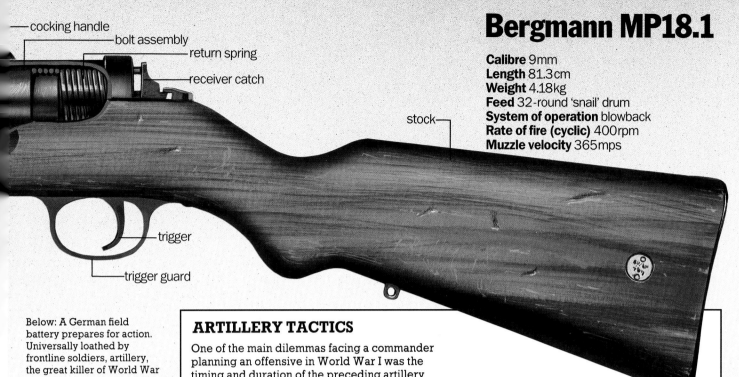

Bergmann MP18.1

Calibre 9mm
Length 81.3cm
Weight 4.18kg
Feed 32-round 'snail' drum
System of operation blowback
Rate of fire (cyclic) 400rpm
Muzzle velocity 365mps

cocking handle
bolt assembly
return spring
receiver catch
stock
trigger
trigger guard

Below: A German field battery prepares for action. Universally loathed by frontline soldiers, artillery, the great killer of World War I, was used to smash trenches, scythe paths through barbed wire and paralyse communications. The level of noise generated by a full-blooded bombardment could drive men insane. During the Michael Offensive, the devastation produced by the opening barrage, enabled the stormtroopers to seize their objectives, but the guns' lack of mobility meant that they could not help to consolidate the gains.

ARTILLERY TACTICS

One of the main dilemmas facing a commander planning an offensive in World War I was the timing and duration of the preceding artillery bombardment. A long, thorough barrage threw away the element of surprise, and rarely achieved its objective of destroying the enemy's machine-gun posts and command headquarters. A short hurricane bombardment sometimes achieved surprise, but lacked the necessary planning for good target registration.

For the Michael Offensive in March 1918, the Germans decided to adopt and adapt the short hurricane bombardment, which they hoped would surprise and paralyse the defenders. The tactics were largely the result of the experience and ideas of Oberst (Colonel) George Bruchmüller, who earned the nickname 'Durchbruchmüller' ('Breakthrough Müller'). Bruchmüller had begun to experiment with short, accurate artillery bombardments during the Verdun battles in 1916, and had then demonstrated his technique in Russia during the attack on Riga in 1917. As a result of this, General Erich Ludendorff, the German First Quartermaster-General, appointed him to co-ordinate the artillery for the offensive.

Bruchmüller's technique emphasised fire in depth throughout the enemy's position, including the *Feuerwalze*, or creeping barrage, which preceded the advancing infantry. Instead of having a blanket bombardment, Bruchmüller devised several stages in a five-hour artillery bombardment. Each battery had to hit specific targets under detailed timetables, 'shooting by the map'. To cause as much confusion in and behind the British lines as possible, German batteries were ordered to make extensive use of gas shells.

Despite the fact that Bruchmüller was to use half the entire German artillery strength on the Western front, some 6473 guns, and had made careful preparations for the bombardment, he realised that he could not destroy or disable every British position. However, he believed that the artillery fire would destroy or paralyse enough to enable the assault infantry to break through. This was largely achieved by German artillery on 21 March, but after that the problem of moving supplies, reinforcements and artillery across devastated ground proved all-but insurmountable.

recruited from around Burton-on-Trent. The battalion
had a high proportion of young conscripts and was
not regarded as a particularly strong unit. There
were few defences in depth, and there was a shortage of trench equipment and supplies.

On the night of 19/20 March, Jünger's company
moved into frontline dug-outs for the assault. Unfortunately, they came under British shellfire and one
shell hit part of the company sheltering in a giant
crater. As a consequence, even before the battle
began, Jünger had lost over 80 men and found
himself commanding only 63 fusiliers. These heavy
pre-battle losses depressed the survivors, who
spent a whole day waiting for the order to attack
under desultory shellfire. However, their excitement was great as they waited out the last five hours
before the onslaught, listening to and watching the
German artillery bombardment.

After Jünger and his fusiliers had crossed the first
line of British trenches, running through smoke and
drifting gas, they reached a railway embankment
and came under machine-gun fire. They then began
to fight their way through a network of trenches and
dug-outs. Junger recounts:

'For the first time in the war, I saw large bodies of
men in hand-to-hand fighting. The English held
two terraced trenches on the rear slope. Shots
were exchanged and bombs lobbed down at a
range of a few metres. I jumped into the first
trench.

'Stumbling around the first traverse, I collided
with an English officer with an open tunic and his
tie hanging loose. I did without my revolver and,
seizing him by the throat, flung him against the
sandbags, where he collapsed. Behind me the
head of an old major appeared. He was shouting
to me, "Shoot the hound dead!" I left this to those
behind me and turned to the lower trench.

'It seethed with English. I fired off my cartridges

so fiercely that I pressed the trigger 10 times
at least after the last shot. A man next to me threw
bombs among them as they scrambled to get
away. A dish-shaped helmet was spinning high
in the air. A minute saw the battle ended. The
English jumped out of their trenches and fled by
battalions across the open.'

The commanding officer of the North Staffords,
Lieutenant-Colonel T.B.H. Thorne, had been hit in
the head and killed during the attack, which broke
up the battalion and left only scattered pockets of
resistance. Jünger's fighting spirit was almost out of
control, and he snatched a rifle from a fusilier and
began to shoot at the retreating British. Killing his
first victim at 150m, Jünger watched him as he
'snapped together like the blade of a knife and lay
still.' But even among such slaughter, there

Left: Wary of being caught in the open by artillery or machine-gun fire, German assault troops forsake the protection of their trenches to make the dash across the shell-blasted moonscape of no-man's land. Despite the scale of the preliminary artillery barrage, they had to cut their way through the enemy's barbed-wire defences.

appeared some ludicrous moments, as when one of Jünger's fusiliers paused to shoot at a hare that had jumped up and was running through their lines.

The Germans had to maintain the momentum of the attack to prevent the British from consolidating their defences. At one point, the 7th Company was held up by two British machine guns, one on each side of a hollow. After a brief pause, Jünger charged them with a few men:

'It was a fight to the death. After one or two springs forward I lay opposite the left-hand machine-gun position, alone but for one man. I could clearly distinguish a flat helmet behind a low mound of earth, and close behind it a thin spiral of steam.

'I approached in quite short springs, so as to allow no chance for aim. Each time I lay down, the man threw me a clip of cartridges and I fired a few carefully aimed shots. "Cartridges.....car-

tridges!" I turned round and saw him lying twitching on one side.'

Jünger leapt forward, and jumped into the trench as the defenders ran off to the machine-gun position to the right. This second obstacle was taken after a light machine gun had been brought up to fire from the flank, enabling another company to move forward. A large number of British troops surrendered and over a dozen were shot by the Germans. Although Jünger despised such action, he did not blame the fusiliers, believing that their blood lust was up and that the British had been happily trying to kill his men only a few minutes earlier. Pushing on, the 7th Company reached the outskirts of the village of Vraucourt. Here, in abandoned British dug-outs, they found provisions that they had not seen for months – white bread, jam and ginger beer.

At this point, the regiment's advance was halted

Michael Offensive
73rd Hanoverian Fusilier Regiment, March 1918

In August 1914 the First World War began with a German advance to within 40 miles of Paris. The French counter-attack began early in September and – after a race for the Channel ports – a stable trench line was established with the British and Belgians in the north and the French holding the line to the south. After the Somme battle of 1916, the German armies pulled back to the 'Hindenburg Line'. By the spring of 1918, after three and a half years of war, the Germans were ready for one last-ditch attempt to defeat the Allies, and on 21 March they launched the Michael Offensive.

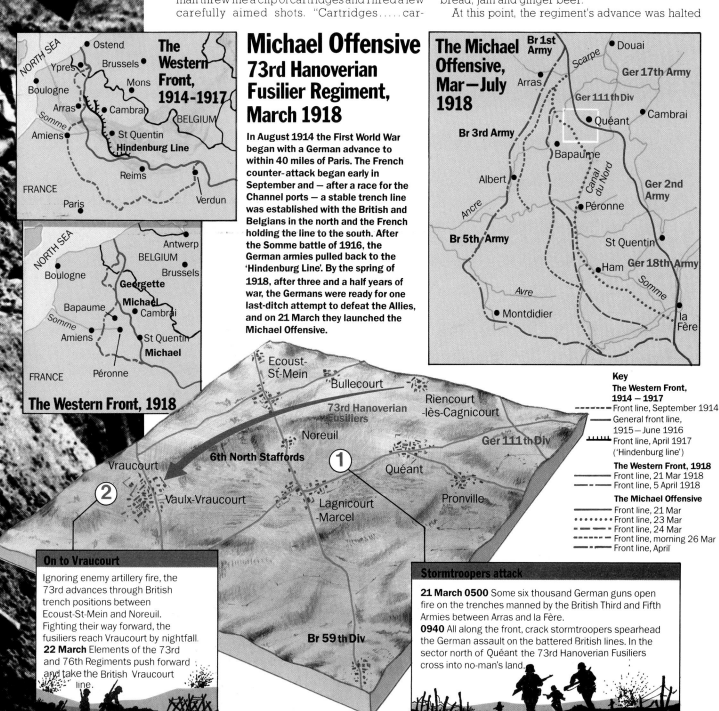

Key

The Western Front, 1914 – 1917
- - - - - - Front line, September 1914
———— General front line, 1915 – June 1916
⊥⊥⊥⊥⊥ Front line, April 1917 ('Hindenburg line')

The Western Front, 1918
———— Front line, 21 Mar 1918
— - — Front line, 5 April 1918

The Michael Offensive
———— Front line, 21 Mar
•••••••• Front line, 23 Mar
– - – - Front line, 24 Mar
- - - - - Front line, morning 26 Mar
— - — - Front line, April

On to Vraucourt

Ignoring enemy artillery fire, the 73rd advances through British trench positions between Ecoust-St-Mein and Noreuil. Fighting their way forward, the fusiliers reach Vraucourt by nightfall.
22 March Elements of the 73rd and 76th Regiments push forward and take the British Vraucourt line.

Stormtroopers attack

21 March 0500 Some six thousand German guns open fire on the trenches manned by the British Third and Fifth Armies between Arras and la Fère.
0940 All along the front, crack stormtroopers spearhead the German assault on the battered British lines. In the sector north of Quéant the 73rd Hanoverian Fusiliers cross into no-man's land.

by their own artillery fire. As they attempted to move forward into the village, the fusiliers were forced back three times by shellfire that they were unable to stop. As darkness fell, Jünger began to collect his exhausted men, and they made themselves comfortable in captured dug-outs.

On the morning of 22 March, Jünger received orders to attack the British defensive line to the right of Vraucourt with his company and elements of the 76th Regiment. As his men waited to attack, they came under artillery fire and were shot up by aircraft of the Royal Flying Corps. When he heard a German attack going in on his left, Jünger led his men forward, penetrating the British line without much opposition. They found that the so-called Vraucourt Line was still in the course of being dug, and that many stretches were only marked out by the removal of turf. However, those areas where trenches had been dug were fiercely defended by Highlanders; Jünger was impressed, saying, 'we had no cowards in front of us'.

Jünger believed that it was in trench fighting that a man's real courage or fear was displayed:

'The bravest push to the front, shooting and bomb throwing. The rest follow on their heels automatically, in a herd. In the hand-to-hand battle the fighters jump back and forward and, in avoiding the murderous bombs of the enemy, they run back on those behind them. Only those in the forefront know what the situation is, while further back a wild panic breaks out in the trench.

'Perhaps a few even jump over the top and get shot, whereat the enemy of course are much encouraged. Indeed, if they seize their opportunity all is lost; and it is now for the officer to show that he is worth his salt, though he too may have the wind up.'

Jünger was just such an officer, and he fought and bombed his way along the trench which led to the Vraucourt-Mory road. By the early evening, he was forced to prepare his fusiliers to hold a defensive position. However, at that moment the German troops to their right broke through the British position and, cheering and aided by the illumination from signal flares, the fusiliers found themselves part of a mad stampede, with the Highlanders fighting and then withdrawing as they tried to escape being surrounded. In the confused mêlée, Jünger felt a sharp blow on his chest and discovered that he had been hit just over the heart. The irony was that he had probably been shot by one of his own men, because he was wearing a captured British trench coat and might have been mistaken for one of the enemy.

With great difficulty, he was persuaded to go back

Below: During the early phase of the German onslaught, the stormtroopers combined speed and firepower to carve a path through the positions held by the British Third and Fifth Armies. While the follow-on waves consolidated the early gains, the assault troops pushed deeper into enemy territory, by-passing pockets of resistance and thrusting into the open countryside beyond the front lines. After three years of bloody stalemate in the trenches, the German army was ill prepared to cope with the demand of mobile warfare and the offensive spirit gradually evaporated. Starved of essential supplies and local artillery support, the men were unable to fully consolidate their initial gains, and in the face of stiffening opposition, gradually conceded ground. Although the offensive was restarted on several occasions, counter-attacks by the British and French recaptured the ground lost in the first days of the Michael Offensive by late August.

and seek medical attention. This meant crossing the line of trenches that had been captured and were under British artillery and smallarms fire. Jünger was wounded once again, this time in the head, a penalty which he paid for wearing his officer's soft hat rather than a steel helmet. He saw the brigade commander and urged him to send forward reserves to support the assault troops. When Jünger reached the field hospital at Souchy-Couchy, he was told by an astonished surgeon that he was very fortunate, because the bullet had passed through the back of his head but had not penetrated the skull.

Jünger was out of the battle and did not return to the 73rd Hanoverian Fusiliers until June. By that time, the Michael Offensive had ended in failure. Despite the fact that the Germans had cracked the British front line and were eventually to punch a 40-mile bulge in the position, practically destroying the Fifth Army, they were unable to do the same thing to the Third Army and thus force a general withdrawal to the coast. Although they had been able to surprise the British and, by using carefully developed artillery tactics and infantry assault tactics, were able to break through the main defensive trench system, the Germans were unable to maintain the momentum of the attack. This was due to a number of factors, not least the dogged defensive fighting of the British.

German casualties on 21 March had not been light. It has been calculated that they suffered 39,929 casualties; the British lost 38,512 men. The 73rd Hanoverian Fusiliers had 12 officers and 132 men killed, and probably four times that number wounded and missing. Jünger's 7th Company had suffered heavy casualties due to the unlucky hit by a British shell even before they reached their start line. When brave and aggressive soldiers like Jünger were killed or wounded, the attacking spirit of the German units was weakened. Replacements lacked enthusiasm or experience, and discipline was liable to break down when they were given the opportunity to loot British supply depots.

However, the best German units, like the 73rd Hanoverian Fusiliers, were experienced and well trained, with considerable tactical initiative shown by junior officers and NCOs. Trained under realistic conditions and taught to reinforce success and exploit opportunities created by the German artillery bombardment, they were a formidable force.

THE AUTHOR Keith Simpson is senior lecturer in War Studies and International Affairs at Sandhurst. He is a member of the Royal United Services Institute and the International Institute for Strategic Studies.

Streaming from their transports, the strike force of Israeli paras tore into the airport at Entebbe to do battle with a group of terrorists

SHORTLY BEFORE dawn on 3 July 1976, specialist units of the Israeli Defence Forces (IDF) loaded their equipment and drove to a nearby airbase, where ground-crews stood ready to lash their vehicles into the bellies of four Hercules transports. Elsewhere on the field, the crew of a Boeing 707, fitted out as a mobile hospital, made their final checks. By early afternoon, the transports were airborne and heading for Ophira on the southern tip of the Sinai peninsula; the Boeing began the first leg of a journey that would take it to the airport at Nairobi in Kenya. Operation Thunderball, the plan to rescue 105 Jewish hostages held by terrorists at Entebbe, Uganda's international airport, was underway.

The crisis faced by the Israelis had begun at 1230 hours on 27 June, when four terrorists, two members of the German Baader-Meinhof gang and two members of the Popular Front for the Liberation of Palestine, hijacked Air France Flight 139, with 12 crew and 246 passengers on board, as it flew from Tel

THUNDERBALL AT ENTEBBE

PREPARATIONS

In the immediate aftermath of the hijacking of Flight 139 on 27 June 1976, the government of Israel began formulating its response to the terrorists' demands. Once it became clear that the lives of the Jewish passengers were in danger, the authorities started to consider a military response. However, before an appropriate course of action could be thrashed out, the Israelis had to build up a detailed picture of the situation at Entebbe.

The first break came on 30 June, when a batch of non-Jewish hostages were released by the hijackers. After arriving at Orly airport near Paris, all were interviewed by undercover agents with regard to the number of terrorists, their weapons, routine and clothing, and the degree of Ugandan involvement.

As agents gathered intelligence, a high-ranking team, consisting of politicians and military chiefs, discussed the range of possible military options. Three main rescue strategies were covered: a paradrop into Lake Victoria followed up by a waterborne assault, a direct assault from Kenya; and an airborne landing on Entebbe. Although the third response was considered most feasible, no firm decision was made until further information was available.

It was discovered that an Israeli firm had constructed several installations at the airport and agents were sent out to 'borrow' the blueprints. Other men paid several visits to travel agencies and airline offices to enquire about the regular flight schedules over East Africa. As the Israeli Air Force had helped to train the Ugandans, several members of the missions were contacted to provide intelligence on the lay-out of Entebbe, the location of other airfields, and the strength of Amin's air force. By early July, the Israelis had a detailed picture of the airport and a workable rescue plan. However, the final decision to launch the rescue bid was not taken until 3 July.

Above left and left: Israeli paras in training.

Entebbe
Israeli paras, July 1976

The Hijack, 27 June 1976

Air France 139 hijacked 1230
Athens
MEDITERRANEAN
Benghazi
27 June 0859
27 June 1450
Tel Aviv
Cairo
LIBYA
EGYPT
RED SEA
Nile
CHAD
SUDAN
CENTRAL AFRICAN REPUBLIC
ETHIOPIA
28 June 0315
Entebbe
UGANDA
KENYA
ZAIRE
Lake Victoria
TANZANIA

Shortly after midday on 27 June a group of German and Palestinian terrorists hijacked Air France flight 139 en route from Tel Aviv to Paris. At 0315 the following morning the aircraft arrived at Entebbe airport in Uganda. Five days later over half of the passengers were still being held hostage in the airport's old terminal — and a force of crack Israeli paras was on its way to Entebbe to attempt a dramatic rescue.

The Rescue, 3-4 July 1976

Athens
MEDITERRANEAN
Benghazi
Tel Aviv
4 July 1101
Cairo
Ophira
3 July 2150
LIBYA
EGYPT
CHAD
Nile
SAUDI ARABIA
RED SEA
SUDAN
CENTRAL AFRICAN REPUBLIC
DJIBOUTI
Djibouti
ETHIOPIA
UGANDA
Entebbe
3 July 2301
SOMALIA
KENYA
Nairobi
ZAIRE
Lake Victoria
4 July 0110
INDIAN OCEAN
TANZANIA

Aviv for Paris via Athens. After the takeover, the passenger jet was diverted to Benghazi in Libya, where it was refuelled, and then flew south, landing at Entebbe at 0315 on the 28th. Uganda's ruler, Field-Marshal Idi Amin Dada, was no friend of the Israelis and welcomed the terrorists, who used the airport's old terminal to hold the hostages. On 29 June, the hijackers, organised and supported by a highly-developed international terror network, demanded the release of 53 of their comrades held in Israel, France, West Germany, Kenya and Switzerland.

Initially, the Israeli government was unwilling to risk the lives of the non-Jewish hostages in a rescue attempt, but when the other passengers were released, senior politicians and military leaders, including Lieutenant-General Mordechai Gur, the chief-of-staff, Prime Minister Yitzhak Rabin and Minister of Defence Shimon Peres, accepted a daring plan proposed by Major-General Dan Shomron, the director of infantry and paratroopers. After a day of intensive preparation, the assault teams left Ophira airbase on 3 July; ahead lay a 3000-mile journey to Entebbe.

Fifteen minutes after the last aircraft left Ophira, a second Boeing was on its way south from an airbase in central Israel. It would also land at Ophira, then follow the transports – three hours behind to allow for its higher speed. On board were Major-General Kuti Adam, another senior officer, and a team of communications officers. Their job was to circle Entebbe, providing a vital radio link between the men on the ground, the planners in Israel and the medical team at Nairobi airport.

In the cockpits of the four transport planes which were now flying low over the Gulf of Suez, beneath the reach of hostile radar surveillance, the pilots

Hercules No. 1
2301 The lead plane touches down. Men detailed to secure the runway disembark, followed by the assault group.

Hercules No. 2
After an interval of several minutes, the second aircraft arrives and further troops deploy.

Hercules No. 3
The aircraft bearing reserve forces touches down as the main runway lighting is extinguished.

Hercules No. 4
2308 The final Hercules is on the ground. Further reserve forces disembark and the aircraft taxies towards the old terminal to pick up rescued hostages.

Group D deploys in APCs to the old terminal.

Group B secures the main runway and takes the new terminal and control tower.

Route of Hercules Nos. 1 - 3
Route of Hercules No. 4

Command Group and Ta move out from the first aircraft and assume con

Group A drives down the taxiway and assaults the old terminal.

Group C, the reserve force, moves down to the old terminal on foot to assist with the evacuation.

Key
Operation Thunderball
Operation Thunderball: routes of Hercules transports
Operation Thunderball: routes of assault groups
Air France flight 139

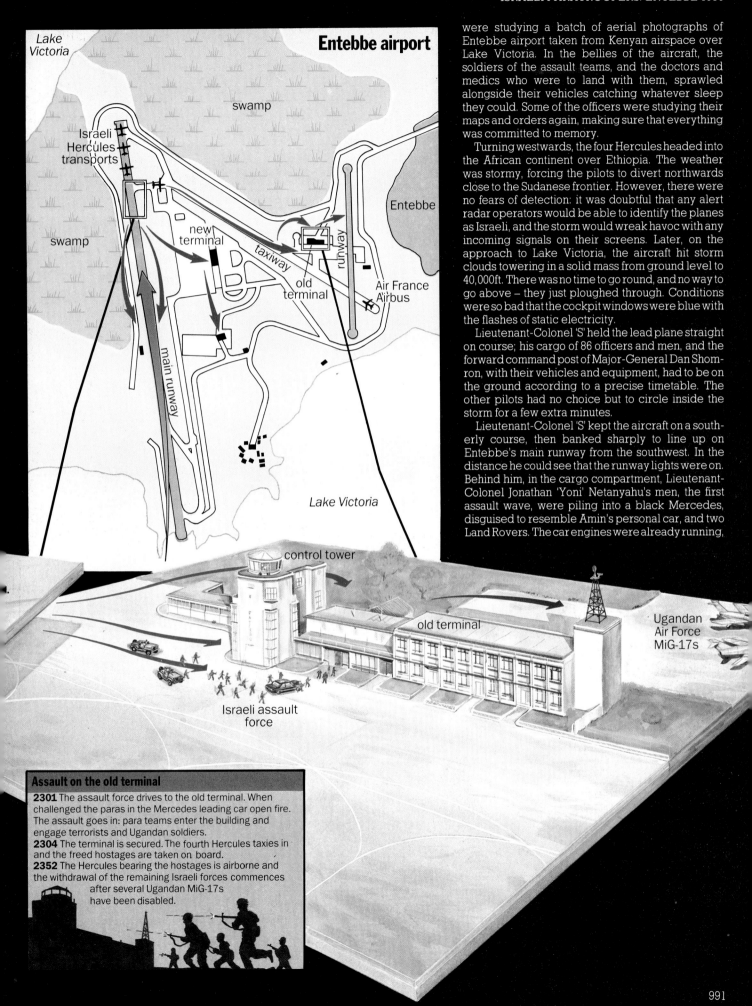

Lake Victoria

swamp

Entebbe airport

Israeli Hercules transports

swamp

new terminal

taxiway

old terminal

runway

Entebbe

Air France Airbus

main runway

Lake Victoria

control tower

old terminal

Ugandan Air Force MiG-17s

Israeli assault force

Assault on the old terminal

2301 The assault force drives to the old terminal. When challenged the paras in the Mercedes leading car open fire. The assault goes in: para teams enter the building and engage terrorists and Ugandan soldiers.

2304 The terminal is secured. The fourth Hercules taxies in and the freed hostages are taken on board.

2352 The Hercules bearing the hostages is airborne and the withdrawal of the remaining Israeli forces commences after several Ugandan MiG-17s have been disabled.

were studying a batch of aerial photographs of Entebbe airport taken from Kenyan airspace over Lake Victoria. In the bellies of the aircraft, the soldiers of the assault teams, and the doctors and medics who were to land with them, sprawled alongside their vehicles catching whatever sleep they could. Some of the officers were studying their maps and orders again, making sure that everything was committed to memory.

Turning westwards, the four Hercules headed into the African continent over Ethiopia. The weather was stormy, forcing the pilots to divert northwards close to the Sudanese frontier. However, there were no fears of detection: it was doubtful that any alert radar operators would be able to identify the planes as Israeli, and the storm would wreak havoc with any incoming signals on their screens. Later, on the approach to Lake Victoria, the aircraft hit storm clouds towering in a solid mass from ground level to 40,000ft. There was no time to go round, and no way to go above – they just ploughed through. Conditions were so bad that the cockpit windows were blue with the flashes of static electricity.

Lieutenant-Colonel 'S' held the lead plane straight on course; his cargo of 86 officers and men, and the forward command post of Major-General Dan Shomron, with their vehicles and equipment, had to be on the ground according to a precise timetable. The other pilots had no choice but to circle inside the storm for a few extra minutes.

Lieutenant-Colonel 'S' kept the aircraft on a southerly course, then banked sharply to line up on Entebbe's main runway from the southwest. In the distance he could see that the runway lights were on. Behind him, in the cargo compartment, Lieutenant-Colonel Jonathan 'Yoni' Netanyahu's men, the first assault wave, were piling into a black Mercedes, disguised to resemble Amin's personal car, and two Land Rovers. The car engines were already running,

4X-FBB

Left: Field-Marshal Idi Amin Dada, Uganda's power-hungry dictator, gave his full support to the hijackers and his intransigence forced the Israeli government to use force to secure the release of the hostages. Ironically, Amin had close links with the Israelis who had trained elements of his armed forces and helped in the modernisation of Entebbe's facilities in the years before the crisis. On ceremonial occasions, as here, he took great pride in wearing the much-coveted Israeli para wings above all other decorations. Above and above right: Speed and deception were the keys to the success of Operation Thunderball. Heavily armed jeeps and a Mercedes, disguised as Amin's personal limousine, were used to fool the Ugandan airport guards. Below: Doctor Jossi Faktor, head of the operation's medical team.

and members of the aircrew were standing by to release the restraining cables.

At 2301 hours, only 30 seconds behind the pre-planned schedule, Lieutenant-Colonel 'S' brought the aircraft in to touch down at Entebbe in the wake of a scheduled cargo flight that unwittingly covered the first landing. The rear ramp of the Hercules was already open, and the vehicles were on the ground and moving away before the plane rolled to a stop. A handful of paratroopers had already jumped out of the aircraft to place beacons next to the runway lights, in case the control tower shut them down.

The Mercedes and its escorts moved down the connecting road to the airport's old terminal building as fast as they could, consistent with the appearance of a senior officer's entourage. On the approaches to the tarmac apron in front of the building, two Ugandan sentries faced the oncoming vehicles, aimed their carbines, and shouted an order to stop. There was no choice, and no time to argue. The first shots from the Mercedes were from silenced pistols. One Ugandan fell and the other ran in the direction of the old control tower. The Ugandan on the ground was groping for his carbine. A paratrooper responded with a burst. Muki, Netanyahu's second-in-command, and his team jumped from the car and ran the last 40yds to the walkway in front of the building. The first entrance had been blocked off; without a second's pause, the paratroopers raced on to the second door.

After a searching debate with Netanyahu, Muki had decided to break a cardinal rule of the IDF. Junior officers usually lead the first wave of an assault, but Muki felt it important to be up front, in case there was need to make quick decisions about changes in

MEDICAL AID

The officer in charge of the medical support team, Doctor Jossi Faktor, recalls his part in the Entebbe operation:

'In addition to our usual medical supplies, we carried [aboard our Hercules transport] lots of 'space blankets' (aluminium sheets used for burn wounds) and large old-fashioned milk pails. Both were useful: the sheets were used to cover the hostages and Air France crew who had insufficient clothing, and the pails were used as giant sick bags.

'Being the last Hercules to land at Entebbe and the first to leave, we spent less than one

As the authorities in Israel considered their response to the hostage crisis, senior military officers began to prepare forces to carry out a rescue mission. In secret, assault teams commanded by Lieutenant-Colonel Jonathan Netanyahu, consisting of the cream of the country's paras and members of the Golani Brigade, gathered at a remote airbase in Israel. Based on available intelligence, a mock-up of Entebbe's old terminal was rapidly constructed and the men practised their assault techniques under the critical gaze of Netanyahu. However, because of the layout of the airport, it became clear that a speedier means of reaching the terminal was imperative. The problem was solved by Netanyahu's second-in-command, who remembered that senior Ugandan officers, and Amin himself, always travelled in black Mercedes limousines. A quick phone call, and a Mercedes was on its way to the airbase. As the assault groups were being put through their paces, the Israeli Air Force's senior officers picked the pilots and aircrews to fly Netanyahu's men to Entebbe. The distance was no problem, Hercules transports had regularly flown to Uganda. However, there were difficulties in landing at night and the crews were ordered to practise landing in darkness. After several sessions at a remote air strip in Israel, the senior air force officers detailed to oversee the raid training were convinced that their men were equal to the task. Unsure as to the physical state of the hostages the Israelis also made provisions for medical staff to accompany the assault force. In the days before the raid both reservists and current military doctors were placed on alert and a Boeing jet was fitted out as a hospital. Although given less than a week to prepare, all the elements of the operation were ready for action by 3 July.

plan. Tearing along the walkway, he was fired on by a Ugandan. Muki responded, killing him. A terrorist stepped out of the main door of the old terminal to see what the fuss was, and rapidly returned the way he had come.

Muki then discovered that the magazine of his carbine was empty. The normal procedure would have been to step aside and let someone else take the lead. He decided against this, and groped to change magazines on the run. The young officer behind him, realising what was happening, came up alongside. The two of them, and one other trooper, reached the door together – Amnon, the young lieutenant, on the left, Muki in the centre, and the trooper to the right.

The terrorist who had ventured out was now standing to the left of the door. Amnon fired, followed by Muki. Across the room, a terrorist rose to his feet and fired at the hostages sprawled around him, most of whom had been trying to get some sleep. Muki took care of him with two shots. Over to the right, another member of the hijack team managed to loose off a burst at the intruders, but his bullets went high, hitting a window and showering glass into the room. The trooper aimed and fired. Meanwhile Amnon identified a female terrorist to the left of the doorway and fired.

In the background, a bullhorn was booming in Hebrew and English, 'This is the IDF. Stay down.' From a nearby mattress, a young man launched himself at the trio in the doorway and was cut down by a carbine burst. The man was a bewildered hostage. Muki's troopers fanned out through the room and into the corridor to the washroom beyond – but all resistance was over.

The second assault team had meanwhile raced through another doorway into a hall where the off-duty terrorists spent their spare time. Two men in civilian clothes walked calmly towards them. Assuming that they were hostages, the soldiers held their fire. Suddenly, one of the men raised his hand and threw a grenade. The troopers dropped to the ground. A machine-gun burst eliminated their adversaries and the grenade exploded harmlessly.

Netanyahu's third team from the Land Rovers moved in to silence any opposition from the Ugandan soldiers stationed near the windows on the floor above. On the way up the stairs, they met two soldiers, one of whom opened fire. The troopers killed them.

While his men circulated through the hall, calming the shocked hostages and tending the wounded, Muki was called out to the tarmac. There he found a doctor kneeling over his commanding officer.

hour on the ground. We spent the short flight to Nairobi evaluating and stabilising the condition of the wounded soldiers and hostages. However, our desperate attempts to resuscitate "Yoni" were to no avail.

'At Nairobi, we were faced with the difficult decision to leave some of the more seriously wounded behind as they required immediate hospitalisation. After refuelling, we took off on the final leg of the journey home, which was medically uneventful. The hostages were shocked and excited; the soldiers emotionally exhausted. Yet only a few managed to doze off after 36 hours without sleep. The rest is now history.'

Netanyahu had remained outside the building to supervise all three assault teams and a bullet from the top of the old control tower had hit him in the back. While the troopers silenced the fire from above, he was dragged into the shelter of an overhanging wall by the walkway.

The assault on the old terminal was completed within three minutes after the lead plane had landed. Now, in rapid succession, its three companions came in to touch down at Entebbe. By 2308 hours, all of Thunderball Force was on the ground. The runway lights shut down as the third plane came in to land, but it didn't matter – the Israeli beacons did the job well enough.

With clockwork precision, armoured personnel carriers roared off the ramp of the second transport to take up positions to the front and rear of the old terminal, while infantrymen from the first and third planes ran to secure all access roads to the airport and to take over the new terminal and control tower. The tower was vital for the safe evacuation of the

Above: After their triumphant return to Israel on 4 July, the assault teams received their nation's grateful thanks from Major-General Dan Shomron, the director of paratroopers and infantry (standing, third from left), and the Minister of Defence, Shimon Peres (standing, far left). Left: Scenes of unrestrained jubilation marked the arrival of the freed hostages at Lod airport. The celebrations were marred only by the sad loss of Lieutenant-Colonel Jonathan 'Yoni' Netanyahu (far left), cut down during the fighting at Entebbe's old terminal. Below: One of the Israeli Air Force's Hercules transports taxis to a halt on a remote airfield.

hostages and their rescuers. In a brief clash at the new terminal, Sergeant Hershko Surin fell wounded. The fourth plane taxied to a holding position near the old terminal ready to take on the hostages. The engines were left running. A team of air force technicians was already hard at work off-loading heavy fuel pumps to transfer Idi Amin's precious aviation fuel into the thirsty tanks of the lead transport – a process that would take well over an hour.

Meanwhile, as planned, the Medical Corps' Boeing had landed at Nairobi, at 2205 hours. General Benny Peled, the GOC Air Force, was able to radio Lieutenant-Colonel 'S' that it was possible to refuel in Kenya's capital. Unable to raise Shomron on the operational radio, and uncomfortable with the situation on the ground – the Ugandans were firing tracer at random, while the aircraft with engines running were vulnerable at the fuel tanks – he decided to make use of the Nairobi option.

Muki radioed Shomron to report that the building and surroundings were secure, and to inform him that Netanyahu had been hit. Although they were ahead of schedule, there was no point in waiting around (possibly allowing the Ugandans the time to bring up reinforcements). The fourth Hercules was ordered to move closer to the old terminal. Muki's men and the other soldiers around the building formed two lines from the doorway to the ramp of the plane; no chances would be taken that a bewildered hostage might wander off into the night or blunder into the aircraft's engines.

As the hostages straggled out, the heads of each family were stopped at the ramp and asked to check that all their kin were present. Captain Bacos, the civilian pilot of Flight 139, was quietly requested to perform the same task for his family – the crew of the airliner. Behind them, the old terminal was empty but for the bodies of six terrorists, among them Gabriele Kröcher-Tiedemann and a blond-haired man, Wilfried Böse, both members of the Baader-Meinhof gang. Seven other terrorists, who were at Entebbe to meet the hostages when they first arrived, also died.

It took seven minutes to load the precious cargo of humanity, while a pick-up truck, brought 3000 miles specially for the purpose, ferried out the dead and wounded, including Netanyahu. The paratroopers made a last check of the main building, then signalled the aircrew to close up and go. At 2352 hours, the craft was airborne and on its way to Nairobi. Inside, doctors worked over seven wounded hostages. Two

had died during the rescue and a third, Mrs Dora Bloch, moved to a hospital in Uganda's capital, Kampala, before the raid, was later murdered.

At the other end of the airfield, an infantry team fired machine-gun bursts into seven Ugandan Air Force MiGs. There was no point in tempting Ugandan pilots into pursuit. The paratroopers reloaded their vehicles and equipment. Their job done, they were airborne at 0012 hours on the 4th.

The tired airmen in the cockpit were astonished to see people in the streets below waving and clapping

Thirty minutes after the final departure, the communications Boeing and the first Hercules touched down at Nairobi and taxied to the fuel tanks in a quiet corner of the airport. Sergeant Hershko, who was seriously wounded, was transferred to the hospital Boeing. Two hostages whose wounds needed immediate care in a fully equipped hospital were loaded into a waiting station wagon and taken into Nairobi. At 0204 the remaining passengers and crew of Flight 139 were airborne on the last leg of their long journey home. In Lieutenant-Colonel 'S's' aircraft, the paratroopers were sunk in their own private thoughts. Despite all the efforts of the doctors, Netanyahu was dead. The mission was later renamed Operation Jonathan in his memory.

Early in the morning, the lead Hercules flew low over Eilat, at the southern tip of Israel. The tired airmen in the cockpit were astonished to see people in the streets below waving and clapping. The plane flew on to land at an air force base in central Israel. Here, the hostages were fed and given a chance to shake off the trauma. The wounded were taken off to hospital, and psychologists circulated among the rest, giving help where it was needed.

In a corner of the same airfield, the three combat teams unloaded their vehicles and equipment. They would return to their own bases, hardly aware of the excitement in Israel over their achievement.

It was mid-morning when a Hercules transport of the Israeli Air Force touched down at Lod airport outside Tel Aviv, rolled to a stop and lowered its rear ramp to release its cargo of men, women and children into the outstretched arms of their relatives and friends, watched by a crowd of thousands. The ordeal was over.

By the rescue of the hostages, the Israelis had gone some way to showing the rest of the world that terrorism could be met and defeated by the clinical application of controlled force.

THE AUTHOR Major Louis Williams, an editor with long experience in publications on military subjects, is a senior press officer with the Israeli Defence Force Spokesman's reserve unit. A fuller version of this article appears in the IDF Journal of May 1985.

WILD WEASELS

In their F-105 Thunderchiefs the pilots of the 44th Tactical Fighter Squadron flew some of the most hazardous missions undertaken by the US Air Force in Vietnam

OPERATION 'Rolling Thunder', the United States Air Force (USAF) bombing offensive against North Vietnam from 1965 until 1968, was carried out in the face of an ever-growing threat from North Vietnamese air-defence systems. Initially, opposition was weak, but by the end of 1967 North Vietnam had deployed a total of more than 6500 anti-aircraft (AA) guns, ranging in calibre from 37mm up to 100mm, about 200 SA-2 Guideline surface-to-air missile (SAM) sites, and 40 interceptor aircraft. The AA guns and fighters could be dealt with using traditional methods: by assigning flak-suppression aircraft to accompany

the bombing force, and providing an escort of air-superiority fighters. The latter measure had proved to be particularly effective, as was shown by the reduction of the North Vietnamese interceptor force from a strength of nearly 100 aircraft in the spring of 1967, to under half that figure by the end of the year. However, SAMs were a comparatively new air-defence system that called for innovative counter-measures.

It was found that the SA-2s could be defeated by jamming their guidance radars and even, under certain conditions, outmanoeuvred in flight, but by far the surest method of dealing with them was to attack and destroy the missiles on their launchers before they could be fired against American aircraft. This defence-suppression mission, code-named 'Iron Hand', was the task of the 'Wild Weasel' crews flying F-105 Thunderchiefs, or 'Thuds' as they were invariably nicknamed in Southeast Asia. 'They had the most demanding job and the most hazardous,' thought Seventh Air Force commander General William Momyer, 'These flights were the first into the target area and the last out.' Moreover, in the autumn of 1967, just as the threat from enemy interceptors had been all but mastered, that from the SAMs intensified . It was at this crucial stage of the air war that the USAF's 44th Tactical Fighter Squadron (44th TFS), nicknamed the 'Vampires', became the 388th Tactical Fighter Wing's specialised Wild Weasel unit at Korat air force base in Thailand.

In December 1964 the 44th TFS became one of the first USAF Thunderchief squadrons to become involved in the war in Southeast Asia when six of its F-105s deployed from Okinawa to Da Nang in the Republic of Vietnam. On Christmas Day, the detachment flew its first combat mission, a dive-bombing attack on North Vietnamese Army barracks at Tchepone in Laos. A larger-scale air strike followed on 13 January 1965, the target being a bridge at Ban Ken, also in Laos. This had been identified as a potential chokepoint on the communications network linking North and South Vietnam through ostensibly neutral territory, which was to become known by the Americans as the Ho Chi Minh Trail. Sixteen F-105s drawn from the 44th TFS and the 67th TFS made up the bombing force. They were accompanied by eight F-100s armed with cluster bombs for flak suppression, one RF-101 Voodoo to act as pathfinder and another to obtain post-strike reconnaissance photos.

The first eight F-105s, armed with 750lb bombs, succeeded in cutting the bridge. Consequently, the following eight Thuds, carrying both bombs and two AGM-12B Bullpup air-to-surface missiles, switched their attack to the enemy's AA gun emplacements that the F-100s had not succeeded in completely silencing. This proved to be a tactical error. Each aircraft needed to make at least three passes to release its ordnance and, moreover, had to descend to within lethal range of the AA fire in order to guide its missiles onto the targets. As a result, one F-105 was shot down and four others were damaged for no

44TH TFS, USAF

The history of the 44th Tactical Fighter Squadron (44th TFS) began in January 1941 when the 44th Pursuit Squadron was activated as part of the 18th Pursuit Group. Operating Curtiss P-40s from Bellows Field, Hawaii, the unit suffered considerable losses during the Japanese attack on Pearl Harbor.
Renamed the 44th Fighter Squadron, it began operations from Guadalcanal in the Solomon Islands at the end of 1942.
In 1944 the squadron re-equipped with P-38 Lightnings, and transferred to the Philippines in 1945.
The war over, the 44th Fighter Squadron remained in the Philippines as part of the 18th Fighter Group, operating the P-51 Mustang, the P-47 Thunderbolt, and its first jet, the F-80 Shooting Star. In 1954 the squadron converted to F-86 Sabres, moving with them to Kadena Air Base on Okinawa the following year. F-100 Super Sabres were received in 1957, and in 1963 the unit, by then designated the 44th TFS, part of the 18th Tactical Fighter Wing (TFW), was re-equipped with F-105 Thunderchiefs.
After the Vietnam War the Vampires rejoined the 18th TFW at Kadena on Okinawa to operate F4-D Phantoms. In 1980 they re-equipped with F-15 Eagle air-superiority fighters, which today proudly carry the unit's vampire insignia (above).

Far left above: F-105 crews of the 44th TFS pose for the camera in front of the squadron's distinctive vampire insignia at Korat air base in April 1967. Left: A line of F-105 Thunderchiefs of the 44th TFS at Korat. Left above: View from a Thunderchief of a knocked-out bridge in North Vietnam.

THUNDERCHIEF

The last aircraft built by Republic before the company became part of Fairchild Hiller, the F-105 Thunderchief was already on the drawing-board when its predecessor, the F-84F Thunderstreak, went into service in 1954. The F-105 was an ambitious and complex aircraft – more than 65,000 components went into the plane and more than five million engineering man-hours were spent in its creation. In compensation, it set standards of performance, ordnance and electronics capability, and mission adaptability which were only to be bettered in the late 1970s.

The prototype Thunderchief, powered by a Pratt & Whitney J57-25 engine, flew on 22 October 1955 and exceeded Mach 1. The Area Rule for shaping aircraft for minimum transonic or supersonic drag was then applied to the F-105 and a new version, incorporating a J75-P-3 engine, flew on 26 May 1956 and achieved a speed exceeding Mach 2. Introduced into service as the F-105B, this version was superseded by the F-105D in 1959, now powered by the new Pratt & Whitney J75-P-19W turbojet.

After 1966 nearly all the USAF's F-105Ds were flying combat missions over Vietnam. Fitted with 17 stores points, they were able to carry virtually every strategic air-to-ground weapon of the USAF. These planes were later joined by two-seater F-105Fs fitted out as Wild Weasel electronic warfare platforms and featuring the new Thunderstick computerised fire-control system.

The F-105s played a major part in air strikes on North Vietnam, and it was only the toll exacted by being constantly in the front line that caused them to be withdrawn in 1970.

worthwhile return, since the bridge had already been destroyed. Yet the mission's greatest mistake was made not by the Thud pilots, whose only fault had been a commendable excess of enthusiasm, but by the staff planners. This became apparent three days later, when the North Vietnamese converted the top of a dam just upstream of the Ban Ken bridge into an alternative route, thus completely negating the results of the bombing.

The 44th TFS remained in the combat theatre on temporary duty until May 1965, moving from Da Nang to Korat air force base in Thailand. One of its most memorable missions during this period was the attack on the Thanh Hoa bridge in Annam Province, North Vietnam, on 3 April 1965. This massive structure, spanning the Song Ma river, was known in Vietnamese as the Ham Rung (Dragon's Jaw). The 79-aircraft strong strike force was led by Lieutenant-Colonel Robinson Risner of the 67th TFS and included 46 F-105s armed with 750lb bombs and Bullpup missiles. The missile-armed aircraft were first into the target area, each Thud having to make two firing passes as the Bullpups needed to be guided individually.

The No.3 pilot in the third flight, Captain Bill Mayerholt of the 44th TFS, was surprised to see that the bridge was still undamaged as he guided his first missile onto the target. However, after watching the

Bullpup's 250lb explosive warhead detonate against the bridge's superstructure and do no more damage than scorch the steel and concrete, he wondered no more. It was like shooting shotgun pellets at a Sherman tank, he later reflected. In all, 32 missiles and 120 bombs had been aimed at the bridge and many of them had hit, yet it remained standing. It was only when laser-guided bombs were employed during the Linebacker I campaign in the spring of 1972 that American airmen succeeded in making any impression on this formidable structure.

In May 1965 the 44th TFS's period of temporary duty in Southeast Asia came to an end and it was not until April 1967 that the unit returned to the combat theatre. The squadron was then assigned to the 388th Tactical Fighter Wing at Korat, and for the following six months was employed in a tactical bombing role against targets in North Vietnam. Enemy interceptors were especially active during this period, and on 13 May one of the 44th TFS pilots was credited with the squadron's only MiG kill of the war. Major Maurice E. Seaver Jr. had just pulled out from his bomb run against the Vinh Yen army barracks when he saw a MiG-17, 1000ft ahead of him at the 10 o'clock position. Pulling in behind it, Seaver opened fire with his 20mm Vulcan cannon. The North Vietnamese pilot had not spotted him and took no evasive action. Seaver's fire took immediate effect. The North Viet-

Left: A flight of F-105 Thunderchiefs roars into action against a North Vietnamese railway bridge in 1965. Ordnance on the aircraft includes conventional bombs and AGM-12 air-to-surface Bullpup missiles. Below: The Princess Cheri, an F-105D of the 44th TFS. The F-105D was the definitive single-seat model of Thunderchief and over 600 of this variant were produced. The F-105D could carry a wide range of stores including bombs, missiles, mines, napalm and rockets. The F-105D was also armed with an M-61 20mm six-barrelled rotary cannon, mounted in the nose.

Thanh Hoa raid
44th TFS, 3 April 1965

Five months after its deployment in Vietnam, the 44th TFS participated in an air strike against the Thanh Hoa bridge. The mission was typical of long-range air-refuelled bombing missions flown from Thailand.

CHINA

NORTH VIETNAM

Lang Son

Dien Bien Phu

Hanoi

Haiphong

Song Ma

LAOS

Thanh Hoa bridge

F-105s

Vinh

GULF OF TONKIN

F-100s

Dong Hoi

DMZ

F-105s and KC-135 tankers

Tchepone

Da Nang

THAILAND

✈ Takhli

✈ Korat

CAMBODIA

SOUTH VIETNAM

Key
Thanh Hoa raid, 3 April 1965

aircraft to detect the SA-2 sites' radar emissions and determine their position so that they could be attacked. It was the duty of the F-105's backseater (officially titled the electronic warfare officer, but more usually known as 'the Bear') to manage this equipment and direct his pilot into an attack. The SAM sites could be dealt with from stand-off ranges, by launching AGM-45A Shrike anti-radiation missiles against their radars. Alternatively, the Wild Weasels could make a direct attack on the entire complex, using free-fall bombs and cannon fire. Often though, the mere threat of a Shrike-armed Wild Weasel was sufficient to cause the North Vietnamese missile crews to shut down their radars. However, an optical tracking device for the SA-2 had recently been introduced as a partially effective counter-measure to the Wild Weasel's Shrike tactics.

Captain Don Carson has written a graphic account of one of the 44th TFS's Iron Hand missions over North Vietnam:

'"SAMs at two and five... guns at three", my Bear, Don Brian, coolly calls over the intercom, telling me where the threat is located.

'I light up the afterburner and our speed approaches 600 knots. I turn towards the SAM site, which is looking at my flight of four Weasels with its radar. We have the green light in the outboard weapons pylon buttons, indicating that

Below: US Thunderchief pilot Clarence H. Hoggard of the 44th TFS prepares to leave the cockpit of Princess Cheri after a mission over North Vietnam in July 1967. By 1967 Hoggard had flown over 100 missions with the Princess.

namese fighter broke sharply to the right and its wing exploded. From first to last, the combat had lasted just 90 seconds. It had been an outstandingly successful day for the USAF's fighter pilots, with a total of seven MiG-17s shot down – five of them by Thud pilots. Although the F-105 had not been designed for fighter-versus-fighter combat, it often proved to be a dangerous antagonist and 25 North Vietnamese fighters were shot down by Thuds during the conflict.

In October 1967 the 44th TFS took over the Wild Weasel missions for the entire 388th TFW, adopting the nickname Vampires which was also used as a radio callsign. They flew the F-105F two-seat version of the Thud, which had been specially modified for the defence-suppression role. Radar-homing and warning receivers were fitted, which enabled the when we're in range and position, we are armed and ready to fire our AGM-45 Shrike anti-radiation missiles.

'"SAMs at 12 o'clock... a three ringer." My Bear now has the SAM battery off our nose and is getting very strong signals on his indicating equipment. We press in, pull up our F-105 at the proper range and hose off a pair of Shrikes just as the SAM site fires at our flight. My skin crawls as the rattlesnake sound in my headset and the flash of the warning-gear light tells me that it is for real this time.

'"Valid launch.... 12 o'clock," yells my Bear. "Vampires... take it down," I call to my flight as I nose over and unload. "Taking it down" is the standard Wild Weasel manoeuvre of rapidly diving in full afterburner and picking up speed to avoid the SAMs being guided onto your aircraft.

'I see clouds of dust and the "telephone poles" [SA-2s] trailing fire as they climb. Our Shrikes are still guiding directly toward the radar van which controls them. Suddenly, however, the SAMs appear to go unguided and streak off well above our flight. This means the radar control van had shut down in hopes of foiling our Shrikes, but it doesn't work. Our Shrikes impact the van, and dust and smoke rises to mark the target area clearly.'

Ignoring the flak from gun emplacements ringing the SAM site, Carson's flight then completed its destruction by bombing, before heading out of the area to

Nor were the enemy air defences less active by night than during daylight. However, Carson thought that because it was easier to see a SAM or AA gunfire at night, the pilot then had more time to react and this balanced out the handicaps of night operations. As the threat from radar-directed SA-2s was just as great during night missions, the Commando Nail F-105Fs were usually accompanied by a Wild Weasel escort. Carson remembered one such night mission in 1968:

'We trolled back and forth along the target area, listening and looking for any enemy SAM or AA activity. This was not unlike trolling for fish, except this time we were the bait. A couple of strobes from a radar-guided gun and a low-pulse repetition-frequency SAM radar light indicated that someone knew we were there. They probably also knew that since we were alone and carried no jamming pods, we were a Weasel bird.'

The Shrike lit off with a roar and left the F-105 with a burst of speed and a trail of brilliant fire

As the first Ryan's Raider approached the target area, enemy activity increased, with heavy fire from 37mm and 57mm AA guns. Then Don Brian picked up a strong SAM signal and his pilot launched a Shrike:

'It lit off with a roar and left the F-105 with a burst of speed and a trail of brilliant fire. I waited for Don to

Below: An F-105G, a twin-seat variant of the Thunderchief, on an 'Iron Hand' anti-SAM mission over Laos in December 1972. The aircraft is armed with two anti-radiation missile types: the outboard station mounts an AGM-45 Shrike and the inboard station carries the larger AGM-78 Standard ARM.

rendezvous with a tanker aircraft in order to top-up their tanks for the flight back to Korat.

As well as controlling the Wild Weasel flights, the 44th TFS was responsible for Ryan's Raiders, a select force of six F-105Fs converted under project 'Commando Nail' to specialised night-bombing aircraft for missions over North Vietnam. The aircraft radars were modified to give an expanded picture of the ground, which was of sharper definition than that obtained by the standard set. Using this information, the backseater was able to direct his pilot into a blind bombing-run against targets with a good radar return. The Commando Nail F-105Fs' weapons circuits had been modified to allow the backseater to release the bombload – the job of the pilot on standard aircraft. Ryan's Raider missions, nicknamed after General John D. Ryan, the C-in-C Pacific Air Forces, who originated the project, could be extremely hazardous. Don Carson thought:

'You've never lived until you've battled the Southeast Asia weather at night. A night thunderstorm, tanker join-up and aerial refuelling – with lightning and St Elmo's fire crackling around your canopy and pitot tube until they glowed with an eerie purple light – could be more frightening than the arcing red balls of 37mm or 57mm guns.'

call the SAM launch, hoping the Shrike would get there first. The Shrike guided and, as we saw it impact, the SAM signal suddenly ceased.'

In April 1968 American bombing was limited to the southern provinces of North Vietnam, thus putting the heavily-defended Hanoi and Haiphong areas out of bounds. This measure was but a prelude to the complete halt of bombing raids against North Vietnam, which came into force at the end of October. During that month, the 44th TFS had been reassigned to the 355th TFW at Takhli air force base in Thailand; a logical move since the other squadrons of the 388th TFW had converted onto the F-4E Phantom, whereas the Vampires' new wing continued to fly Thuds. The transition also marked the end of the 44th TFS's service as a Wild Weasel squadron. Because US strike forces no longer penetrated into the high-threat areas, the Weasels' services could be delegated to specialised flights within each squadron. Accordingly, the Vampires reverted to the tactical bombing role until the squadron was withdrawn from the combat theatre in March 1971.

THE AUTHOR Anthony Robinson was formerly on the staff of the RAF Museum, Hendon and is now a freelance military aviation writer. He has edited the books *Aerial Warfare* and the *Dictionary of Aviation*.

Above: Personal insignia were popular with the 44th's pilots and aircraft were decorated with a variety of jokey motifs.

CARLSONS

RAIDERS

MARINE RAIDERS

During the 1930s, the US Marine Corps experimented with the idea of using raider forces to carry out unconventional activities behind enemy lines, and in January 1942 the concept reached fruition when the 1st Battalion, 5th Marines was retitled the 1st Separate Battalion; a month later, a Marine officer, Lieutenant-General Evans F. Carlson, was ordered to raise men to form the 2nd Separate Battalion. Lieutenant Merritt A. Edson, a World War I veteran and ex-pilot, was placed in charge of the 1st Battalion.

In the following month, the units were redesignated the 1st and 2nd Raider Battalions, and prepared for action. Each battalion consisted of over 850 officers and men divided between six rifle companies, and a small headquarters. Apart from standard infantry weapons and equipment, the raiders used shotguns, bangalore torpedoes, chainsaws and rubber dinghies.

The raiders were formed to carry out three specific types of operation: spearheading amphibious landings; undertaking hit-and-run attacks on enemy-held islands; and launching long-term guerrilla-style sorties behind enemy lines. By mid-1942 both battalions were in the field. In August Carlson's raiders hit Makin Island and Edson's men fought on Tulagi. The success of the raiders encouraged certain officers to request the formation of other units. Although there was official opposition to the creation of further 'elites within an elite', other units were raised and formed into the 1st and 2nd Raider Regiments. *Above: The badge of the 1st Raider Regiment.*

In November 1942 the 2nd Marine Raider Battalion landed on Guadalcanal to begin a savage month-long battle against the Japanese

ON 20 SEPTEMBER 1942, Carlson's Raiders, the 2nd Marine Raider Battalion, landed at Espiritu Santo in the New Hebrides, some 400 miles short of their destination, the embattled island of Guadalcanal, part of the Solomon Islands in the south Pacific. After a final reconnaissance flight over the area, Carlson briefed his company commanders on their mission:

'Soon, my small command group and two companies, C and E, will board two destroyers and sail for Aola bay, 40 miles east of the island's Lunga river. From there, we will advance inland and provide security for a naval construction battalion building an airfield. This mission is to last two days and then we will return to Espiritu Santo.'

Nobody at the meeting believed that the job would be over so quickly, as the forces on the island needed all the help they could get in the face of a stubborn foe. US troops had been on Guadalcanal since early August when, in the first American offensive of the Pacific campaign, the 1st US Marine Division under Major-General Alexander Vandegrift had made a relatively unopposed landing. Since then, however, the Japanese had flooded the island with reinforcements, and launched a series of counter-blasts to throw the Americans back into the sea.

The raider companies earmarked for the job reached Guadalcanal on 4 November, a day later than planned as the Japanese had landed a strong body of reinforcements in the area on the previous day. On the 5th, Carlson's men were relieved by army units and ordered to patrol inland to the village of Reko, lying some 16 miles away. In the meantime, my company, B, and D Company had sailed for Aola, landing on the 7th. There were now four companies ashore and these would soon be reinforced by A and F Companies.

Ordered to join Carlson, B and D Companies set off

RAIDERS ON MAKIN

At 0300 hours on 17 August 1942, two US submarines, *Nautilus* and *Argonaut*, hove to some 500m off the shore of Makin, a tiny atoll in the Gilbert Islands. Aboard the boats were 13 officers and 208 men of the 2nd Raider Battalion under the command of Evans Carlson; their mission was to hit the Japanese garrison, estimated at 70 men, gather intelligence, destroy installations and then withdraw.

The landings on the south shore of Butaritari Island in the atoll were unchallenged and Carlson ordered A Company to push inland where they seized key buildings and dock facilities. The company then moved south, but ran into stiff opposition.

By early afternoon, Carlson ordered his raiders to fall back on the re-embarkation beaches. However, heavy surf prevented the assault teams from reaching the subs and Carlson was forced to stay on the island. On the following morning, resigned to another day ashore, Carlson despatched patrols to scour the island. One team uncovered an enemy supply cache, which they destroyed. Other patrols recovered the bodies of 11 raiders and polished off the remnants of Japanese resistance. By nightfall, the raiders were reunited with the submarines. Mission accomplished.

Page 1001: A month after landing on Guadalcanal (below), members of Carlson's Raiders display their captured war trophies (above). Above, far left: Marines escort Japanese prisoners back to base. Far left: Prior to Guadalcanal, Carlson's men hit enemy installations on Makin. Top: The objective seen through the periscope of the US submarine *Nautilus*, used to carry the raiders to Makin. Above: A gruelling pre-raid route march. Left: Carlson (left) is congratulated after the Makin mission.

THE RAIDER'S LEADER

Evans F. Carlson, (below) the famed leader of the 2nd Raider Battalion in World War II, was born in 1896 and enlisted in the US Army at the age of 16. Seeing action in the Great War, he was awarded the Purple Heart for battle wounds.

He joined the Marines as a private in 1922 and was commissioned as a second lieutenant during the following year.

During a tour of duty in China at the end of the decade, he was awarded the Yangtze Service Medal and the Expeditionary Medal. In 1930 he was ordered to Nicaragua where he won his first Navy Cross for leading a dozen men against 100 bandits.

Carlson left the Marines briefly in 1939 after a particularly hazardous third tour of duty in which he won the China Service Medal. Recommissioned as a major in 1941, Carlson was placed in charge of the 2nd Raider Battalion, a unit he led until its disbandment in 1944. Carlson won a Gold Star in lieu of a second Navy Cross for his part in the attack on Makin Island in 1942. Three months later, a further Gold Star was awarded for his heroism and leadership on Guadalcanal.

After being forced to retire on 1 July 1946 as a result of wounds received on Saipan, where he won a second Purple Heart, Carlson was promoted to the rank of brigadier-general on the retired list, for his outstanding combat record.

into the jungle only to be hit by enemy smallarms fire. D Company deployed to deal with the threat while the other raider company continued to Reko. After four hours of hard going, we crossed the Bokokimbo river, the last barrier between us and Carlson's base.

During the night, a few Japanese tried to penetrate our lines, but all were shot. On the morning of the 8th, three raider companies were sent out on patrol to the north, west and south of our base and all had brushes with the enemy. The next day the raiders moved up to the village of Kema. From there were sent out the usual patrols, but one company was sent to the village of Tasimboko to pick up much-needed supplies delivered by sea from Aola. Escorted by parties of raiders, local natives back-packed the rations to our camp. Each man filled his extra socks with food and blocks of thick chocolate.

At dawn on the 9th, we moved forward to Binu, a village on the Balesuna river, south of where the Japanese were engaging the 7th Marines and 164th Infantry. Although exhausted, our gourmet cooks put some spark in the air with their activities. Rice was prepared with raisins, fatback and chocolate – every way a raider could dream up. That night was a really special occasion: the 167th anniversary of our corps' foundation.

We had several encounters with the enemy on the next day. It was B Company's turn to provide base security and stand ready to assist any raiders in trouble; other companies were sent out on the usual patrols. It was not long before they bumped into the Japanese. C Company had hardly cleared our lines before one Japanese soldier ran into our outpost and got killed for his pains. He seemed healthy, unlike the weak and anaemic Japanese we had seen before, and was probably a member of the reinforcements that had just landed on the island. Within the hour, all the patrols were engaged and our base was under direct attack.

D Company ran into trouble. Pinned down by accurate mortar fire, casualties mounted

The first radio message came in from C Company. The CO reported that his men had run into a battalion-sized enemy unit armed with machine guns and mortars. Although the raiders had surprised the Japanese, inflicting heavy casualties, they had lost five men killed and several wounded. Carlson believed that the enemy was moving south from the mouth of the Metapona river, where the 7th Marines and 164th Infantry had given them a bloody nose. Carlson ordered Captain R.E. Washburn, the leader of E Company, to move his men south along the river, and moved C Company along the river's eastern bank. Both company commanders were told to rendezvous at a point north of Asamana village.

Washburn was fortunate. Catching two Japanese companies in the process of crossing the river, he ordered Lieutenant Evans Carlson, the CO's son, to position his heavy weapons on the river bank in plain view of the unwary enemy. Opening fire, his men inflicted heavy casualties, but after a few minutes they came under accurate machine-gun fire. Washburn then committed Lieutenant Clelland Early's platoon to the fight and it quickly silenced the Japanese fire.

Elsewhere, D Company ran into trouble as it was crossing a wide, flat clearing. Pinned down by accurate mortar fire, casualties mounted. After much scurrying around, identifying the dead and admi-

nistering first-aid to the wounded, Platoon Sergeant George Schrier began to evacuate his men. Carlson ordered my men to assist the withdrawal, but we had gone less than 100yds before we sighted Schrier leading the remnants of D Company back to base.

During the night I received orders to move the rest of B Company up to Washburn's position. A heavy rain was falling and, although the first leg of our journey was less than two-and-a-half miles, it was through thick jungle. The trail wound around banyan trees and briars, but just after daybreak we left the jungle and entered Carlson's base, sited in a coconut grove. After a short break, Carlson and Major John M. Mather, an Australian officer in charge of Sergeant Major Vouza and his natives, joined B Company and we continued on into Asamana. F and C Companies returned to Binu, where E Company was preparing to join us for the march into Asamana.

Near the river, some raiders spotted three Japanese in a canoe. As it reached the right spot, the lead team jumped the canoe, killing one man and capturing the other two. A short time later, Lieutenant Bill Does' platoon skirmished through the village, receiving sporadic smallarms fire. The rest of my company came up and was assigned defensive positions; Washburn's men took charge of the other half of the village. With Corporal McCall's squad, I went back across the river to organise some defences and then hiked back to my command post.

Dead tired, I ate a D-bar, unrolled my shelter, poncho and blanket, and then fell into a deep sleep. About midnight, a rifle shot cracked through the hut, but I was too tired to be bothered. Later, however, several rounds came through the walls and I got on my knees to dig a prone foxhole. Whilst digging, I uncovered the body of a dead Japanese. Firing was pretty general by this stage; most of it came from around McCall's position.

At daybreak, Gunnery Sergeant Cone, Corporal Needham and I made our rounds of the village. Because of heavy rainfall during the night, the river was too swollen to wade. Captain Green gave it a try and almost drowned, but Private Royal, our best swimmer, swam across with a rope in his mouth and tied it to a boat. We ferried across the river; later, our demolition experts felled a tree to make a permanent bridge. McCall's squad had killed 13 Japanese during the night, and by the afternoon of the 13th, Green's platoon had accounted for seven and Doe's nine. Washburn had also killed a similar number.

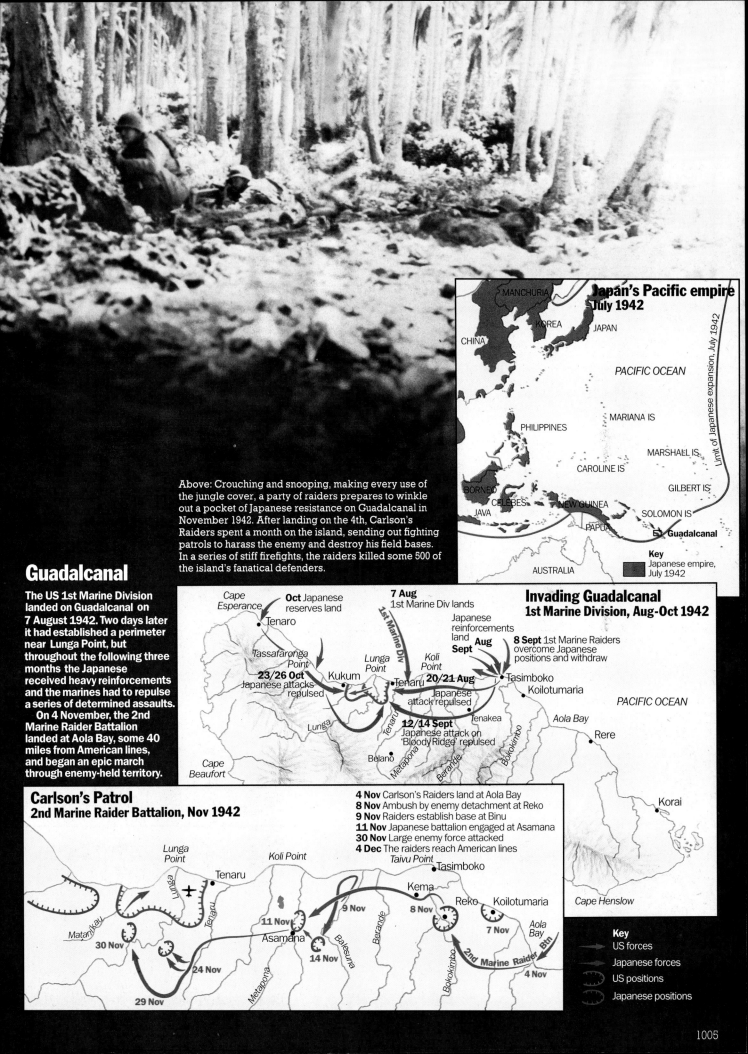

Above: Crouching and snooping, making every use of the jungle cover, a party of raiders prepares to winkle out a pocket of Japanese resistance on Guadalcanal in November 1942. After landing on the 4th, Carlson's Raiders spent a month on the island, sending out fighting patrols to harass the enemy and destroy his field bases. In a series of stiff firefights, the raiders killed some 500 of the island's fanatical defenders.

Japan's Pacific empire
July 1942

MANCHURIA
KOREA
JAPAN
CHINA
PACIFIC OCEAN
Limit of Japanese expansion, July 1942
MARIANA IS
PHILIPPINES
MARSHALL IS
CAROLINE IS
GILBERT IS
BORNEO
NEW GUINEA
CELEBES
JAVA
SOLOMON IS
PAPUA
Guadalcanal
Key
Japanese empire, July 1942
AUSTRALIA

Guadalcanal

The US 1st Marine Division landed on Guadalcanal on 7 August 1942. Two days later it had established a perimeter near Lunga Point, but throughout the following three months the Japanese received heavy reinforcements and the marines had to repulse a series of determined assaults.

On 4 November, the 2nd Marine Raider Battalion landed at Aola Bay, some 40 miles from American lines, and began an epic march through enemy-held territory.

Invading Guadalcanal
1st Marine Division, Aug-Oct 1942

Cape Esperance
Oct Japanese reserves land
7 Aug 1st Marine Div lands
Tenaro
Japanese reinforcements land
Aug
Sept
8 Sept 1st Marine Raiders overcome Japanese positions and withdraw
Tassafaronga Point
1st Marine Div
Lunga Point
Koli Point
23/26 Oct Japanese attacks repulsed
Kukum
Tenaru
20/21 Aug Japanese attack repulsed
Tasimboko
Koilotumaria
PACIFIC OCEAN
Lunga
Tenakea
Aola Bay
Rere
12/14 Sept Japanese attack on 'Bloody Ridge' repulsed
Belano
Metapona
Berande
Bokokimbo
Cape Beaufort
Korai

Carlson's Patrol
2nd Marine Raider Battalion, Nov 1942

4 Nov Carlson's Raiders land at Aola Bay
8 Nov Ambush by enemy detachment at Reko
9 Nov Raiders establish base at Binu
11 Nov Japanese battalion engaged at Asamana
30 Nov Large enemy force attacked
4 Dec The raiders reach American lines

Lunga Point
Koli Point
Taivu Point
Tasimboko
Tenaru
Kema
Lunga
Tenaru
9 Nov
11 Nov
Reko
Koilotumaria
Asamana
Berande
8 Nov
7 Nov
Aola Bay
Matanikau
30 Nov
Balesuna
14 Nov
Bokokimbo
Cape Henslow
24 Nov
2nd Marine Raider Btn
29 Nov
Metapona
4 Nov

Key
US forces
Japanese forces
US positions
Japanese positions

Just after noon, we saw a flight of enemy dive-bombers and fighters overhead; our naval and shore-based anti-aircraft shells filled the sky. Our Wildcats were dogfighting with Japanese Zeroes. Ashore it was relatively quiet, aside from artillery and anti-aircraft fire. However, our naval guns were blasting away and, shortly after midnight, a huge flash lit up the night sky. We imagined that the powder room of a ship had exploded. It seemed that a big naval battle was taking place and that the Japanese were trying to land more reinforcements.

During the morning of 14 November, three companies and Carlson's small headquarters patrolled back to Binu where we drew rations. With security posted, we all went down to the river to wash our clothes and get rid of the stench of the jungle. Under the supervision of Mather, some 200 natives were also drawing rations and being briefed for their next assignment. Two native guides were posted to each raider company while the rest, some armed with Lee Enfield and Japanese rifles, were used to bring up supplies under the watchful eye of Vouza.

Later, we heard that one scout had seen 15 Japanese camped just off the trail that led south from our base, and Carlson ordered Schwerin's F Company to patrol the area. Meanwhile, B Company escorted Carlson to the village of Volimuva, the headquarters of the 7th Marines, to see their commander, Colonel Sims. After a discussion, Carlson was given permission to move back to Asamana and patrol to the south and west of the village, while the 7th Marines covered an area to the east of the Metapona river.

When Schwerin returned to base, he had a remarkable story to tell. His scout had led the company to a natural defile that was guarded by a lone sentry. From a safe point, they had observed the camp until the sentry went for chow, and then slipped in, killing every Japanese in sight. Schwerin's men also picked up some valuable intelligence, including the personal effects of Major-General Kawaguchi, the senior Japanese officer in the area.

On the 17th Carlson led D Company, by this stage under the command of Captain Joe Griffith, into unexplored territory, to a point some 10 miles west of our base. After being ordered to rendezvous with the 1st Marine Division, Carlson and his men double-timed back to our base. Wet with sweat, dirty and exhausted, they refreshed themselves and then started out again, heading for the beach five miles away. There, Carlson was taken to the division's HQ. He returned on the next day with his orders: his mission was to establish a base on the Tenaru river and then patrol around that area and the Lunga river.

We placed two machine guns on a line with the enemy and started firing

On the following day, all the raiders, with the exception of B and F Companies, started out for the upper Tenaru. After spending the night on the trail near the upper Nalimbiu river, the column then moved into the new camp, a few miles south of Henderson airfield. Later, B and F Companies moved up. Between the 20th and 24th, the raiders set up their defences and received the occasional visitor. Lieutenant-Colonel 'Chesty' Puller visited Carlson, and I received a large can of fruit cocktail from Captain Don Peppard – it was delicious beyond words. However, patrols were sent out and on the

26th members of B Company brought in 100 enemy rifles and seven pistols.

On the 28th, after we had moved our base four miles to the west, B and D Companies went out to interdict a Japanese supply route known as the east-west trail. After crossing the upper Tenaru, the columns climbed the steep side of Mombula mountain by a twisting, turning, slippery trail. While B Company established positions across this route, Griffith's men set up positions along the same path but nearer the river, at the base of the mountain. After a quiet night, we started back to base, but we met a friendly scout en route and he guided us to where F Company was fighting a strong enemy force.

One squad, led by Corporal John Yancey, had already advanced through one Japanese position and was tackling another when we finally arrived. Yancey's men accounted for most of the enemy's 75 dead. Later I heard that the company had stumbled into a row of stacked rifles in the dark and killed most of the Japanese as they were running for their weapons. While F Company tidied up, I went over to see the 75mm mountain gun, known as 'Pistol Pete', which had been shooting down our aircraft on Henderson Field. It was still in good shape, as was a 37mm anti-aircraft gun located nearby. The rain poured down during the night, and the mountain air was cold and bitter. After many attempts, we got a fire going to fight off some of the chill.

The next morning, we started patrolling. I led a small patrol team up the Lunga river. At the end of a gorge, we sighted several Japanese sitting in a circle on a sand spit, jabbering away. Without being noticed, we placed two machine guns and several automatic weapons on a line with the enemy and started firing. After a couple of minutes, we moved in

Left: A patrol hacks a path through dense undergrowth on Guadalcanal. Below left: After a vicious exchange of fire, wary raiders enter an abandoned Japanese camp to search for vital intelligence. Below: Marines examine the bodies of enemy troops cut down during an abortive attempt to reinforce the island's beleaguered garrison. Suicidal bravery was no match for US firepower.

and examined the results. The Japanese were a pitiful sight: skinny, pale and sickly. One had a crutch and another had a rough splint on an injured leg. Our return to base was quick and without problems.

After dark, Carlson issued orders for 3 December. Washburn was told to move C, D and E Companies down the Lunga trail into the division's main perimeter. Captain Gary's recently-arrived A Company, along with Carlson, B and F Companies, were to patrol Mombula mountain.

About midday, the lead fire team reached the summit of the mountain and deployed to provide security, while the rest of the column climbed the steep slopes to reach their position. A Japanese combat patrol passed the fire team's perimeter and was engaged. Covered by their comrades, Lieutenant Miller and several raiders hurried forward but were caught by Japanese fire. Miller and three of his men were seriously wounded before the enemy troops were eliminated.

Carlson's Raiders had carried out a 150-mile trek and fought over a dozen actions against the Japanese

Bright and early the next morning, B Company led the way back to our main base. The lead fire team had advanced about 100yds beyond our perimeter when it was hit by heavy machine-gun fire. The lead raiders, Privates Farrar and Matelski, were killed instantly. Private Van Buren, trying to take out the enemy guns, jumped off the trail and into a gully. He was also hit. One man, Corporal Croft, had identified the enemy position, and suggested that Sergeant Potter should shake a branch to draw the unfriendly fire. Potter carried out this ploy several times, and each time the enemy fired, he accused Croft of ducking and not being able to spot the machine guns. After another try or two, however, Croft killed the gunner.

Before we moved off, B Company buried the dead, so A and F Companies took the lead. We had not gone far before the battalion surgeon, Dr Charles Robinson, asked to halt the column as Lieutenant Miller was failing fast. A little later, he was dead, and Carlson made his way from the front of the column, pulled a bible and US flag from his pack, and performed a short ceremony.

Slowly, B Company led the rear of the column down the trail and into the low ground near the Matanikau river. We were met by several ambulances on the way in and our stretcher cases were given a ride to the division hospital. We still had a few more miles to hike before reaching our bivouac area. On the morning of 5 December we reached the beach where our transport back to Espiritu Santo was waiting. After a long, tiring month on Guadalcanal, we were pulling out for a well-earned rest. In a period of four weeks, Carlson's Raiders had carried out a 150-mile trek through the jungle and fought over a dozen actions against the Japanese, killing 500 and driving the rest into the interior of the island. Although the battle for Guadalcanal was to last until 9 February 1943, by which stage the Japanese had suffered 25,000 dead, the raiders' operations had undermined the enemy's belief in final victory.

THE AUTHOR Major-General O.F. Peatross served with Carlson's Raiders in World War II, and saw service in Korea and Vietnam. During his long military career he was awarded seven personal decorations including three Legions of Merit.

NO.249 (GOLD COAST) SQUADRON

Formed in 1917 as Royal Naval Air Squadron, Killingholme, it was not until 18 August 1918 that the unit became No.249 Squadron, Royal Air Force. No.249 operated from Dundee until being disbanded on 8 October 1919. Brought out of retirement on 16 May 1940, No.249 was re-formed as a gift fighter squadron from the Gold Coast at Church Fenton. After flying Spitfires for only a month, the squadron was equipped with Hurricanes, and on 3 July became operational, moving to Boscombe Down in August in time for the Battle of Britain. On 16 August 1940, Flight Lieutenant James B. Nicolson of No.249 won the only Victoria Cross ever awarded to Fighter Command when, although wounded and with his Hurricane ablaze, he proceeded to destroy his attacker, a Bf 110.
On 21 May 1941, the squadron was transferred by aircraft carrier to Malta where it played a decisive role in the air battles there. No.249 converted back to Vickers-Supermarine Spitfires in March 1942, and in October 1943 moved to Italy, carrying out sweeps over Albania and Yugoslavia. In September 1944 No.249 converted to Mustangs. Following a short spell in Yugoslavia, the squadron returned to Italy and was disbanded on 16 August 1945, having destroyed 244 enemy aircraft.
Above: The badge of No.249 Squadron: the motto translates as 'With fists and heels'.

BATTLE FOR MALTA

In the defence of Malta during World War II the pilots of No. 249 Squadron made a heroic stand against the might of the Axis air forces

BETWEEN MARCH and late June 1940, the air defence of Malta relied solely upon four Gladiator biplanes. On 21 June some Hurricanes arrived and were used to bolster Malta's defences against the Italian Regia Aeronautica's bombing raids. Six weeks later 12 Hurricanes of No. 148 Flight landed at Luqa. These and Malta's surviving fighters were formed into No. 261 Squadron.

In May 1941, following heavy engagements with both the Aeronautica and the Luftwaffe, the squadron's remaining Hurricanes were quickly incorpo-

rated into the newly-formed No. 185 Squadron. On 28 June, No. 126 Squadron was also reformed, operating from Ta'Qali airfield. A third squadron, No. 249, arrived from Britain when the aircraft carriers *Ark Royal* and *Furious* delivered several Fleet Air Arm Fulmars and 46 Hurricanes during Operation Splice on 21 May 1941.

During its service in Malta, No. 249 Squadron was to become a highly cosmopolitan unit. It came to lose its British identity, becoming an informal, if not casual, mixture of nationalities. Yet, as was often the case with such units, No. 249 continued to do its job, and to do it very effectively indeed. From May 1941 until it left Malta at the end of October 1943, No. 249 Squadron built up an impressive tally of Axis aircraft destroyed. Out of Malta's 10 top-scoring fighter pilots, five flew with the squadron, and between

Background: Takali airbase on Malta is pounded by Ju 88s operating from Sicily. The Regia Aeronautica and the Luftwaffe never succeeded in grounding Malta's air defence, however, even when it numbered only a handful of fighters. Far left: Flight Lieutenant Johnny Plagis, veteran pilot of No. 249 Squadron. Below: Although it was believed that Pilot Officer 'Screwball' Beurling had shot down the 1000th Axis aircraft over Malta, that distinction was finally accredited to Squadron Leader John Lynch, also of No. 249 Squadron, on 28 April 1943. Right: Pilots of the squadron's A Flight with a Hurricane.

them these pilots, hailing from Australia, New Zealand, Rhodesia and Canada, notched up a total of 62 confirmed 'kills'.

In his papers, Field Marshal Rommel was prompted to write of Malta that the island 'has the lives of many thousands of German and Italian soldiers on its conscience.' Both Britain and the Axis powers knew that control of Malta would have a crucial bearing on the campaigns in North Africa. Consequently, from 1940, Malta and the convoys which served her were subjected to relentless aerial attacks by German and Italian bombers based in Sicily. The Axis objectives were to sever the garrison's supply lines, thereby ensuring safe delivery of fuel and ammunition to Rommel in North Africa, and to destroy the Allied defences prior to an invasion of the island.

The heroic defence of Malta lasted three years, and the aerial warfare above her shores during 1941-42 must rank as the most vicious and uncompromising of the entire war. For the RAF, heavily out-numbered and short of supplies, it was a desperate fight for survival. Between March and May 1942 there were 803 air-raid alerts. According to II Fliegerkorps, 345 reconnaissance and 11,474 bomber/fighter sorties were flown against the island during the period 20 March to 28 April 1942. For a time the RAF could barely muster more than six fighters to counter the onslaught. In the face of such adversity the tenacity of No. 249 Squadron was to

become almost legendary. With the anti-aircraft defences, the RAF exacted a heavy toll of enemy machines. As an indication of Malta's incredible fighting spirit it is known that Field Marshal Kesselring confided to Maresciallo Ugo Cavallero, Chief of the Italian General Staff, that Luftwaffe aircrew who were engaged in daily sorties over Malta invariably developed a state of extreme tension, known to the Germans as 'Maltese sickness'.

On the RAF side, the veteran No. 249 pilot Squadron Leader Johnny Plagis is quoted as saying that he did not believe '... the Battle of Britain had anything over Malta!' No. 249 found itself fighting a ruthless battle, and one unpleasant aspect of it was the occasional practice on both sides of finishing off aircrew who had abandoned their aircraft. Wing Commander P.B. 'Laddie' Lucas, DSC, DFC, CBE, witnessed one such incident involving a Rhodesian pilot officer, Douglas Leggo:

'Bounced out of the sun by the German ace Neuhoff, whom 249 then shot down, Leggo rolled his Spitfire onto its back and parted company. His parachute opened immediately. As he descended earthwards, a lone Messerschmitt, appearing seemingly from nowhere, sprayed the canopy with tracer bullets in a callous gesture of murder. It was over in seconds...'

Less than a week later, Leggo's death was avenged by a Canadian pilot of No. 249. Laddie Lucas recalled:

'A Junkers 88 had been shot down southwest of the island. The aircraft had ditched in the sea, and now the crew of three were in a dinghy 10 miles or so from Delimara Point... as we headed home for Takali, my eye caught sight of a single Spitfire away to my left, at the bottom of a shallow, fast dive, heading straight for the dinghy. A sustained burst of fire sent geysers of sea water creeping up on the tiny inflated boat. Not content with one run, the pilot pulled up into a tight climbing turn to the left and dived again...'

MALTA

By virtue of its proximity to Sicily (60 miles), the European mainland (140 miles), and Africa (180 miles), the island of Malta provided a crucial air and naval base for British control of the Mediterranean during World War II. Malta-based aircraft, submarines and ships took a vast toll of Axis convoys to Rommel's Afrika Korps. The cost, however, was high.

Only 18 miles long and nine miles wide, Malta was subjected to 3340 air raids in which 1540 civilians lost their lives and nearly 4000 more were injured. Over 14,000 tons of bombs rained down upon the island's population, airfields and dockyards. In the capital, Valletta, 75 per cent of the houses were destroyed or damaged. A total of 1252 Axis and 707 RAF aircraft were reported lost, and hundreds more were damaged.

Supplies had to be brought in by sea, through the Axis blockade. The Royal and Merchant Navies made 17 convoy runs between August 1940 and December 1942, delivering over 395,000 tons of essential provisions. Of the ships on convoy duty, 37 were sunk and a further 37 rendered unserviceable.

At the height of the campaign, Malta's anti-aircraft guns were firing 13,000 rounds per day, and during the 283 alerts in April 1942, her formidable box barrage shot down 102 Axis aircraft. Ammunition supplies ran desperately short and anti-aircraft guns had to be rationed to six rounds a day, but Malta held out.

On 15 April 1942 the islanders were awarded the Commonwealth's highest civilian honour; the George Cross. Their ordeal continued for another seven months; then, on 20 November 1942, the siege was finally lifted.

Pilot Officer George 'Screwball' Beurling (top right) was shot down during an intense aerial dogfight on 14 October 1942. He had just succeeded in disrupting a force of eight Bf 109s which had been in hot pursuit of a Spitfire flown by Pilot Officer Eric Hetherington (above right).

Ditched aircrew were not entirely safe even when fortunate enough to be picked up by one of the marine craft and Air Sea Rescue launches. In fact, High Speed Launch 129 had had to be written off following a vicious attack in February 1942 when German fighters shot up the vessel, killing several of the crew.

By 1942, fighter pilots on both sides were using extreme measures in the air. Some pilots would go to any length in order to destroy an enemy, even at the risk of sacrificing themselves. One such incident involving a No. 249 pilot occurred when Raoul Daddo-Langlois attacked a Bf 109 head-on. Neither pilot broke, and the two aircraft struck each other in mid-air, breaking a wing off the German fighter and leaving the Spitfire without a wing-tip. Daddo-Langlois crash-landed on Malta and, with enemy fighters attempting to finish him off, leapt from his machine and ran for the nearest available cover.

Shortly after, Johnny Plagis found himself involved in a similar close shave off the coast of Sicily. At sea level and separated from the rest of his squadron, he became surrounded by 10 or so Italian fighters. Not surprisingly, Plagis thought his last moment had come. So, determined to sell his life as dearly as possible, he flew straight at the nearest machine, fully intending to ram it. The pilot of the Macchi was obviously horrified and desperately took violent evasive action, only to stall and crash into the Mediterranean. Plagis survived to escape back to Malta where, five days later on 16 May 1942, No. 249 celebrated its hundredth Axis aircraft destroyed

Above: The Spitfire VC in which Pilot Officer 'Screwball' Beurling was shot down off Malta in October 1942.

Left: Spitfire VCs ranged on a rough Maltese airstrip. This type of Spitfire featured the Vokes filter housing beneath the nose and the universal 'C' wing.

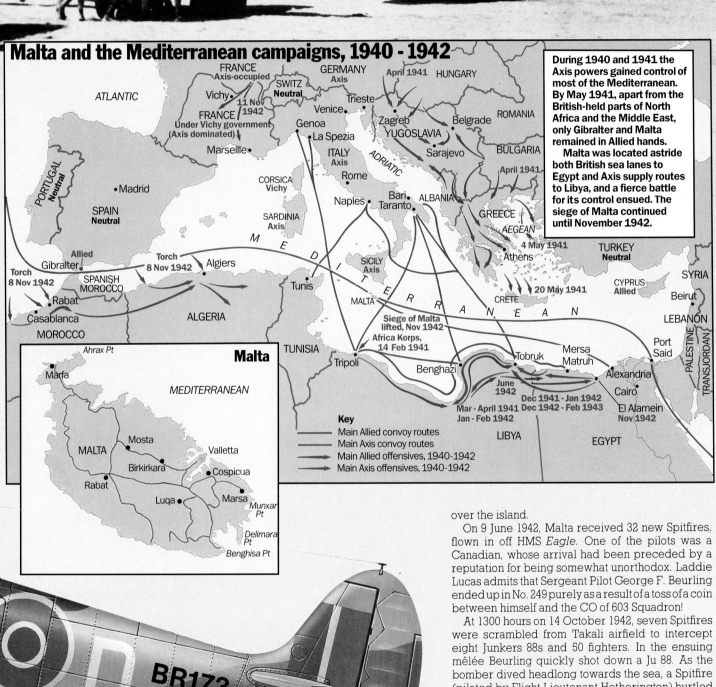

Malta and the Mediterranean campaigns, 1940 - 1942

ATLANTIC

FRANCE
Axis-occupied

Vichy
11 Nov 1942
FRANCE
Under Vichy government
(Axis dominated)

Marseille

SWITZ
Neutral

GERMANY
Axis

April 1941   HUNGARY

Trieste

Venice

Genoa

La Spezia

ITALY
Axis

Rome

Zagreb
YUGOSLAVIA

Sarajevo

Belgrade

ROMANIA

April 1941

BULGARIA

PORTUGAL
Neutral

Madrid

SPAIN
Neutral

CORSICA
Vichy

SARDINIA
Axis

Naples

Bari
Taranto

ALBANIA

ADRIATIC

GREECE

AEGEAN

Athens
4 May 1941

TURKEY
Neutral

Allied
Gibraltar

Torch
8 Nov 1942   Algiers

Tunis

SICILY
Axis

MALTA

CRETE
20 May 1941

CYPRUS
Allied

SYRIA

Beirut

Torch
8 Nov 1942

SPANISH
MOROCCO

Rabat

Casablanca

MOROCCO

ALGERIA

TUNISIA

Tripoli

MEDITERRANEAN

Siege of Malta
lifted, Nov 1942
Africa Korps,
14 Feb 1941

Benghazi

Tobruk

Mersa
Matruh

LEBANON

Port
Said

Alexandria

Cairo

El Alamein
Nov 1942

PALESTINE

TRANSJORDAN

June
1942

Mar - April 1941
Jan - Feb 1942

Dec 1941 - Jan 1942
Dec 1942 - Feb 1943

LIBYA

EGYPT

During 1940 and 1941 the Axis powers gained control of most of the Mediterranean. By May 1941, apart from the British-held parts of North Africa and the Middle East, only Gibralter and Malta remained in Allied hands.

Malta was located astride both British sea lanes to Egypt and Axis supply routes to Libya, and a fierce battle for its control ensued. The siege of Malta continued until November 1942.

Malta

Ahrax Pt

Marfa

MEDITERRANEAN

MALTA

Mosta

Birkirkara

Valletta

Rabat

Cospicua

Luqa

Marsa

Munxar
Pt

Delimara
Pt

Benghisa Pt

Key

———	Main Allied convoy routes
———	Main Axis convoy routes
——→	Main Allied offensives, 1940-1942
——→	Main Axis offensives, 1940-1942

BR173

over the island.

On 9 June 1942, Malta received 32 new Spitfires, flown in off HMS *Eagle*. One of the pilots was a Canadian, whose arrival had been preceded by a reputation for being somewhat unorthodox. Laddie Lucas admits that Sergeant Pilot George F. Beurling ended up in No. 249 purely as a result of a toss of a coin between himself and the CO of 603 Squadron!

At 1300 hours on 14 October 1942, seven Spitfires were scrambled from Takali airfield to intercept eight Junkers 88s and 50 fighters. In the ensuing mêlée Beurling quickly shot down a Ju 88. As the bomber dived headlong towards the sea, a Spitfire (piloted by Flight Lieutenant Hetherington) hurtled past under Beurling with eight Bf 109s on its tail. The Canadian flung his machine towards the leading German fighter and in doing so passed the burning Junkers he had just shot up. The resolute rear gunner of the doomed aircraft was quick to take this last opportunity to shoot at Beurling's Spitfire. One round nicked the middle finger of the Canadian's throttle hand, and another pierced his left forearm. Beurling

Above: The pilot of this downed Ju 88, trapped alive in the burning wreckage, was mercifully shot after it proved impossible to save him. Above right: Aircrew at Takili airbase. On the right is Raoul Daddo-Langlois, who survived a head-on crash with a Bf 109. Right: Wing Commander P.B. 'Laddie' Lucas, one of No. 249's commanding officers. Far right: A German photograph showing a tanker blazing after a strike on Valletta in the summer of 1942.

afterwards recounted:

'What was more important and inconvenient at the moment, however, was that I'd picked up two Messerschmitts on my own tail and still had Hether to worry about. I had to shoot in one hell of a hurry to clean Hether up and salvage my own neck, so I took a chance and tried for a long shot, from about 450yds from above and to port. I got the bastard in the engine and he dove into the sea, streaming smoke and shedding pieces...'

But while Beurling was intent on shooting down this second aircraft, one Messerschmitt on his tail had riddled his port wing:

'...like a sieve, and put a couple of bullets through the perspex hood, right over my head, while the other Schmitt blasted my starboard wing full of holes...Well, Hether was out in the clear again...'

Moments later Beurling answered a call for assist-

ance. In characteristic fashion he dived from 24,000ft straight into the action below:

> 'I went down vertically, hitting almost 600mph in my riddled crate, and at 14,000ft pulled up under a Messerschmitt, just as he was all set to pot Willie the Kid (Pilot Officer Williams)...just as I pulled up from the dive and was going up vertically I gave the [Bf 109] a two-second burst and blew his whole left wing off at the root... Willie's ship... was just about able to cart him home...'

With its controls shattered and the throttle jammed wide open, the Spitfire went into a full-power spin

But in rescuing Williams, Beurling had made the cardinal error of failing to look behind before going in to attack. (Perhaps he had good cause for his mistake. Not only had he been wounded, he was weakened by the island's poor diet and by the bouts of dysentery that the British called 'Malta Dog', and had lost close to 50lb in weight.) He was now wounded again as a Bf 109 sent a burst of cannon fire into the belly of his Spitfire. This time he was hit in the right heel, left elbow, ribs and left leg. With its controls shattered and the throttle jammed wide open, the Spitfire went into a full-power spin. Desperately Beurling threw back the cockpit hood, but when he tried to climb out he found himself pinned to the seat by centrifugal force With the Merlin engine streaming flame the Canadian fought to escape his doomed machine:

> 'Somehow I managed to wriggle my way out of the cockpit and out onto the port wing, from which I could bale into the inside of the spin. By the time I got out onto the wing I was down to 2000ft. At about 1000 I managed to slip off. Before I dared pull the ripcord I must have been around 500.'

Beurling landed in the Mediterranean several miles south of Malta. As a pair of Bf 109s hovered nearby, Pilot Officer Robert Seed circled around the Canadian until he climbed into his dinghy. Twenty minutes later Beurling was rescued by High Speed Launch 128. The following day the *Times of Malta* reported that:

> 'It was disclosed by the Air Ministry on Wednesday (13 October 1942) that the Axis lost its 1000th aircraft over or near Malta soon after dawn on Tuesday to 20-year-old Canadian ace fighter pilot Pilot Officer Beurling... The Air Ministry says his sense of positioning is instinctive and he must be one of the best marksmen in the RAF...'

Before leaving Malta at the end of October, 'Screwball' Beurling was awarded the DSO, DFC, DFM and Bar, and he became the highest scoring RAF ace in the entire Mediterranean theatre of war. He destroyed 26⅓ aircraft, probably destroyed another, and damaged seven. That he did not account for more than he did can be attributed to the fact that for a month after his arrival in Malta there was an unusual lull in aerial activity. There followed three hectic weeks with Beurling in his element, shooting down 16 aircraft over six separate days. Then for six weeks there was another lull. Thereafter Beurling, now a pilot officer, enjoyed only a few more days of activity. In all, he flew 27 sorties that resulted in contacts with the enemy. Nineteen of these, spread over 14 separate days, led to the impressive tally run up by this unique fighter pilot.

August 1942 had witnessed the arrival of the famous Pedestal convoy, bringing sufficient rations to the island to ward off starvation. The first three merchant vessels arrived in Grand Harbour on 13 August, followed on the 14th by another, and on the next day by a battered tanker, lashed between two destroyers and with her decks almost awash. Loaded with oil and aviation fuel essential to the maintenance of Malta's air defence, the tanker, *Ohio*, had arrived at a most critical period of the siege. With the arrival of Pedestal, and with Malta now fairly brimming with fighters, the Germans were reluctant to risk losing more bombers. The Luftwaffe, therefore, took to sending over 100 fighters as escort for only 14 bombers, preferring to use the Bf 109 in a fighter-bomber role. No. 249 Squadron, always in the forefront of battle, often succeeded in intercepting the enemy before they could even reach Malta.

A new concept of warfare was initiated in August, when Spitfires were fitted with improvised bomb racks and used for the first time on bombing missions from Malta. Modified to carry two 250lb GP bombs slung directly underneath their two outboard cannon, Spitfires of No. 249 Squadron were soon carrying out offensive sorties against Sicily.

On 27 August the whole Spitfire force on Malta attacked the airfields of Comiso, Biscari and Gela. Contemporary wartime accounts claim that between 22 and 39 Axis aircraft were destroyed on the ground and in the air. There were two RAF casualties; one pilot who crash-landed and was captured, and the Takali station commander Group Captain Churchill who was hit by anti-aircraft fire and killed over Biscari.

The battle over Malta reached a climax when, for 10 days in October 1942, the enemy flew 2400 sorties against the island. But gone were the days when Malta could muster only a handful of worn-out Hurricanes in its defence. July and August had seen the arrival of 125 Spitfires, and whereas Malta had often received inexperienced fighter pilots in the past, this time the quality of the new pilots was of a satisfactorily high standard.

Suddenly, unbelievably, it was over: the battle for Malta had been won

On 20 October the Axis air offensive came to an abrupt halt when nearly all of its aircraft were transferred from Sicily to North Africa. Suddenly, unbelievably, it was over: the battle for Malta had been won. Enemy attacks did continue, but never with the same tenacity as before. The Regia Aeronautica carried out its last raid on 26 February 1943, and intermittent raids were carried out by the Luftwaffe even after the surrender in May of the Afrika Korps in Tunisia.

On 10 July 1943 the Allies landed in Sicily. The Spitfires of No. 249 Squadron left Hal-Far airfield the following month, flying north to their new base in Italy in order to resume operations with fighter sweeps and bomber escorts on the east coast. Behind them they left many comrades, lost in the depths of the Mediterranean, or buried in military cemeteries on the islands over which No. 249 had flown and fought during two-and-a-half years of operations.

THE AUTHOR Anton Sammut has researched aspects of the history of Malta for many years, and has a particular interest in the island's defences during World War II.

'THE PHILISTINES'

Within the South African Defence Force (SADF) in the early 1980s, a number of British, Rhodesian and American troops were jocularly known as 'the Philistines' on account of their cavalier attitude to counter-insurgency warfare. These former members of the Rhodesian Army had joined the SADF following the creation of Zimbabwe in April 1980. Some were absorbed into 32 Battalion, a unit containing ex-FNLA guerrillas. In addition, Colonel Carpenter, commander of the SADF's 44 Parachute Brigade, had recruited a force of, mainly Rhodesian, professional soldiers to act as a new fighting arm of the brigade. Its name was the Pathfinder Company.

The role of the Pathfinder Company was to conduct mobile, fighting patrols deep inside Angola. Already highly trained in counter-terrorist operations, the pathfinders were totally self-sufficient and independent of the rest of the SADF.

After passing a selection course, the company's volunteers underwent further training in bush warfare and conventional pathfinding techniques, and then moved to their permanent base at Ondangwa in South West Africa (Namibia). From there the pathfinders launched operations against SWAPO, sometimes on foot, but more usually utilising a convoy of Landcruisers, Land Rovers and Unimog trucks. Led by Colonel Carpenter, the force was highly successful throughout its short and controversial history. The Pathfinder Company was disbanded when Colonel Carpenter left 44 Parachute Brigade in early 1982. Above: The silver wings worn by SADF paras who have completed 50 jumps.

BUSH
PATHFINDERS

Battle-hardened veterans from all over the world, the men of the Pathfinder Company, 44th Parachute Brigade acted as a spearhead in a raid against guerrillas in Angola

THE PATHFINDER Company of 44 Parachute Brigade, South African Defence Force (SADF), was activated in early 1980, and, along with many other foreign troops, I was recruited direct from service in Support Commando of the Rhodesian Light Infantry. During 1980, 44 Para Brigade had been fully reorganised. Based at Bloemfontein, 1 Parachute Battalion (1 Parabat) consisted of national servicemen doing their two-year call-up, and one company was permanently based at Ondangwa in South West Africa (Namibia). Two and 3 Parabats comprised Citizen Force personnel who had completed national service but were still required to attend a yearly camp, often for active duty in South West Africa (Namibia) or Angola. The permanent headquarters of the three parabats was 44 Para Brigade.

By early 1981, two pathfinder selection courses had produced sufficient personnel to be deployed on active service and a convoy of vehicles was being prepared for their use in the workshops of the South African Department of Scientific and Industrial Research. The convoy consisted of three Toyota Landcruisers, two mounting 0.5in Browning machine guns and one with a 20mm cannon bartered from the South African Air Force (SAAF); three Land Rovers which would carry twin FN MAG light machine guns mounted at the rear, plus a single machine gun for the commander, and three Unimog trucks were to carry

Left: A 'Philistine' in the flesh – an ex-Rhodesian Army pathfinder in FAPLA uniform and carrying a Soviet 7.62mm AK assault rifle. Above: An SADF Unimog, armed with a captured Soviet 14.5mm machine gun, and (top) a Unimog after the short, sharp shock of a SWAPO landmine.

the fuel, rations and ammunition needed for long-range patrols. All the vehicles were fitted with smoke dischargers and winches, as well as foam-filled tyres as a precaution against puncturing from thorns.

The convoy was delivered to Murrayhill, the pathfinders' permanent base, only days before we set off

JOINING THE PATHFINDERS

Every volunteer for the Pathfinder Company, 44 Parachute Brigade, was required to turn up at the SADF headquarters in Pretoria for preliminary vetting and medical examination. Successful candidates were issued with kit and sent to the unit's South African base at Murrayhill, an abandoned farm at Hammanskraal on the Pretoria highway. Training commenced immediately under Captain Botha and Company Sergeant Major McDonald (an ex-member of the British SAS who had commanded mercenaries in the FNLA after the capture of the infamous 'Colonel' Callan). The men then transferred to the para brigade's bush camp at Mabilique on the Limpopo river. There, bushcraft, infantry skills and pathfinding were taught, with continual emphasis on the development of peak physical fitness. For instance, a full ammunition box was carried on every run, and a 5-10km run rounded off every day's training. All fire practice was conducted with live rounds.

The determination and endurance of the men under selection were put to the test in the Drakensburg mountains in Natal. They had to cover a fixed distance of mountainous terrain within a time limit, carrying measured weights and the heavy ammo box. Each leg of the route had its own time limit and weight loading, and failure to complete any section on time meant an immediate end to the candidate's hopes of inclusion in the Pathfinder Company. However, such was the calibre of the men volunteering for the unit that only a few were defeated by the high standards of entry. Above: The beret badge of the South African paras.

for Sector 10, the operational area in South West Africa (Namibia) that borders Angola. The pathfinders took two weeks moving up through the Kalahari Desert along the Botswana border, trying out ambush and anti-ambush drills, patrol formations and types of laagers along the way. It was decided that two-vehicle sections worked best, the commander riding in a Landcruiser and the second-in-command in a Land Rover. This combination also provided a satisfactory blend of firepower. For communication between vehicles, VHF radios were carried, and contact with base camp was maintained with HF sets.

Our first operation in Angola turned out to be a dawn attack on a known SWAPO (South West Africa Peoples' Organisation) base. Following a preliminary SAAF air strike, the camp was to be assaulted by 32 Battalion with the pathfinders providing close support with machine guns.

The company received its orders and prepared kit. There was no standard dress, and South African brown uniform mingled with Rhodesian camouflage and any other uniform available. Webbing was also left to individual preference. Personal armament consisted of the South African version of the Israeli Galil, the R-4 rifle. This weapon was not as popular with the men as the old Rhodesian issue FN FAL, however, as most disliked its smaller calibre and 'tinny' feel. Some of us took along hand guns, both privately-owned models and the issue 9mm Star automatic. Each vehicle carried a quantity of M79 grenade launchers and an RPG-7 rocket launcher.

The day before the attack, the company crossed the 'cut line' (the border with Angola). Aided by aerial photographs, we struck north, seeking a route through the scrub. When the bush became dense, hampering progress, a Unimog was called to the fore and this marvellous workhorse would crash, bend and batter a road through for the others to follow. At last light we linked up with 32 Battalion.

Before dawn the next day, the terrorist camp began to buzz with activity. The enemy had discovered that something was up and soon speculative fire was being laid on likely approach routes with BM-21 multiple-barrel rocket launchers. The air strike went in on schedule, and met anti-aircraft fire from several points around the camp. The ground forces then commenced their advance into the camp area. A well-disciplined sweep-line was formed by 32 Battalion, with the pathfinder vehicles spaced at intervals along it. We moved forward, firing into likely enemy cover. There was no return fire, however, and it soon became apparent that apart from the anti-aircraft gunners, everyone else had fled.

While 32 Battalion dealt with two unexploded bombs which had been dropped by Mirages on the initial strike, the Pathfinder Company moved out to clear the anti-aircraft positions. Supporting helicopters had reported seeing terrorists wheeling off heavy machine guns, but we managed to locate one position with three 14.5mm machine guns still intact. When we arrived a guerrilla, wounded in one leg and unable to escape, chose to shoot himself in the head. After checking for booby traps, the guns were lifted out by Puma helicopter. (Later Colonel Carpenter, commander of 44 Para Brigade, managed to retrieve one and it was mounted in a Unimog for our own use.)

Because the element of surprise had been lost, the attack was only a partial success, but we were satisfied that the pathfinders had done well on this, our first operation.

In total secrecy an invasion force was being gathered and formed into battle groups and task forces

During the summer of 1981, the Pathfinder Company mounted ceaseless combat patrols into Angola, but all the time the men were waiting for 'the big one'. This was to be a large-scale invasion of Angola that would destroy SWAPO's ability to mount incursions into South West Africa (Namibia), as well as give FAPLA (Popular Armed Forces for the Liberation of Angola) such a bloody nose that they would have to reconsider the support they gave SWAPO. Unknown

to the pathfinders, the SADF hierarchy had already planned the op and was putting it into action. Its codename was Operation Protea.

Throughout South Africa men were reporting as usual for their annual camps and boarding aircraft, expecting to be flown to various training areas. Instead, they found themselves landing at Grootfontein in South West Africa (Namibia), where in total secrecy an invasion force was being gathered and formed into battle groups and task forces. Without informing us of the operation, the Pathfinder Company was ordered to leave Ondangwa and head south. We departed at 0800 hours on 19 August.

The training area was bushland near Omuthiya. A vast amount of men and equipment had been gathered and rehearsals had already reached an advanced stage. Upon arrival, the men were required to fill out medical and next-of-kin forms. It was standard practice for the pathfinders to include a note requesting that next of kin be notified only in the

Below: The Pathfinder Company crosses the cut line into Angola. Top and above: The pathfinders' ambush of an FAPLA convoy on the night of 25 August 1981 yielded a fine haul of valuable vehicles and weaponry.

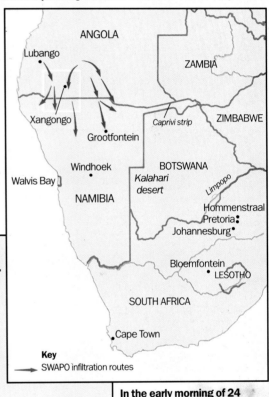

Key
→ SWAPO infiltration routes

Operation Protea
44 Parachute Brigade, SADF, August 1981

Key
→ 44 Para Bde
→ Other South African forces
✳ South African airstrikes
▪ SWAPO/FAPLA encampments

**In the early morning of 24 August 1981 the South African Defence Force moved against SWAPO insurgents in one of its largest ever cross-border operations into Angola. While a mechanised force crossed the border at Ruacana falls, a second task force – with the 44 Para Brigade's Pathfinder Company attached – moved on Xangongo.
As the force swept forward through southern Angola, a South African Mirage strike went in at Xangongo and at the radar station outside Cahama. The Pathfinder Company penetrated as far as Chibemba and was involved in two sharp engagements with the enemy.**

1017

Left: The Pathfinder Company rejected heavy armoured vehicles in favour of fast, light, adaptable platforms for a formidable range of offensive armament. The Landcruiser in the foreground carries a 0.5in Browning machine gun, with a light machine gun for the commander, while the Unimog has a 60mm mortar mounted on its flat-bed. Bottom left: A pathfinder foot patrol in Angola. No man is dressed alike, and their weapons come from both Western and Communist sources. Bottom right: Amongst the early casualties of Operation Protea was this Soviet-made BRDM-2 scout car. Below: This guerrilla, wounded in a raid on a SWAPO base, chose to finish himself off rather than surrender to the South Africans.

event of death. Nobody wanted their families worried unnecessarily.

The next day the company began practising camp attacks with Task Force Alpha. We were to specialise in tank hunting, and for this our RPG-7s were replaced by French 89mm rocket launchers. Men of 32 Battalion made up a prominent part of the attack force and many of our old Rhodesian friends came over. At night, many of us who had been recruited from outside South Africa would gather around a blazing fire and, with the help of a few beers and lusty singing, celebrate the coming events. The South Africans, who could not understand our enthusiasm, had already nicknamed us 'the Philistines'. It was a name everyone quickly took to their hearts.

On 21 August we were ordered to be ready to move any time after 1700 hours. The following day, at 1100 hours, the company was given its final briefing: Task Force Alpha would attack target 'Yankee', which was the town of Xangongo, and the FAPLA armoured brigade positioned there. As tank hunters, the Pathfinder Company would remain uncommitted, but ready to be deployed as required. By 1745 the task force was heading for its form-up point (FUP), and at midday on 23 August, it had reached Okalongo, 30km from the cut line, where a major refuelling programme was carried out. The FUP was

to Battle Group 30. Joining up with Ratel infantry combat vehicles, the Pathfinders hared along the tarmac road towards an FAPLA camp, 80km northwest of Xangongo, but the camp was already deserted by the time the column reached it.

At last light the battle group units dispersed for the night, one Ratel company remaining on the road to halt any FAPLA vehicles coming down from Cahama in the north. The pathfinders camped 200m off the road, about a kilometre down from the Ratels.

Corporal David Beam was the gunner on Colonel Carpenter's Landcruiser. Due to his wealth of knowledge gained serving in US Marine helicopters in Vietnam, Beam was responsible for all our heavy machine guns. At 2200 hours he was on guard when a convoy of petrol-driven trucks passed by, heading north. As all the friendly forces had diesel engines, Beam quickly woke the sleeping crews. By now the convoy had reached the Ratels blocking the road and a sharp engagement was heard to take place, lasting between five and 10 minutes. It was followed by a silence, broken only by the sound of the FAPLA convoy now driving back the way they had come. By chance they stopped again, right next to the pathfinders who were now stood-to at their vehicles.

At a command from Colonel Carpenter, all the vehicles on the side nearest the road opened fire. Men from the far side assisted with rocket launchers and their 60mm mortar. An incredible amount of red and green tracer streaked across the sky, while a nearby artillery unit added to the surreal scene by firing illumination shells.

Both lorries exploded, hit by 89mm rockets, and after only a few minutes Botha's men ceased firing

The FAPLA stopped firing and all was quiet again. The pathfinders had suffered no casualties or damage, but noises coming from the far side of the road indicated that the terrorists could now be setting up mortars. A patrol, under Captain Botha, was quickly formed and, armed with 89mm rocket launchers, the men silently inched their way towards the sounds.

On the other side of the road they saw two Russian GAZ lorries and several FAPLA soldiers setting up mortars. Unseen, the pathfinders crossed the road and formed a firing line. At a signal from Captain Botha they opened fire. It was dramatically effective. Both lorries exploded, hit by 89mm rockets, and after only a few minutes Captain Botha's men ceased firing. There was neither sight nor sound of the enemy, but recognising the dangers of sweeping a contact area in the dark, the patrol returned to the camp. With the action over for the night, sentries were posted while the rest caught up on some long overdue sleep. Exploding ammunition in the burning vehicles made a din for some time to come.

By early morning the Pathfinder Company was up and ready to move. To everyone's great satisfaction, the entire FAPLA convoy was found deserted and almost intact on the road. It consisted of a fully equipped radio jeep, two BTR armoured cars, two BM-21 multiple rocket launchers and four other GAZ trucks, each with twin 23mm anti-aircraft machine guns mounted on the back. These nine vehicles captured, plus the two lorries destroyed, made a successful night's work. Although no enemy bodies were found, trails of blood showed that casualties had been removed.

After returning to Xangongo for a quick clean-up, the company set off on an independent mission,

reached shortly afterwards.

The move from the FUP to the target started at 0230 on the next morning. Crossing the cut line, a Unimog carrying a multiple rocket launcher detonated a mine and became the first casualty of Operation Protea. Then, at exactly 1200 the SAAF Mirages struck Xangongo. The ground forces, including the pathfinders, were already on the outskirts and 32 Battalion provided the assault troops, supported by artillery fire from 155mm G-5 guns. By 1900 the town was firmly in South African hands.

All was quiet by midday on the 25th, so Colonel Carpenter arranged for his men to become attached

Above: A pathfinder patrol north of Xangongo unleashes a hail of fire into a suspected SWAPO encampment. Below: The author (with sergeant's stripes) and a Landcruiser fitted with twin 0.5in Brownings. The vehicle was later destroyed during a raid in Angola.

heading north to the town of Chibemba where reports indicated an FAPLA force of unknown size. Deliberately making our presence known in the town area, we then lay in ambush along the road, hoping to catch any patrols reckless enough to come after us. This tactic showed no results, so it was decided to visit known SWAPO and FAPLA camps. Before entering a camp area we called over helicopter gunships, but no enemy force was encountered.

The camps had been empty for a number of days.

By 29 August all possible enemy positions outside Chibemba had been checked and found deserted, so it was decided to enter the town itself. As one of our Land Rovers had broken down, Colonel Carpenter elected to leave the mechanics behind, protected by two other vehicles, while he approached the town with seven vehicles and 26 men. The column had got no further than the kraals on the town outskirts before the colonel's Landcruiser was destroyed by a landmine. Two crewmen, myself and Corporal Beam, had to be casevaced by helicopter. The former US Marine later had to have both legs amputated. The colonel and his American driver were shaken, but able to carry on. However, when our helicopters reported at least 1000 SWAPO and FAPLA guerrillas in Chibemba, the colonel made a tactical withdrawal in order to reorganise.

The pathfinders continued their checks on suspected enemy camps, but fought only one engagement. This occurred when the leading vehicle emerged from the bush right onto a group of resting guerrillas. Taking the only course of action possible, it charged straight into them, shooting on all sides. In a moment all the terrorists were dead, either shot or run down. For the pathfinders this marked the end of Operation Protea, and they returned home to Murrayhill and leave.

In October the Pathfinder Company joined a 2 Parabat force in an operational parachute jump into Angola as part of a camp attack. This was to be their last action as a unit. Changes were taking place at 44 Para Brigade and Colonel Carpenter was moving on to Military Intelligence. After his departure the pathfinders found themselves involved in giving instruction to the Citizen Force paras. Upon completion of their one-year contracts some men chose to leave the army, while others, the majority, transferred to 32 Battalion. Thus the Pathfinder Company was disbanded.

THE AUTHOR Graham Gillmore served in the Grenadier Guards and the Rhodesian Light Infantry. He was an SNCO in the Pathfinder Company, 44 Parachute Brigade, until he was wounded during Operation Protea in 1981. He now works for a London security firm. All names used in this article, have been altered to protect those still involved in sensitive work in Africa.

THE PARAS GO IN

Suez crisis, November 1956: the men of 3 Para jumped into the teeth of fierce Egyptian resistance on the narrow airfield at Gamil

'PREPARE FOR ACTION! Stand up, fit equipment! Check equipment! Tell off for equipment check!' The orders came in sequence as the men went through their final pre-jump drills, checking their helmets, their 120lb equipment containers, each man checking the parachute of the one in front. Then came the warning, 'Red on! Stand in the door!'

THE BRITISH PARAS AT SUEZ

After World War II, the parachute formations of the British Army were gradually whittled down until all had been disbanded except the 16th Independent Parachute Brigade Group. This group, formed in 1948 with a nucleus from the old 2nd Parachute Brigade, had been named the 16th in honour of the wartime 1st and 6th Divisions which had fought at Arnhem and Normandy.

The British government's intention to deploy an airborne force at Suez caught the military establishment off guard. When the crisis began, the 1st and 3rd Battalions of The Parachute Regiment were serving in Cyprus in counter-terrorist operations against Colonel Grivas and his EOKA organisation. In this role their parachute training had lapsed, and as soon as the 2nd Battalion arrived in Cyprus with the brigade's supporting arms, both battalions were returned to England for urgent practice. Still unaware that an air assault was in the offing, the paras returned to Cyprus and resumed operations which continued right up to the end of October.

The battalion selected for the initial assault, 3 Para, had been welded into a tight, purposeful unit by the hard campaigns in Cyprus. It contained a number of veterans of The Parachute Regiment's historic battles, including the Rhine crossings and Arnhem, and these men had created a strong esprit de corps among the battalion's national servicemen. Brought up to standard by their rushed refresher course in England, 3 Para gained the distinction of making the last combat jump conducted by the regiment to date.

Above: Para wings awarded to qualified men in the early 1950s.

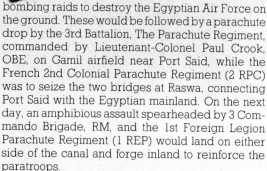

The sticks of men squeezed together, lining up behind Number One, who stood at the port trooping door of the Valetta transport. The joint British and French fighting force raised for Operation Musketeer was about to go into combat.

The British paras had taken off at 0415 hours from Nicosia airfield in Cyprus on 5 November 1956. Their operation was designed to gain control of the Suez Canal, owned by the Anglo-French Suez Canal Company, but recently nationalised by Egypt's head of state, President Gamal Abdel Nasser.

Operation Musketeer involved about 80,000 men, spearheaded by the British 16th Independent Parachute Brigade, commanded by Brigadier M.A.H. Butler, DSO, MC, and 3 Commando Brigade, Royal Marines; leading the French forces were their 10th Parachute Division and 7th Mechanised Division, both of which were fresh from service in Algeria. The operational plan entailed a series of preliminary bombing raids to destroy the Egyptian Air Force on the ground. These would be followed by a parachute drop by the 3rd Battalion, The Parachute Regiment, commanded by Lieutenant-Colonel Paul Crook, OBE, on Gamil airfield near Port Said, while the French 2nd Colonial Parachute Regiment (2 RPC) was to seize the two bridges at Raswa, connecting Port Said with the Egyptian mainland. On the next day, an amphibious assault spearheaded by 3 Commando Brigade, RM, and the 1st Foreign Legion Parachute Regiment (1 REP) would land on either side of the canal and forge inland to reinforce the paratroops.

Perhaps Lieutenant-Colonel Crook's greatest problem was the drop zone (DZ) on which the 3rd Battalion (3 Para) would land. Gamil airfield lay on a narrow spit of land between the Mediterranean Sea

Suez
3rd Battalion, The Parachute Regiment
5-6 Nov 1956

Spearheading the Anglo-French effort to reopen the Suez Canal after its closure by President Nasser of Egypt, 3 Para carried out a successful assault on Gamil airfield, to the west of Port Said, early on 5 November 1956. As the amphibious assault on Port Said was launched the following day, 3 Para provided vital covering fire from its positions to the west and was heavily engaged throughout the day's fighting.

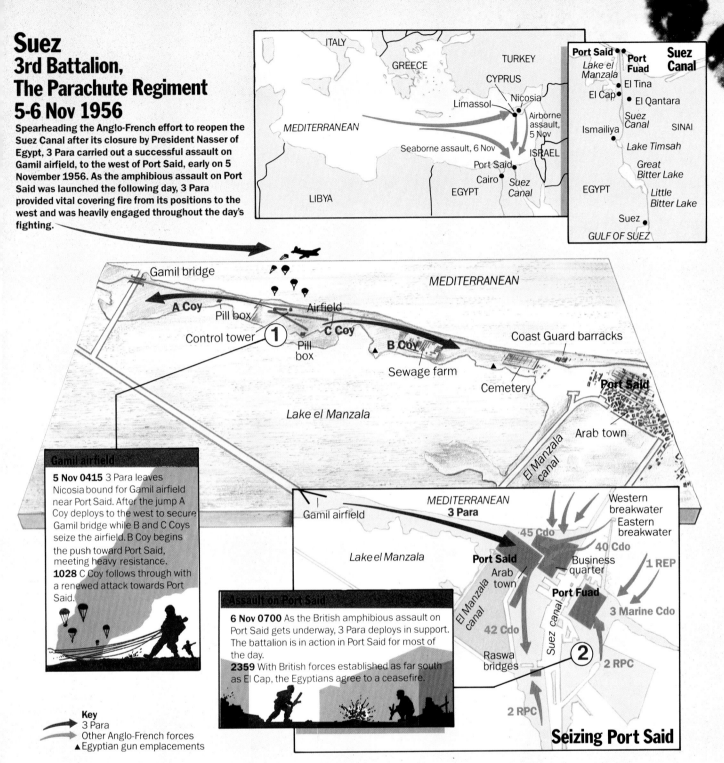

Gamil airfield

5 Nov 0415 3 Para leaves Nicosia bound for Gamil airfield near Port Said. After the jump A Coy deploys to the west to secure Gamil bridge while B and C Coys seize the airfield. B Coy begins the push toward Port Said, meeting heavy resistance.
1028 C Coy follows through with a renewed attack towards Port Said.

Assault on Port Said

6 Nov 0700 As the British amphibious assault on Port Said gets underway, 3 Para deploys in support. The battalion is in action in Port Said for most of the day.
2359 With British forces established as far south as El Cap, the Egyptians agree to a ceasefire.

Seizing Port Said

Key
→ 3 Para
→ Other Anglo-French forces
▲ Egyptian gun emplacements

---

and Lake el Manzala. It was less than a mile long, and the paras would have to drop in tight sticks of about 20 men from each aircraft run over it. Cross-winds would mean men dropping into the sea or the lake, while an overshoot would land men on an Egyptian-held sewage farm at the airfield's eastern end. In addition, the beaches on the spit were strewn with mines, and well-sited machine guns covered the whole area. Crook decided to drop A Company at the western end to seal it off. C Company was to seize the southern perimeter, and B Company was to gain control in the east in preparation for an advance into Port Said itself. In support of the companies, Crook had elements of the 33rd Parachute Light Regiment, Royal Artillery, and the 9th Parachute Squadron, Royal Engineers, with a field surgical team and an

RAF forward air control team. Defending the airstrip was a battalion of Egyptian troops and an unknown number of National Guardsmen with four SU-100 self-propelled guns.

In the British Valetta transports, nervously fingering the quick-release boxes of their X-type parachutes, the men of 3 Para waited for the signal to jump. There ahead of them was the airfield. A Canberra had just dropped a smoke flare to mark the jump point of the paratroops, and a gentle breeze was blowing it out to sea. The paras moved rapidly down the aircraft and, to prevent themselves being thrown against the side of the fuselage by the slipstream, each threw himself in a strong dive, chest leading, from the door. For the paras the world briefly became a kaleidoscope of blue sky, sand and

OUTMODED EQUIPMENT

The Suez crisis in 1956 clearly demonstrated how unprepared the British were for a full-scale airborne assault. Unlike the French parachute regiment which landed on Port Fuad from modern Noratlas aircraft, the British were obliged to use obsolescent Hastings and Valettas, both old designs with tail wheels and side cargo doors. The French could drop 17 men in 10 seconds from their tail ramps, while the British were limited to 15 men over 20 seconds.
Expecting eventual delivery of Beverley and Argosy planes, the British had already adapted their ancillary gear in readiness for the new transports. Their Austin Champ vehicles, designed to be carried by the Beverley, were too big for the Hastings, and World War II jeeps and trailers had to be sought out all over Cyprus. The dropping-beams to which the underslung jeep crash-pans were attached also had to be found, and one was actually collected from an airborne forces museum.
For use against the Egyptian T-34 tanks and SU-100 self-propelled guns the paras had only six 106mm recoilless rifles. Much of their armament predated even such World War II innovations as the Sterling sub-machine gun, and included .303in No. 4 Lee-Enfield rifles, Sten guns, Bren light machine guns and even .303in Vickers medium machine guns.
The weapons, ammunition and other supplies were all dropped in containers, meaning that, unlike the French paras who had guns with folding stocks for use as they came down, the British were defenceless until they reached the ground.

trailing khaki parachutes, until at last all the canopies had billowed open. Below them they could hear the hammer of anti-aircraft fire. The light battery beside the Gamil bridge, A Company's first objective, was hacking at the aircraft as they roared over, and soon the machine guns of the pillboxes at each end were spitting hot metal at the aircraft and the vulnerable men dangling under their canopies. .

Captain Sandy Cavenagh, 3 Para's medical officer, took a splinter in the left eye when a shell came through the equipment container hanging below him, severing its suspension cord. Major Geoff Norton, commander of the paras' Support Company, found himself all but entangled in severed rigging

lines as machine-gun fire slashed through his canopy. One sapper's 'chute was shredded by an anti-aircraft round and he broke both legs on landing. Private Neal from the Medical Section landed in the sewage farm. Private Lamph landed in the sea and managed to gain the rare distinction of making a parachute assault and yet also being the first amphibious soldier ashore, all in about 10 minutes and in both cases under heavy fire. Another soldier landed in one of the minefields.

The fire was murderous, and for the first 30 seconds or so, until they could retrieve their containers, the paras had no weapons with which to fight

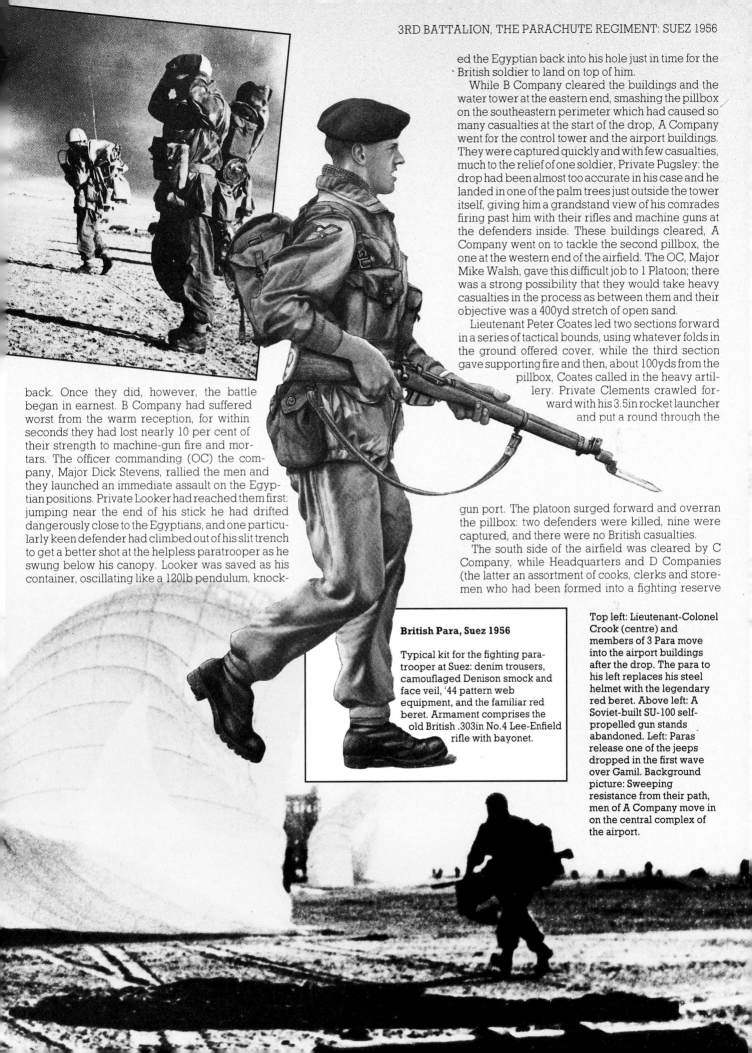

ed the Egyptian back into his hole just in time for the British soldier to land on top of him.

While B Company cleared the buildings and the water tower at the eastern end, smashing the pillbox on the southeastern perimeter which had caused so many casualties at the start of the drop, A Company went for the control tower and the airport buildings. They were captured quickly and with few casualties, much to the relief of one soldier, Private Pugsley: the drop had been almost too accurate in his case and he landed in one of the palm trees just outside the tower itself, giving him a grandstand view of his comrades firing past him with their rifles and machine guns at the defenders inside. These buildings cleared, A Company went on to tackle the second pillbox, the one at the western end of the airfield. The OC, Major Mike Walsh, gave this difficult job to 1 Platoon; there was a strong possibility that they would take heavy casualties in the process as between them and their objective was a 400yd stretch of open sand.

Lieutenant Peter Coates led two sections forward in a series of tactical bounds, using whatever folds in the ground offered cover, while the third section gave supporting fire and then, about 100yds from the pillbox, Coates called in the heavy artillery. Private Clements crawled forward with his 3.5in rocket launcher and put a round through the

back. Once they did, however, the battle began in earnest. B Company had suffered worst from the warm reception, for within seconds they had lost nearly 10 per cent of their strength to machine-gun fire and mortars. The officer commanding (OC) the company, Major Dick Stevens, rallied the men and they launched an immediate assault on the Egyptian positions. Private Looker had reached them first: jumping near the end of his stick he had drifted dangerously close to the Egyptians, and one particularly keen defender had climbed out of his slit trench to get a better shot at the helpless paratrooper as he swung below his canopy. Looker was saved as his container, oscillating like a 120lb pendulum, knock-

gun port. The platoon surged forward and overran the pillbox: two defenders were killed, nine were captured, and there were no British casualties.

The south side of the airfield was cleared by C Company, while Headquarters and D Companies (the latter an assortment of cooks, clerks and storemen who had been formed into a fighting reserve

British Para, Suez 1956

Typical kit for the fighting paratrooper at Suez: denim trousers, camouflaged Denison smock and face veil, '44 pattern web equipment, and the familiar red beret. Armament comprises the old British .303in No.4 Lee-Enfield rifle with bayonet.

Top left: Lieutenant-Colonel Crook (centre) and members of 3 Para move into the airport buildings after the drop. The para to his left replaces his steel helmet with the legendary red beret. Above left: A Soviet-built SU-100 self-propelled gun stands abandoned. Left: Paras release one of the jeeps dropped in the first wave over Gamil. Background picture: Sweeping resistance from their path, men of A Company move in on the central complex of the airport.

force, in accordance with the regiment's insistence that every man in the battalion should be a trained paratrooper) collected the heavy drop equipment and set up both Lieutenant-Colonel Crook's headquarters and a rudimentary HQ for Brigadier Butler, who had also jumped with the battalion. Then a problem presented itself: the DZ was so soft that the crash-pans to which the jeeps were fitted had not worked properly. On impact these were supposed to crumple, cutting the canopies free automatically and releasing the vehicles so that they could be driven off immediately. Sweating and swearing under a growing volume of mortar fire, now interspersed with salvoes from Russian-built Stalin Organs – multi-barrelled rocket launchers – which the Egyptians had deployed, they struggled to free the vehicles, while others rushed to the containers nearby which held their 106mm recoilless rifles, machine guns and mortars, and the precious ammunition.

With the sun glinting on their bayonets and winged cap badges, the men were ready to move

The loads carried by the men made fast movement impossible. The men actually had too much to carry, a common problem in the British Army, but always an unavoidable part of airborne operations when each man has to carry all his kit on his back. Once they reached their initial rendezvous (RVs), however, they could ditch their bergens and join the battle in earnest.

With the initial objectives secured, it was now the task of B Company to exploit forward. Their decimation in the earliest stage of the battle had been sudden and brutal and, while Crook was happy with Dick Stevens' progress, he nevertheless went up to

offer the men some moral support, accompanied by Brigadier Butler. The two men arrived, looking like directing staff on an exercise in their maroon berets, and the effect they had on the men was very positive. Steel helmets were still being worn because there had been no time to take them off, but soon the paras' berets appeared and, with the sun glinting on their bayonets and winged cap badges, the men were ready to move. The mortar fire had not slackened, however, and Dick Stevens was wounded minutes after Crook's arrival.

The battalion's mortars were in operation and a short vicious 'stonk' preceded the assault

His second-in-command, Karl Beale, assumed command of B Company and sent Sergeant Norman down the road to the north of the sewage farm, with a section from that NCO's platoon, to blast out another pillbox which had been giving trouble. The battalion's mortars were in operation now, and a short, vicious 'stonk' preceded Norman's assault, leaving the way clear for another platoon, led by Lieutenant Chris Hogg, to probe forward under the watchful eyes of the anti-tank platoon, who were ready with their recoilless guns. As Hogg led his men through the sewage farm to the empty buildings at the far end, the 106mm guns destroyed a self-propelled gun, a success which cheered the paras. Meanwhile, François Collet and his staff were calling down air strikes from the carriers offshore, and one of these was nearly Hogg's undoing. Ordered only to make contact with the enemy and then report back, he and his men came under fire from the cemetery beyond the sewage farm and withdrew to the concrete troughs of the sewage farm. Two French Mystères saw them below and made a strafing run which had the platoon diving into the troughs for cover. A thick crust on the sewage supported their weight – just – and they made it into the dense reeds in front of B Company's position. A terse message from Collet to his airborne compatriots informed them that, yes, 3 Para had got beyond the sewage farm already, and targets were to be engaged when ordered, not before!

C Company now took over from B Company: at 1028 hours a massive air strike, supported by the battalion's mortars, medium machine guns and recoilless rifles, pulverised the enemy position that Hogg had found in the cemetery and, at 1030 precisely, the company rose as one man from its shell scrapes and advanced steadily across the 300yds of low sand dunes to the cemetery wall. The Egyptian positions were in a shambles, but many of the defenders were still entrenched and the fighting was savage, with few prisoners taken on either side.

Below: Following the initial assault, helicopters were used in a full-scale troop drop.

Above: British paras consolidate the Canal road leading into Port Said. Top: Members of the assault force wait to be airlifted out of Egypt following the ceasefire agreement.

It seemed to take an age for the cemetery to be cleared. Fighting at close quarters with their grenades and Sten guns, the younger soldiers had to summon immense nerve and provide mutual support to get through. C company's commander, Major Ron Norman, MBE, MC, had fought on Crete against the invading German paratroopers in World War II, and he couldn't help feeling a grudging respect for those Egyptians who stood and fought so hard against the intimidating parachute assault.

Finally the defenders retreated, many of them joining the women and children who were fleeing from Port Said on the *feluccas* which plied the El Manzala Canal between Port Said and Gamil. As C Company consolidated, many of the men threw away their Stens, which had proved unreliable in many cases, and replaced them with Egyptian Berettas, Schmeissers, Russian-made SKS Simonov rifles and PPSh sub-machine guns which had been left behind. Back at the airfield's control tower, despite the attention of an SU-100 self-propelled gun in Port Said which had found the range, the Headquarters staff were organising the next stage of the assault. Naval helicopters had already flown casualties out of the airfield and 9 Parachute Squadron had cleared the runways of the empty oil drums used by the Egyptians to block them. Colonel de Fouquieres, the French commander's liaison officer, now arrived in a Dakota, ignoring the mortar and machine-gun fire which periodically raked the airfield, and after a short conference with Brigadier Butler, took off again for Akrotiri bearing eight more casualties and 3 Para's medical officer, Sandy Cavenagh, who had been ordered to leave.

As C Company fought eastwards it came under fire from a block of flats on the outskirts of Port Said. However, continual air strikes had eroded Egyptian morale, and the four SU-100 self-propelled guns in the defended apartment block had been abandoned. Machine-gun fire from the flats was holding up the company's advance when Lieutenant Mike Newall, OC Machine Gun Platoon, spotted both the guns in the ground-floor flats and an abandoned Bren-gun carrier lying in no-man's land. Leaving his platoon, for whom he had been scouting out better fire positions, he ran to the carrier through a storm of fire and, assisted by a C Company sergeant, got the thing working. The two men drove straight at the machine-gun post, overran it and returned in triumph to what they thought was the front line. The company had been under sniper fire for some time and knew that there was no British armour for miles; on hearing the carrier coming down the road, B Company's anti-tank detachment

prepared for action, the first ranging shot from their spotting rifle hitting fair and square. Only a quick-witted NCO prevented the loss of the two men.

As D-day came to an end, C Company pulled back to the airfield, leaving B Company to hold any Egyptian attacks at the sewage farm. Next day the paras expected to see a major naval bombardment to mark the beginning of the second stage of the operation, the amphibious assault on Port Said. All the 3rd Battalion's objectives had been secured, and their comrades in the French 2nd Colonial Parachute Regiment had completed their tasks at Port Fuad with typical panache. Their commander, Colonel Conan, had made telephone contact with the Egyptian commander and he was confident that a surrender could be negotiated without further military action; Conan, therefore, ordered all air strikes to cease at 1700 hours. Brigadier Butler took a helicopter to join Conan in the French positions, and from 1800 to about 2030 hours an uneasy peace reigned.

As night fell, the 2nd Battalion came ashore with a squadron of Centurion tanks

A quick peace settlement was too much to hope for, however, and after a fairly quiet night 3 Para was deployed on 6 November in support of the amphibious invasion of the port. Following a series of air strikes and a naval bombardment of the beach-head, 40 and 42 Commandos, Royal Marines, hit the beaches just before 0700 hours, with 3 Para's medium machine guns helping to give them a clear run from their craft. A little later, 45 Commando, RM, was landed by helicopter in the town, and the 1st Foreign Legion Parachute Regiment was coming ashore alongside Port Said's eastern breakwater. Elements of 3 Para were in action throughout the day, and, as night fell, the 2nd Battalion (2 Para) came ashore with a squadron of Centurion tanks. Joined by the brigadier, 2 Para forged out to El Cap, 19 miles down the Suez Canal, and at 2359 hours the Egyptians agreed to a ceasefire.

The 3rd Battalion, The Parachute Regiment, came out of Suez quite well. In military terms, the operation was an outstanding success, and for 3 Para to have done so well with so little support or specialised equipment against an enemy strong in numbers and armour, especially in the confusion of an airborne assault, was no mean feat. Operation Musketeer taught a great many lessons: one of the most important was that a parachute battalion is more than the sum of its parts – and, if given the right support, it is nearly invincible.

THE AUTHOR Gregor Ferguson is the editor of *Defence Africa and the Middle East* and has contributed to several other publications. His most recent work is a short history of The Parachute Regiment in which he served in the 10th (Volunteer) Battalion.

2ND MARINES

The 2nd Marines, vanguard of the 2nd Marine Division in the assault on Tarawa, traces its lineage to the 1st Advance Base Regiment, which was formed at Philadelphia in 1913 and saw action in Mexico, Haiti and the Dominican Republic. The regiment was disbanded in 1934. On 1 February 1941 it reformed as the 2nd Marines and trained at San Diego until the outbreak of war with Japan the following December. After a period of coastal defence duty and further training, the regiment was deployed to the southwest Pacific in July 1942 in preparation for the Guadalcanal campaign. B Company, the first Marine unit to land during the operation, went ashore on Florida Island to protect the left flank of the forces landing at Tulagi. Soon afterwards the remainder of the regiment was landed to participate in mopping up Japanese forces on Tulagi and its neighbouring islands. The 2nd Marines then moved to Guadalcanal itself to join the 1st Marine Division's offensive along the north coast. At the end of January 1943, the regiment was withdrawn to New Zealand and trained with its parent division for several months.
The 2nd Marine Division, whose shoulder sleeve insignia is shown above, provided the bulk of the forces used in taking Tarawa and the rest of the Gilbert Islands, and also saw action in the Mariana Islands in 1944. After the surrender of Japan, the division became part of the occupying forces before returning to the United States. Since 1945 the division has had special responsibility for amphibious operations in the Caribbean and Mediterranean areas.

Lashed by Japanese machine-gun, mortar and artillery fire, the US 2nd Marines fought to the death on the beaches of Tarawa

JUST BEFORE dawn on 20 November 1943, a Japanese coastal battery on Betio Island, at the southwestern end of Tarawa Atoll, part of the Gilbert Islands in the central Pacific, opened fire at a range of about six miles. Its target was an American naval force consisting of three battleships, four cruisers, and several transports supported by minesweepers and destroyers. Shortly afterwards, two battlewagons, the task force's flagship, the *Maryland*, and the *Colorado*, deployed for counter-battery work, bombarding the shore batteries with 16in shells. The battle for Tarawa was on, and the men of Major-General Julian Smith's 2nd Marine Division, hardened veterans of the gruelling Guadalcanal campaign, were back in the war against Japan.

Elsewhere in the Gilberts, other American forces were going into action. The attempted seizure of the islands, Operation Galvanic, was the vital first step in a new offensive in the central Pacific aimed, eventually, at establishing bases in the Marianas from where strikes against the Japanese homeland could be launched. But Tarawa, a bracelet of tiny coral islands that was to become a part of US Marine Corps history, was the toughest objective in the campaign for the Gilberts, and was the most important strategically. On Betio Island itself, there was a heavily-defended airstrip suitable for fighters and light bombers. No thrust northwestwards to the Marshalls and Marianas could be considered until Tarawa had been taken.

The Japanese had established a main defensive

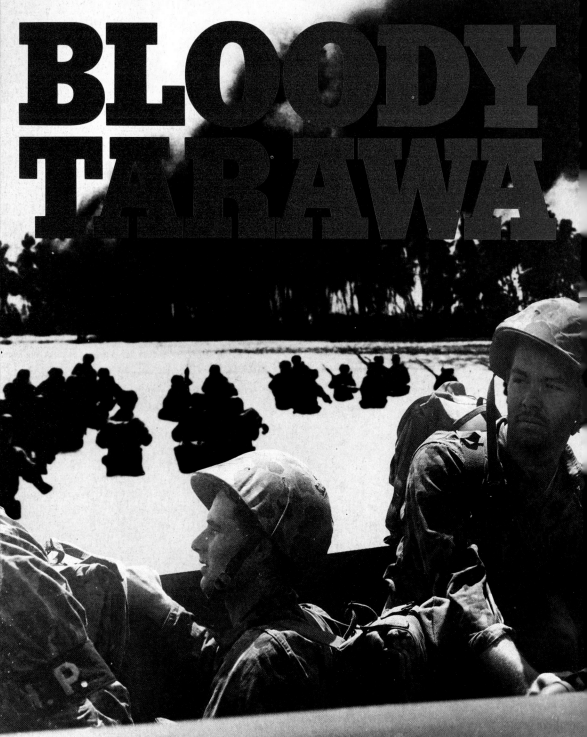

BLOODY TARAWA

of defences: mines, concrete obstacles and barbed wire were disposed offshore to channel attackers into pre-arranged killing grounds, and a four-foot-high sea wall – sufficient to halt even tracked landing vehicles – was defended by enfilading machine-gun posts able to spray a murderous hail of bullets on any assault force attempting to claw its way off the beaches. The coastal defences included four eight-inch guns and several smaller pieces, and a network of bunkers, built with reinforced concrete roofs up to six-and-a-half feet thick, served to protect the defenders. Nor was the quality of the Japanese garrison in doubt: over half of the 4800 men under Rear Admiral Meichi Shibasaki were elite Special Naval Landing Force troops.

However, the greatest obstacle that the marine assault force had to overcome was Tarawa itself. In the words of the American Central Pacific Commander-in-Chief, Admiral Chester Nimitz, 'The ideal defensive barrier has always been the one that could not be demolished, which held up assaulting forces under the unobstructed fire of the defenders and past which it was impossible to run, crawl, dig, climb or sail.' The barrier reef at Tarawa fulfilled these conditions to the letter:

The assaulting forces consisted of the 2nd Marine Division under Major-General Julian Smith. The attack would be spearheaded by Colonel David Shoup's 2nd Marines and the 2nd Battalion, 8th Marine Regiment, while the remaining two battalions of the 8th Marines were held as a divisional reserve. Additionally, a corps reserve of three battalion landing teams of the 6th Marines was held to cover the entire operation in the Gilberts and would be released to the division if needed.

As the US naval force closed on Tarawa, more of the warships joined in the bombardment, raining down ton after ton of high-explosive and high-trajectory armour-piercing shells on the Japanese defences. Some three-and-a-half miles off Betio, the assault teams transferred to their landing craft. While the larger warships stayed on station to the

Below right: Hitting the beaches. On 20 November 1943, troops of the 2nd Marine Division, under Major-General Julian Smith, pounced on the Japanese-held island of Tarawa in the Pacific. The assault was preceded by a ferocious naval bombardment, yet the marines coming in (below) were under no illusion as to the task they faced. Main picture: The shallow lagoon around Tarawa could not be navigated by the US landing craft and the men had to wade ashore, sitting targets for heavy enemy fire. Above: Battlefield conference. Colonel David Shoup (centre, holding map), commander of the 2nd Marines, confers with Lieutenant-Colonel Evans Carlson (seated), and Colonel Merritt Edson (centre, standing with hands on hips).

CLEARING THE GILBERTS

Early in 1943, the Allied forces under General Douglas MacArthur in the southwest Pacific had taken Guadalcanal and were poised to advance on Japan through the Solomons, New Guinea and the Philippines. During the months that followed, US Naval and Marine Corps forces in the central Pacific, under Admiral Chester Nimitz, prepared for a new island-hopping offensive. The offensive was designed to step up pressure on the Japanese, secure MacArthur's right flank, and eventually provide forward bases from which bombing operations, and ultimately a decisive amphibious landing in Japan itself, could be mounted.

On 20 November 1943, the central Pacific campaign opened with the launching of Operation Galvanic – the retaking of the Gilberts at the outer edge of Japan's new Pacific island empire.

The forces for Operation Galvanic comprised the US Fifth Fleet, under Vice-Admiral Raymond Spruance, and V Amphibious Corps under Major-General Holland Smith. As the 2nd Marine Division moved on Tarawa, an army landing force consisting of the 165th Infantry (reinforced) went ashore on Makin Island further north, securing it by 23 November. The day after the Tarawa and Makin assaults, the Corps Reconnaissance Company landed and captured Apanama Atoll. With the end of mopping up operations on Tarawa, on 28 November, it only remained for the 2nd Division's Reconnaissance Company to sweep the neighbouring atolls for Japanese outposts. None were found. The Gilberts were safely in American hands – and within two months V Amphibious Corps was back in action, pushing forward into the next objective, the Marshall Islands.

west, giving support fire and ready to meet any Japanese naval intervention, the marines began the long, tense journey to the assault beaches on the lagoon side of the island. Only the first three waves had LVTs (landing vehicle tracked); the remainder travelled in LCVPs (landing craft vehicle, personnel) and LCMs (landing craft mechanised) – assault craft that risked going aground on the edge of the reef lying several hundred yards offshore.

Two minesweepers were already at work in the lagoon clearing a channel, with two destroyers in close support. By 0823 hours on 20 November, when the first wave of LVTs arrived, one of the minesweepers was marking the line-of-departure and would function as a control vessel from then on. H-hour was timed for 0830, but it was already obvious that the vehicles were making slower progress than had been hoped.

As the first wave of LVTs crossed the reef, the fire support lifted. The effect of the naval bombardment seemed devastating: a cloud of smoke and coral dust hung in the air and many of the enemy's gun emplacements had been disabled. In the words of the naval gunfire support commander, Admiral Kingman, 'It seemed almost impossible for any human being to be alive on Betio Island.' But Kingman had underestimated the strength of the Japanese defensive works.

Only the destroyers in the lagoon were close enough to give accurate suppressive fire during the final run-in. Taking advantage of the lull, the defenders of Tarawa returned to their posts and opened up with 75mm airburst shells and machine-gun fire.

At 0855, just as the supporting bombardment lifted, the first team of marines went into action. The scout and sniper platoon of the 2nd Marine Regiment under Lieutenant William Hawkins reached the end of Betio's long pier by LCVP and took it by storm. Clambering up a ramp to the pier deck, Hawkins' men fought a fierce action against some 10 or 12 Japanese, destroying two wooden huts with flame-throwers and securing a flanking position that might have proved troublesome to the landing forces.

The first marines hit the beaches at 0910. Those LVTs of the first three waves that got across the reef were in most cases unable to cross the barriers sited along the shore. Their occupants reached the beaches, rolled out of the landing craft and raced for what cover they could find in front of the coastal wall. Then, pinned down by cross-fire from enemy machine guns, they began taking heavier losses. Moving forward from the beach would be an inch-by-inch, yard-by-yard, bunker-by-bunker struggle. And the struggle was going to be bloody.

The situation in the water was even worse. Some of the LVTs were destroyed by enemy fire before reaching the shore, and the non-tracked craft were unable to cross from the lagoon to the beaches. The following waves of marines had to walk ashore across several hundred yards of treacherous reef, their landing craft grounded by a tide that was lower than predicted. Lashed by withering machine-gun, mortar and artillery fire, the marines had no cover and no choice but to wade on, undaunted, through the blood-darkened water, past the bodies of their comrades. Robert Sherrod was a journalist with the Marines who faced the full fury of the Japanese fire on the approach to the beaches:

'No sooner had we hit the water than the Japanese machine guns really opened up. There must have been five or six of them concentrating their fire on us – there was no nearer target in the water at the

Below: The grisly aftermath of 'Bloody Tarawa'. Lifeless bodies, abandoned equipment and smashed amphibians litter the shoreline of Red 2 beach, the objective of the 2nd Battalion, 2nd Marines under Colonel Herbert Amey. Amey and many of his men were cut down by withering machine-gun fire from carefully hidden enemy bunkers.

Tarawa
2nd Marine Division
November 1943

On 20 November 1943 the American central Pacific campaign opened with Operation Galvanic — the retaking of the Japanese-held Gilbert Islands. The most difficult objective in the Gilberts was the heavily fortified island of Betio, part of a ring of coral islands known as Tarawa Atoll. The assault on Tarawa by marines of the 2nd Marine Division cost 1000 American lives, but by 28 November the atoll was secure.

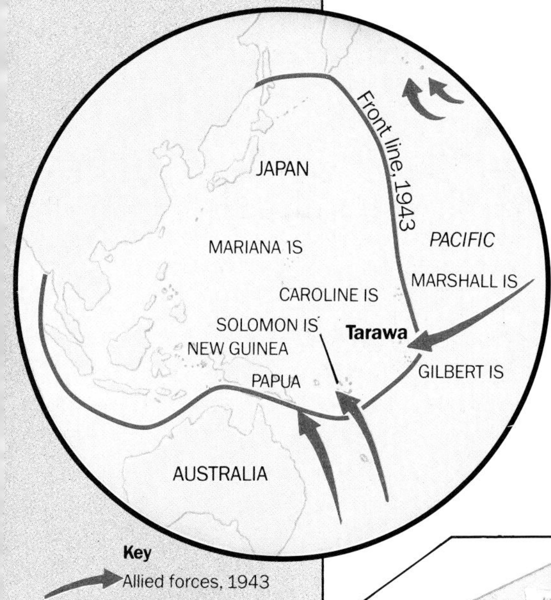

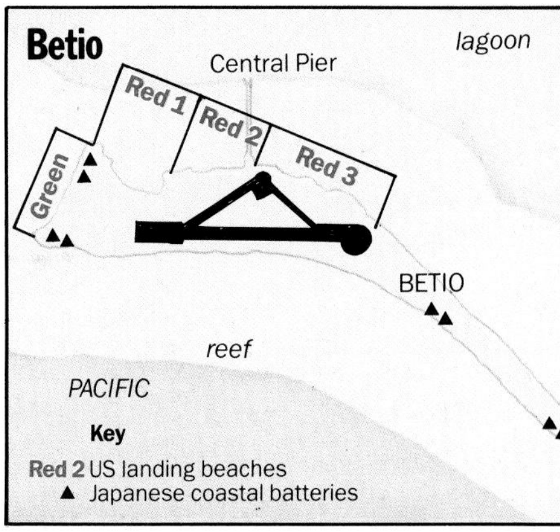

Betio

lagoon
Central Pier
Red 1
Red 2
Red 3
Green
BETIO
PACIFIC
reef

Key
Red 2 US landing beaches
▲ Japanese coastal batteries

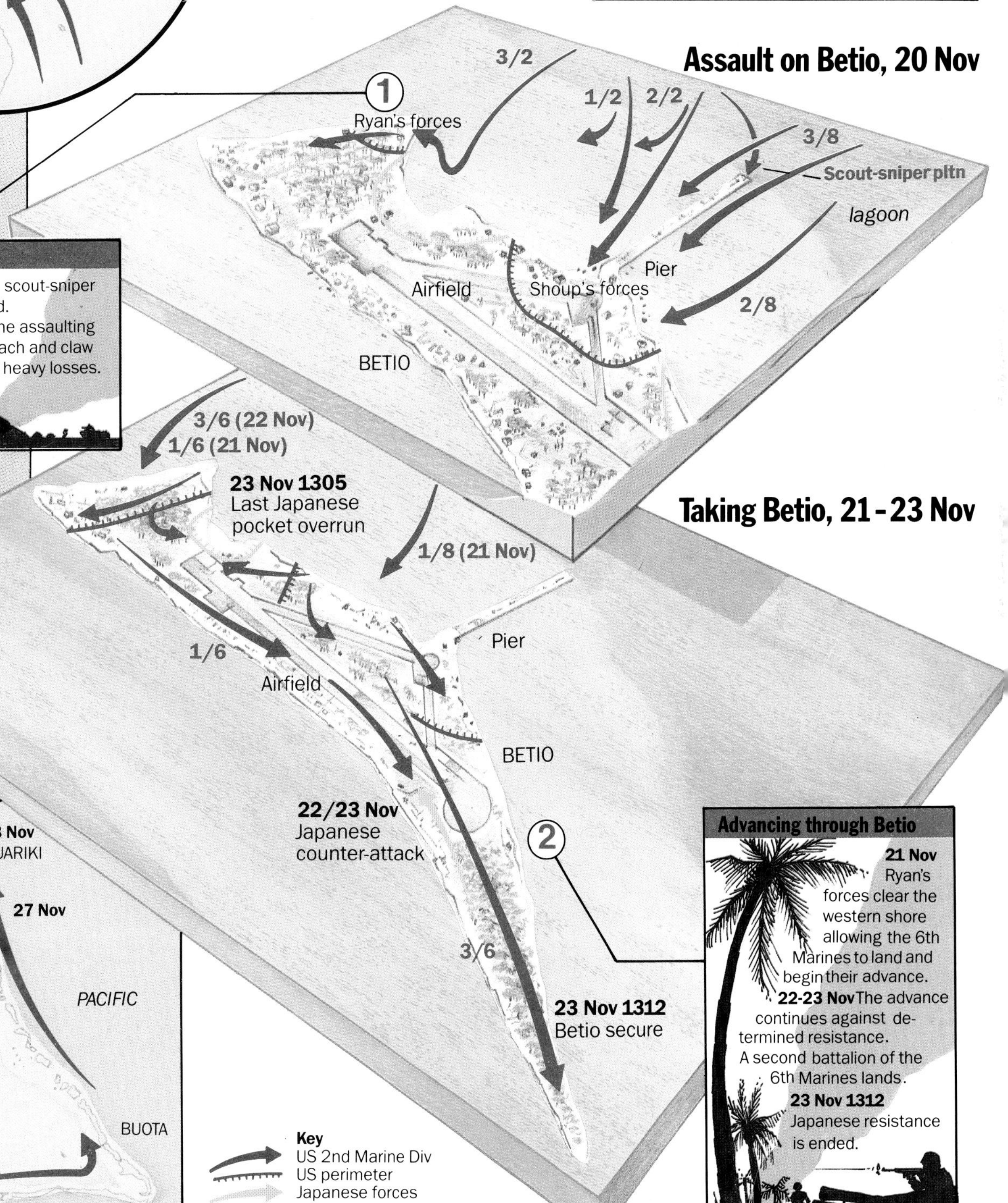

Across Betio beach

20 Nov 0855 The 2nd Marines' scout-sniper platoon storms Betio's pierhead.
0910 Laced by enemy fire, the assaulting battalions reach Betio beach and claw their way forward taking heavy losses.

Assault on Betio, 20 Nov

3/2
1/2 2/2
3/8
Scout-sniper pltn
lagoon
Ryan's forces
Pier
Airfield
Shoup's forces
2/8
BETIO
①

Taking Betio, 21-23 Nov

3/6 (22 Nov)
1/6 (21 Nov)
23 Nov 1305 Last Japanese pocket overrun
1/8 (21 Nov)
1/6
Airfield
Pier
BETIO
22/23 Nov Japanese counter-attack
②
3/6
23 Nov 1312 Betio secure

Advancing through Betio

21 Nov Ryan's forces clear the western shore allowing the 6th Marines to land and begin their advance.
22-23 Nov The advance continues against determined resistance. A second battalion of the 6th Marines lands.
23 Nov 1312 Japanese resistance is ended.

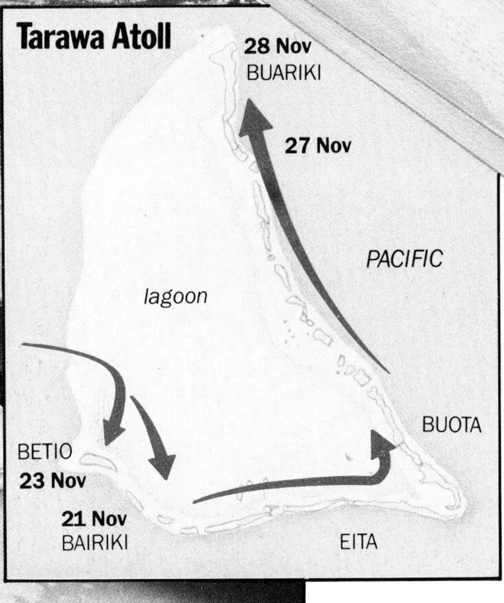

Tarawa Atoll

28 Nov BUARIKI
27 Nov
PACIFIC
lagoon
BETIO 23 Nov
BUOTA
21 Nov BAIRIKI
EITA

Key
→ US 2nd Marine Div
US perimeter
Japanese forces
Main Japanese positions
1/6 US Marine units (battalion/regiments)

(world map)
JAPAN
MARIANA IS
PACIFIC
CAROLINE IS
MARSHALL IS
SOLOMON IS
NEW GUINEA
Tarawa
PAPUA
GILBERT IS
AUSTRALIA
Front line, 1943

Key
→ Allied forces, 1943

time. I don't believe that there was one of the 15 men who wouldn't have sold his chances for an additional 25 dollars added to his life-insurance policy. It was painfully slow, wading in such deep water. We had 700yds to walk slowly into this machine-gun fire, looming into larger targets as we rose onto higher ground.'

Each of the three assault beaches was the objective of one battalion landing team. East of the pier, Red 3 beach was the target of Major Henry Crowe's 2nd Battalion, 8th Marines. Red 2, the centre beach immediately west of the pier, was the objective of Colonel Herbert Amey's 2nd Battalion, 2nd Marines. Amey was an early casualty and his command was taken over by Lieutenant-Colonel Walter Jordan. The westernmost objective, Red 1, was assigned to Major John Schoettel's 3rd Battalion, 2nd Marines.

Not one of the battalions arrived intact. Each suffered heavy casualties during the landing, and only one arrived on the correct beach with its commander.

Crowe's battalion

Far left: Reinforcements from the 1st Battalion, 2nd Marines wade ashore on 21 November to help their comrades pinned down on Red 2 beach. Left: Under a sky blackened by smoke from a blazing fuel dump, marines radio for further orders. Main picture: A lone marine lines up on a Japanese bunker. Below left: Forsaking the reassuring protection of Tarawa's sea wall, marines move inland to flush the enemy from their positions near the airstrip.

US Marine, Tarawa 1943
This weary marine wears the two-piece herringbone-twill fatigue suit, brown boots and M1 helmet with 'beach' camouflage cover. He is armed with the M1 Garand semi-automatic rifle.

got ashore on Red 3 under the excellent covering fire provided by the destroyer *Ringgold*. Only in the fourth and fifth waves did his casualties mount to 10 per cent. By noon Crowe had a platoon of medium tanks available and he fought aggressively, deploying 37mm guns in defence, and pushing inland with infantry, tanks and demolition teams in close mutual support.

On the other two beaches the position was less favourable. On the centre beach, Jordan took command of the 2nd Battalion, 2nd Marines, establishing a command post in a shell crater on the shore at about 1000 hours. Few of his officers had gained the beach. Many of his men were still in the water; he received a report that they could not advance due to machine-gun positions to their front and flanks, and sniper fire from trees in their immediate vicinity. Jordan was acutely aware of his precarious position, 'At this time there was no contact between elements on my right or left and I could not find out how many men of each company had landed.'

The Japanese strongpoints that were wreaking such havoc on Jordan's men were part of a chain that extended along the right half of the centre beach and covered the cove that formed most of Red 1 on the right flank. These positions ensured that neither of the two battalions on the right could establish themselves intact on their respective beaches. At least 100 of Jordan's men had been driven way over to the far right, reaching the shore on the extreme western edge of the island, where they linked up with the remnants of the 3rd Battalion, 2nd Marines.

Under deadly fire from the Japanese strongpoints along the Red 1 cove, Kyle's men crossed the reef

Major Schoettel, the 3rd Battalion's commander, had withdrawn from Red 1 under heavy fire. There were no friendly troops in position ashore and he believed that the first three waves of his landing force had been wiped out. Schoettel reported to Colonel Shoup, now embarked in a landing craft at the line-of-departure and watching the assault anxiously, that his battalion was taking heavy losses. Shoup radioed that he was to come in on the centre beach. Schoettel's last message to his commander was, 'We have nothing left to land.'

Shoup decided to reinforce the centre beach, Red 2, where Jordan's men were dangerously understrength. He deployed the remaining battalion of the 2nd Marines, the 1st Battalion under Major Wood Kyle, with orders to land on Red 2 and push to the right. Under deadly fire from the Japanese strongpoints along the Red 1 cove, Kyle's men crossed the reef, reaching Red 2 between 1130 and 1200 hours. The battalion lost some 200 men on the way and a further 100 were forced off course by enemy fire, joining elements of the other battalions that were cut off at the western edge of Red 1.

By noon, Shoup himself had waded ashore and had established his command post on Red 2 next to a Japanese bunker. As he recalled later, 'I was never off my feet for 50 hours, standing for the most time by an enemy pillbox with 26 live Japs therein.' The situation was perilous.

Matters gradually improved, however. Shoup was soon in contact with Crowe's forces on Red 3. An attack with medium tank support was mounted across the airstrip taxiway and a joint perimeter, some 300yds deep, was established. But there were strong Japanese forces on both flanks and the possi-

TARAWA'S BLOODY LESSONS

The capture of Tarawa in late 1943 marked the beginning of the end for Japanese military supremacy in the Pacific war, but the heavy casualties suffered by the Marines, over 3000 men, forced US planners to review their island-assault tactics in the light of harsh experience.

The Tarawa landings had been preceded by a naval barrage of considerable ferocity, yet when the Marines made their run-in to the beaches they were hit by heavy fire from machine guns and artillery that had escaped the worst of the bombardment. In future operations, the scale and duration of the softening-up process would be much greater to smash the enemy's heavily fortified bunkers and trench systems.

Once on Tarawa, the Marines found it difficult to co-ordinate their actions: radio links between the assault troops and the command ships lying offshore were poor, making it extremely difficult to call up reinforcements to help relieve a hard-pressed sector or bring down air and artillery support on an enemy position.

During the critical battles fought as the Marines pushed inland from the beaches, they faced a succession of defences that could not be silenced by the relatively inaccurate fire provided by the supporting naval units. The Marines, short on heavy weapons, had to close with the enemy, and in doing so suffered. It was soon recognised that 'go-anywhere' amphibians, some equipped with bunker-busting weapons, would provide an effective counter-measure to this problem.

The lessons of Tarawa were well learnt. In later operations, the Marines had both the back-up and equipment to tackle even the most stubborn Japanese defences.

Bottom left: Leathernecks of Major Henry Crowe's 2nd Battalion, 2nd Marines on Red 3 beach, plaster enemy positions with machine-gun fire. Centre left: Shrouded by the acrid smoke of battle, a marine throws a grenade at a Japanese pillbox while his buddies take a break.
Left: Enemy dead lie where they fell in defence of Tarawa.

bility of a counter-attack at night could not be ruled out. Accordingly, one of the divisional reserve battalions was committed to the centre beach, the 3rd Battalion, 8th Marines, commanded by Major Robert Ruud. Ruud's men came in on both sides of the pier, taking casualties from the still-murderous fire from Japanese positions on the left and right.

Meanwhile, on the extreme right flank of Red 1 at the western edge of Betio Island, Major Michael Ryan assumed command of those elements of the 1st, 2nd and 3rd Battalions of the 2nd Marines that had been forced westwards by the ferocity of the Japanese defences in the cove that comprised most of Red 1. Two medium tanks arrived on the shore within Ryan's perimeter and by 1630 he had mounted an attack southwards along Green Beach, the western coast of Betio. His men pushed some 500yds along the coast, but the tanks were soon knocked out by enemy action and, lacking the flame-throwers and heavy equipment needed to take out the Japanese bunkers they encountered, Ryan's marines could not hope to hold the ground they had gained. They withdrew to a defensive position at the north end of the western beach for the night.

As night drew on, the marines and their commanders waited apprehensively for the expected counter-attack. It failed to materialise, probably because Japanese communications had been wrecked by the naval bombardment and the various strongpoints were unable to co-ordinate their actions or assess the overall position.

Ryan had two medium tanks and flame-throwers to take out enemy artillery along the coast

The following morning, Julian Smith committed the remaining divisional reserve, the 1st Battalion, 8th Marines under Major Lawrence Hays, which had spent the night on board their LCVPs at the line-of-departure. Before dawn on 21 November, the battalion set off for the reef and then began the long walk ashore. Again, the marines suffered terrible casualties, and the remnants of a shattered battalion joined the right flank of Shoup's forces in the centre of the island. An artillery battalion of the 10th Marines had also got ashore with five 75mm pack howitzers. But the combined efforts of artillery and the survivors of two Marine battalions were unable to shift the determined enemy resistance on the right and there seemed to be no chance of linking up with Ryan's forces. Crowe and Ruud, on the left, had also made no progress.

However, the tide was about to turn. Ryan's forces were reinforced during the morning: he now had two medium tanks and flame-throwers and air strikes were organised to take out enemy artillery along the western coast. At 1100 hours, with supporting naval gunfire softening up Japanese resistance, Ryan's marines once more began a southward advance. This time, properly equipped, they were able to take out the remaining enemy positions. Green Beach, never part of the original assault plan, was secured shortly after 1200. General Smith could at last think in

terms of getting whole battalions ashore with minimal casualties and with their organisation, command and equipment intact. He had already obtained the release of the corps reserve to division, and the 6th Marines were on their way.

The 2nd Battalion, 6th Marines was deployed with artillery from the 10th Marines on the neighbouring island of Bairiki to contribute its firepower to the final assault and prevent a Japanese retreat across the narrow stretch of water separating the two islands. By the late afternoon of 21 November, the 1st Battalion, 6th Marines under Major William Jones was coming ashore on Green Beach.

In the centre, Shoup's forces had also made progress after resupply during the morning. Elements of Shoup's battalions had advanced across the airstrip and reached the south coast of the island. At the end of the day, Shoup had cause for renewed optimism. He reported the position to General Smith aboard *Maryland*, 'Casualties many; percentage dead not known; combat efficiency: we are winning.'

At 0805 on the morning of 22 November, Major Jones, commander of the first battalion landing force to arrive on Betio intact, began his advance along the island's south coast. He made rapid progress, although for lack of a sufficient number of medium tanks, he experienced difficulties in taking out some of the enemy bunkers. The 8th Marines under Crowe and Ruud made progress during the afternoon, advancing slowly along the northern shore in the teeth of fierce Japanese resistance. General Smith was now ashore to direct the final operation, and by nightfall Jones' marines had linked up with the 8th Marines to their left, forming a line across the island.

During the evening, the long-expected counter-attack came. But it was now too late. As the Japanese massed for the assault, naval gunfire and artillery from Bairiki and Betio were called down to devastating effect. The marines held off firing until the last moment, and the Japanese casualties were heavy as they surged into the attack.

During the following morning, 23 November, one more fresh battalion was deployed, the 3rd Battalion, 6th Marines. Under Lieutenant-Colonel Kenneth McLeod, the new forces pushed forward, renewing the attack to the eastern end of the island, while the exhausted remnants of the initial assault force concentrated on the remaining enemy pocket, along the cove of the original Red 1 beach. At around 1300, this pocket was finally eliminated. McLeod's forces reached the eastern end of the island at about the same time, and at 1312 General Julian Smith pronounced Betio secure.

The following day, the battered, depleted and exhausted 2nd and 8th Marines left Betio Island. With only Betio and Bairiki captured, the 6th Marines were left with the task of tracking down the few remaining enemy forces. On the northern island of Buariki some 175 Japanese made a final stand, but by 28 November the bitter struggle for Tarawa was over. Of the original Japanese garrison of over 4800 men, only 146 prisoners were taken. Taking Tarawa cost the Marine Corps over 1000 dead and 2000 wounded, but the lessons learned there had far-reaching effects on the conduct of future amphibious assaults in the Pacific war. And the bloody assault across Betio reef has passed into legend.

THE AUTHOR Barry Smith has taught politics at Exeter and Brunel Universities. He is a contributor to the journal *History of Political Thought* and has written a number of articles on military subjects.

PATU, the Rhodesian police anti-terrorist unit, waged a tough campaign against infiltrating guerrillas in the Zambezi valley

ON 17 MAY 1966 a white farming couple, Mr and Mrs Viljoen, were killed on their Nevada Farm, situated near Hartley in central Rhodesia. The Viljoens were the victims of a raid that followed a large incursion by ZANU (Zimbabwe African National Union) guerrillas across the Zambezi river from neighbouring Zambia in late April. Soon after the guerrillas had crossed the border, part of their force had been located by the security forces on the outskirts of Sinoia and elimin-

reservist force, but one man in particular, Bill Bailey, a regular officer with the BSAP, was far-sighted enough to realise that the threat posed by the unconventional style of rural warfare favoured by the guerrillas, would have to be met with a more specialised response than the ordinary pattern of everyday police work.

Bailey himself had a great deal of experience of special-operations work: during World War II he had served in the Western Desert with the Long Range Desert Group (LRDG) and had then gone on to work with partisan groups in Albania.

In 1964, realising that the growing terrorist threat might take hold of his own district of Lomagundi, which lay between the Rhodesian capital, Salisbury, and the Zambezi crossing points, Bailey established

WAR IN THE BUSH

ated by a combined police, army and air force operation, code-named Pandora; but the gang responsible for the killing of the Viljoens had got through. The Sinoia and Hartley incidents were to prove a turning point in what was now beginning to look like a war in Rhodesia.

In the early 1960s trouble had already begun to ferment in Rhodesia's African townships and by 1963 this unrest was augmented by terrorist attacks mounted by dissident nationalist guerrillas who were based and being trained outside the country. At first, these raids were on a modest scale and not particularly successful, but by 1966 the guerrillas were better organised and equipped, and had begun to launch large-scale incursions into the country. To combat the growing security problem, the British South Africa Police (BSAP) were recruiting a police

a small military-style outfit within the police known as the Tracker Combat Teams. Senior police officers in Salisbury, however, took a very dim view of this paramilitary approach and Bailey was ordered to disband what they regarded as his 'private army'.

But Bailey kept his concept alive and his team members volunteered to a man for the officially-tolerated Volunteers for Advanced Training (VATs). Known in those days as 'Bailey's Bloody Bush Babies', the VATs, most of them police reservists, concentrated on really getting to know their areas. Many of them were farmers and, working in pairs, they checked out their own farms and the surrounding territory, keeping a sharp eye open for evidence of terrorist movement in the area. Knowledge of the terrain, the local villages and the people, Bailey knew, was the key to counter-insurgency work.

In April and May 1966 the VATs played a significant part in Operation Pandora and the search for the Nevada Farm gang. Opposition within the army and from senior police officers to the police being involved in anti-terrorist work began to melt and Bailey's ideas suddenly became far more acceptable. In July, Police General Headquarters (PGHQ) issued instructions that all regular policemen, from the rank of chief superintendent down to constable, were to be trained in the basics of anti-terrorist work. As the training officer, Bailey was installed in an office at PGHQ with Reg Seekings, a member of the Marlborough Police Field Reserve, to assist him.

Together, Bailey and Seekings took on the task of

PATU volunteers train with a light machine gun (top) and FN FALs (above). Weapon instruction formed part of an SAS-style regime of back-breaking training instituted by Inspector Reg Seekings. Above right: PATU stalwarts take a break during a patrol. On the left is Bob Mansill and in the centre, Herby Gibbon, winner of the Mr Rhodesia and Mr South Africa body-building awards. Right: Jerry Cleveland of PATU prepares rations in the bush.

forming a new police section, specifically trained and organised to meet the terrorist threat, and on 1 August 1966 the Police Anti-Terrorist Unit (PATU) officially came into being. A desperate shortage of equipment and facilities, however, meant that only 32 volunteers could be accepted at the outset. Only the men who passed a rigorous selection course devised by Bailey and Seekings would be taken on.

Seekings, who had served with the British SAS from its very beginnings to the end of World War II, had been a close friend of Bailey during the desert days and, together, they resurrected the notoriously demanding style of training that has always been the hallmark of the SAS. 'Reg's PT', as this regime soon became popularly known among the PATU volunteers, was designed to cream off only the very best from the ranks of the police reserve. Seekings' approach was quite straightforward:

'You've got to hammer these people in training. I'll always remember Jock Lewis, going back to the SAS days, saying, "Training must be made as hard as is humanly possible, so that when you go on an operation you find that it's easier than your training." It gives a man confidence and a confident man, with a little bit of luck, will always come through. It was very hard to put across all those drills, and I had to drive it in and be really set in my ways, because it was hard to make a man understand that I wasn't asking him to win a VC. It was to save his own bloody life. He must attack without question, without hesitation, go in.'

With minimal equipment, a rucksack and a rifle each, scrounged from the quartermaster, the first volunteers began their basic training. Seekings describes the qualities he was looking for:

'We took them out into the field to see how a man reacted physically, how he could find his way around, how good he was at bushcraft and how he was going to fit into the picture. How was he going to get along with his mates? Could he mix in? Could he take authority? And could he keep his mouth shut? The biggest thing in all this was making a man keep quiet. When you're in the bush you've got movement going on all the time. Elephants and other animals are moving around, but once you get the sound of metal, the chink of a rifle, or a voice, the game's up.'

Having ascertained whether a man was suitable material for PATU advanced training, Seekings then sent the selected recruits on an endurance course and gave further instruction in weapons handling and map reading. The trainees were deliberately taken out to areas where they had to cope with all the hardships of rough terrain, extreme heat, and water shortage. Survivors of advanced training were selected to make up the operational PATU teams.

Bailey and Seekings took the training regime on a tour of the police districts and within six months PATU was operational. But PATU still had more than just the enemy to contend with. Despite PGHQ's acceptance of the necessity for anti-terrorist personnel after the Sinoia and Hartley incidents, many officers continued to view PATU's existence as a radical departure from the traditional values of police work and found the emphasis on weapon proficiency particularly hard to swallow. PATU also met with considerable animosity from within the ranks of the regular army, who regarded the PATU men as 'coppers' who should stick to police work and leave the task of hunting down armed and dangerous terrorists to men who knew what they were doing. Subsequent events were to alter these opinions.

Above: PATU members receive their first issue of camouflage uniform. This picture was taken during a PATU operation and legend has it that the quartermasters were far from happy at having to enter the war zone. Right: Inching forward through thick bush, a PATU stick moves into the attack. Below: A very early photo of PATU men, taken before the issue of camouflage and when FNs were in very short supply. Several of the group are armed with old .303s. Far right: Inspector Reg Seekings, the driving force behind the PATU training regime.

Rhodesia

(map labels: ZAMBIA, Zambezi, Chirundu, Lake Kariba, Kariba, Maramba, LOMAGUNDI, Sinoia, Salisbury, Hartley, Wankie, Gatooma, Que Que, R H O D E S I A, Umtali, Gwelo, Fort Victoria, Bulawayo, Shabani, Francistown, B O T S W A N A, Beitbridge, MOZAMBIQUE, S O U T H A F R I C A)

While PATU weathered this friction and protest undeterred, such opposition made it hard for the teams to get hold of the weapons and kit they needed for their anti-terrorist role. At the outset, there were very few modern FN rifles to be had and many men had to make do with old bolt-action .303s, a fine weapon but not well-suited to close-quarters contacts with an enemy fielding AK automatic assault rifles, RPD and RPG machine guns. Uniform was also a problem. Camouflage kit was not forthcoming and the patrols were forced to take to the bush in police 'riot blues'. Only when it was found that many of the guerrillas operated in similar blue clothing were camouflage jackets issued.

It was on this precarious footing that the first PATU patrols went into action in the Zambezi valley, right on the front line where the guerrillas made their incursions. The patrols, organised into sticks of five men made up of four Europeans and one African, were dropped off at police stations in the area and then escorted down into the valley by local police officers. Down in the valley it was a war of nerves. Reg Seekings, who participated in many of the operations, describes the conditions PATUs faced:

'You could have a flurry of contacts and then there would be long periods with no contact at all. That was the trouble. It was really ball-aching for the chaps going in, and then there would be a new incursion with new groups coming into the country and all of a sudden the place would come alive.

'The plan was for us to be seen as often as possible on the river banks by the opposition, the

INSPECTOR REG SEEKINGS

In January 1939 Reg Seekings joined the British Territorial Army, mainly for the boxing, and that year won the East Anglian light-heavyweight championship. When war broke out, he volunteered for sea raiding operations and was attached to No. 7 Commando.
After training in Felixstowe and Scotland, he was sent with Layforce to the Middle East, where he took part in several missions, including the seaborne landing at Bardia. When Layforce was disbanded, Seekings was recruited by David Stirling as a founder member of 'L' Detachment of the SAS and went on to serve with great distinction in 1 SAS in North Africa, Italy, France and northwest Germany.
After the SAS was disbanded in late 1945, Seekings spent several years as a publican in Ely before emigrating to Rhodesia, where he managed a tobacco farm and a chain of stores.
In the early 1960s, as violence flared in Rhodesia's African townships, the government decided to strengthen its security forces by creating a police reserve. Seekings joined the Marlborough Field Police Reserve and became a section leader. When armed incursions began in 1966, he joined forces with an old Long Range Desert Group friend, Bill Bailey, who was the Chief Superintendent of the British South Africa Police, to form the Police Anti-Terrorist Unit (PATU). Seekings became the unit's chief instructor. He served with PATU until its disbandment on 31 July 1980, when he retired from police duty.

idea being to stop them having a clear run. Instead of having a clear passage across the valley at night, if they saw us here, there and everywhere, they would never know where we were going to be and they had to proceed with caution. The longer it took them to cross that valley, the less likelihood there was of them being an active force when they reached the other side. They'd be physically buggered and short of food and water, and suffering. Mentally, too, they'd be in trouble and that was when we picked them up.

'We had cleared the Zambezi valley of what local population there was and it became a killing area. Anything we saw in there, we knew it was a terrorist group. During the day we'd move down to the river and be seen on the banks. Then we'd move out again and be seen a few miles further up, back on the dirt road checking for new spore. The whole idea was that they knew that the area was being patrolled, and they couldn't tell whether it was just one or a dozen patrols.

'In a 100-mile area, we'd have only one stick operating and we even went to the extent of changing the dress of our patrols. We'd turn our hats inside out and change the make-up of our kit and the way it was slung. They couldn't distinguish our faces. At times they attacked us, but their main aim was to get through, so it was a case of us attacking them.'

For several years PATU fought this dangerous game of cat-and-mouse in the sweltering heat of the Zambezi valley, operating without army and air force support. By 1970 PATU numbered some 1000 men distributed around the country. Their actions in the

Above: Bill Bailey, the ex-LRDG Rhodesian police officer who first introduced the idea of a police anti-terrorist unit. Below: A PATU stick. Second from right is Section-Leader Campbell-Watt who was once ambushed by mistake by an army patrol, but wiped them out before the error was discovered. Bottom: PATU men with a personnel carrier in the bush.

border areas earned them a great deal more respect from the regular army, and PATU groups would often operate in conjunction with the military. Essentially, PATU was a tracker/reconnaissance force, and if a large contact was made, the stick was supposed to call in the army and helicopter support in the form of the Rhodesian Light Infantry (RLI) 'fire forces'. Frustration at this procedure, however, often got the better of the PATU men and, depending on the level of indoctrination with police procedure and the characters of the men involved, they would 'do a Nelson' and take on the guerrilla group themselves.

Sticks were deployed to protect convoys carrying vital supplies

In the early 1970s the guerrilla war escalated sharply, and by 1973 the guerrillas had firmly ensconsed themselves in the north and northeast of the country. The bush war had also begun to spread into other areas of the country and PATU operations had extended to the southeastern border areas where Rhodesia met Mozambique. As PATU zones of operation expanded, so did its role. In the south, sticks were deployed to protect convoys carrying vital supplies from South Africa to an economically blockaded Rhodesia, and all over the country PATUs' regular police training proved invaluable for the gathering of intelligence as Reg Seekings outlines:

'At this time, the enemy had infiltrated a lot of political commissars who were holding meetings in the villages. PATU was used to try and break up these meetings, but we found this very difficult. The problem was trying to separate the terrorists from the locals and there was always a big danger of innocent civilians getting hurt. It was a very thankless task. We eventually got down to trying to ambush the terrorists as they left the village after the meeting but that also had its problems. Most villages had a number of exits so selecting the ambush point was a bit hit or miss. Also, if the contact was initiated too soon, the terrorists would not hesitate to use the villagers as a fireguard.

'Another job we had to do was to find out who was feeding them and where they were feeding, so that we could set up ambush points at these places. We tried to get round to villages that had suffered atrocities at the hands of the terrorists and find out from the villagers the whereabouts of the terrorists, their habits, and also get a description of them. All this information was then passed to all the army personnel and patrols in the area.'

During the latter stages of the war in Rhodesia, PATU's role became closely integrated with that of the military. Although they were still policemen, many of the barriers that had isolated them from the armed forces had evaporated and they were widely respected for their experience in the field, their ability to beat the guerrillas at their own game and their professionalism in action.

Although the war in Rhodesia had spawned several highly professional anti-terrorist units such as the RLI fire forces and the Selous Scouts, PATU had been in the thick of the action since the very beginning and had steadfastly maintained that when faced with a threat to internal security, the police had a major role to play. Their actions proved that point.

THE AUTHOR, Jonathan Reed and the publishers would like to thank Reg Seekings, former chief training officer of PATU, for his invaluable assistance in the preparation of this article.

To get to grips with the Japanese Pacific strongholds, the US Marines were issued with a wealth of close combat and landing equipment

LEATHERNECK KIT

DURING THE battles for control of the Pacific islands in World War II, the United States Marine Corps (USMC) faced a skillful foe capable of turning even the most insignificant piece of real estate into a strongly fortified bulwark to protect Japanese territorial gains. Realists recognised that the recapture of the enemy-held islands would be a bloody and time-consuming business, and that specialised equipment would be needed to give the Marines a combat edge in their island-hopping campaigns.

Two particular aspects of this type of warfare stood out as needing attention. First, the assault forces would need specialised craft to deliver the troops to the beaches and then provide firepower capable of taking out enemy bunkers and pillboxes. Second, the Marines themselves would require smallarms appropriate to close-quarters combat in confined spaces and jungle, such as the M3 'Grease Gun', where volume of fire, rather than accuracy, might be the telling factor.

Officially, the Marine Corps was supposed to be armed in conformity with the rest of the US armed forces, particularly the regular infantry. In reality, however, it did not quite work out that way. The Marines were increasingly involved in a particular brand of warfare and, inevitably, there were times when they had requirements that could not be met from army sources. When these problems arose, the Marines would take whatever they could find for the job and, if it measured up in combat, it would become a standard part of their arsenal. In some cases, however, the USMC retained older, tried-and-trusted weapons of war like the M1 Garand rifle because they were familiar or their replacements were not up to much.

The first and most important requirement was for amphibious transport. Following the chaos that attended waterborne landings in World War I, in particular the Gallipoli fiasco of 1915, most military authorities were of the opinion that amphibious assault was no way to fight a war. Ships converted to carry out landings proved a liability and few strategists seemed willing to experiment with more appropriate landing craft. The Marine Corps, however, felt differently. Appreciating that any war in the Pacific would involve amphibious assaults, far-sighted officers studied possible techniques and equipment. Their first requirement was to get the troops onto the beaches with as few casualties as possible. By the 1930s, pioneering work on amphibious craft was underway in the United States.

In 1933 Donald Roebling, a retired manufacturer, developed a unique vehicle for performing rescues in the Florida Everglades, a swampy area untouched by roads, in southeast America. His revolutionary

Right: A marine recruit, his face blacked with cam cream, learns the finer points of operating a flame-thrower.

LANDING CRAFT

Although tracked amphibians played a crucial role in the Pacific campaign, the build-up of men, machines and equipment could not have been achieved without the sterling work done by the humble landing craft. The pioneer of this type of logistical support vessel was Andrew J. Higgins who developed the 'Eureka' boat for the use of fur trappers in Louisiana's swamps in the mid-1920s. To overcome the shallow, weed-infested waters of the region, the boat had a shallow draft and protected 2rpropeller.

In 1934 Higgins approached the Marine Corps with his idea; the Marines were interested but had no money to fund a long development project. Nevertheless, Higgins continued to work with the corps.

By 1939 he had completed a more suitable landing craft and in a series of trials over the next few years his design consistently outperformed any comparable vessel. Only one potentially serious problem remained: any troops using the craft had to disembark by jumping over the side.

In April 1941 Higgins visited Quantico Marine base and, after a round of discussions, agreed to partially redesign the boat with a ramp bow.

By the end of the year, Higgins, in conjunction with Brigadier-General Moses, the head of the corps' Equipment Board, had a design that fulfilled the specifications laid down by the Marines. A short time later, the Navy's Bureau of Ships authorised full-scale production of the Higgins Boat.

Landing craft were, in many ways, less flexible in their application than tracked amphibians, but without their vital contribution in the days after the initial assault on an island, the Marines might not have been able to maintain the initiative gained during the opening stages of their onslaught.

Above: A heavily-laden landing craft heads for the beaches of Tarawa. Below: Marines debouch from an LSI (Landing Ship, Infantry). Above right: An LVT4 armed with 12.7mm and 7.62mm machine guns. Right: A line of LVTs, including an LVT(A)2 (foreground) and LVT4s, ferrying troops to Iwo Jima. Below right: An LVT2 (right foreground) and LVT1s on Tarawa's Red 2 beach.

design comprised an aluminium hull fitted with tracks that, by paddle-wheel action, propelled the amphibian through water and also allowed it to move on land. He built several versions of this vehicle, known as the 'Alligator', and in 1937 they came to the attention of the Marine Corps. An officer, Major John Kaluf, went to Florida to see Roebling's brainchild in action and was sufficiently impressed to recommend the Alligator to the Marine Equipment Board, who authorised further tests. In 1939, the board ordered three Alligators and put them through their paces at Quantico Marine base. Satisfied by their performance, the Marine authorities provided Roebling with funds to make some minor modifications, and then gave him a contract to produce the vehicles in quantity. Thus the first Landing Vehicle Tracked (LVT) was born.

Having seen that the basic idea was sound, the Navy Bureau of Ships began working on a design of its own, passing their blueprints to the Borg-Warner Corporation for manufacture. The principal changes were the adoption of a sprung suspension and the installation of the engine and drive train from the M3 tank. Both modifications were intended to speed up

the manufacturing process; the vehicle, christened the LVT2, went into production in June 1942. Weighing 11,000kg unloaded, the LVT2 had a land speed of 32km/h and a water speed of 12km/h. Its radius of action was 161km in water and 241km on land.

Meanwhile, the executive officer of the Marine Equipment Board, Major Ernest E. Linsert, was working on the plans for an armoured amphibian adapted from the basic Alligator design. His idea was to build a vehicle, some 20ft long, 12ft wide and six-and-a-half feet high, in structural steel. Turrets, made of steel castings, housed the amphibian's main armament. Fitted with a 37mm gun and a single 7.62mm machine gun in a turret taken from the M3 light tank, one 12.7mm gun in each of its two side turrets and two fixed 12.7mm guns fired by the driver manipulating buttons on his steering levers, the design was capable of tackling even the most stubbornly defended enemy bunker. Roebling accepted the board's idea with modifications and the Marine Corps headquarters approved production in November 1940. The first vehicles, known as the Landing Vehicle, Tracked (Armoured) began rolling off the lines a short time later.

The LVT2 was quickly followed by an improved design, the LVT3. This model was an attempt to solve the main drawback of the LVT1 and 2: the problem of having to lift cargoes over the side. To offset this weakness, the LVT3 had the engine moved to the front compartment and a bottom-hinged ramp fitted to the rear, allowing a jeep and trailer to be driven into the cargo space and ferried ashore. The LVT3, fitted with two Cadillac V-8 engines and the M5 light tank's automatic transmission, first saw service at Okinawa in April 1945. The LVT4 was very similar to its predecessors, but was built by the Food Machinery Corporation. First used during the assault on Saipan in June 1944, over 8000 were built before the end of the war.

Other armoured amphibians, produced with the benefit of experience, were modifications of the basic LVT design. The LVT(A)2 was simply an armoured version of the standard cargo-carrier, and a later model, confusingly termed the LVT(A)1, was the A2 with a covered cargo space and the turret of the M3 light tank mounted behind the driver's cab. The LVT(A)4 was the LVT4 with a roofed cargo hold, fully armoured, and the turret of the M8 Howitzer Motor Carriage, fitted with a short-barrelled gun, mounted to the rear of the driver. This craft also had its debut during the landings on Saipan, and was later modified to carry the turret of the M24 light tank, complete with its 75mm main armament.

LVTs were first used during the assault on Guadalcanal in August 1942. However, their deployment was entirely logistical, ferrying ammunition and other supplies to the men on the beaches. It was not until the bloody landings at Tarawa in November 1943 that they were used in the tactical role, delivering the assault waves to their objectives. Their new role came about almost by accident: a coral reef surrounding the main objective of the landings, Betio Island, prevented any deep-draughted vessels from reaching the shoreline. Consequently, LVTs were used to ferry the Marines ashore as the craft were able to swim from their 'mother ships', clamber across the barrier reef and then swim over the intervening lagoon to land on the beaches. The success of the LVTs at Tarawa helped to resolve the argument over their use, and each Marine division was allocated 300 amphibious craft.

LVTs gave the US Marine Corps an invaluable edge in its island-hopping operations

The Marines' assault craft proved to have somewhat limited lives in action, having to face the full fury of the defenders' fire during the final approach to the objective. Yet, many of the first losses were due to design faults and poor organisation, rather than enemy fire. One of the major problems was that the LVTs' bilge pumps were driven by the engine, and if it failed for any reason, the LVT would rapidly sink. Another fault lay in the organisation of the amphibious assault units. Mother ships, used to deliver LVTs within range of their objective, would frequently refuse to repair or assist craft from other ships, condemning them to float off and eventually founder because of some minor defect.

In due course, however, these niggling shortcomings were ironed out and the LVTs played a dominant and crucial part in the battles for the control of the Pacific. Losses remained high, with over 18,000 of the various LVT models being built between 1942 and 1945. The importance of the Marines' landing

and assault craft to final victory over the Japanese cannot be overestimated. By enabling the assault troops to reach the beaches relatively unscathed and providing them with their own heavy firepower, the LVTs gave the US Marine Corps an invaluable edge in its island-hopping operations.

Once ashore, however, the Marines had to get to close-quarters to deal with the enemy, and needed smallarms capable of tackling even the most resolute defenders. Many of their arms were standard issue, but others were peculiar to the Marine Corps. In early 1942, when they began expanding their strength, the Marines were unable to obtain sufficient quantities of the standard 7.62mm M1 Garand rifle to equip every man. There were plenty of bolt-action M1903 Springfields available, but it was thought unwise to mix bolt and automatic rifles because of difficulties in ammunition supply. What was needed was an alternative automatic rifle, and as luck would have it, one was readily available.

In 1936 a captain in the Marine Reserve, Melvin M. Johnson, had developed a 7.62mm semi-automatic rifle working on the short-recoil principle. After designing a staggering 23 prototypes, he had a sound product, but whenever it was tested against the Garand, it always came second. Although rebuffed by the Marines, Johnson found a buyer in the Dutch who ordered 50,000 of his rifles. However, events overtook the Dutch before the contract was half finished. The Japanese invaded the East Indies, and Johnson was left with several thousand rifles on his hands. It was at this point that the Marines were looking for weapons and adopted the Johnson rifle.

The rifle was the only short-recoil design ever to see military service. The barrel, supported in bearings, recoiled for a fraction of an inch after firing, whereupon the bolt rotated and unlocked. Recoil sent the bolt back to cock the hammer and load a spring, while the barrel returned to its forward position. The return spring then thrust the bolt back,

M3A1 SMG

rear sight — guide rod and return spring
guide rod retaining plate
stock (retracted)
magazine filler
stock catch
trigger
trigger spring
grip
oil cap

Below far right: A marine, cradling a Browning automatic rifle, takes a break from the fighting. Right: In full equipment and armed with a Garand rifle, a marine prepares for action.

safety recess · finger hole (for cocking)

ejector cover
bolt
spent case

connector
guard
sear
magazine

guide rod locating plate

Calibre .45in
Length (stock extended) 75.7cm
(stock retracted) 57.9cm
Weight (loaded) 4.52kg
Feed 30-round box magazine
Rate of fire (cyclic) 450rpm
Muzzle velocity 280mps
Maximum effective range 200m

chambering a fresh cartridge from the rotary magazine as it did so. A unique feature of the Johnson was that the 10-shot magazine could be 'topped up' with a fresh five-round clip or with single rounds at any time during a pause in firing. This facility was a distinct advantage over the Garand, which could only be loaded with its 8-shot clip when it was empty and could not be topped up.

However, the truth of the matter was that the Garand was the better of the two weapons: the Johnson was less robust, and since the Garand was well into mass production before the Johnson appeared, it made no sense to change horses in mid-stream. The Marines abandoned the Johnson after a year when they had a sufficiency of Garands.

To accompany his rifle, Johnson had also designed a 7.62mm machine gun, the M1941, which worked on more or less the same principles, but used a side-mounted 20-shot magazine. Again, a shortage of what then passed for a light machine gun in the USA, the Browning automatic rifle, made the Marines turn to Johnson, and they bought sufficient machine guns to arm one or two battalions in the Pacific in 1942. In general the troops were enthusiastic. The M1941 proved reliable, but the magazine was somewhat small in capacity and, sticking out at the left side as it did, usually banged against the legs of the man who carried the gun. So when sufficient Browning guns appeared, another Johnson design was retired.

The Marines had used the Thompson sub-machine gun since the 1920s; indeed, they were probably the first military force to adopt the weapon, using it in Nicaragua in 1928. But the Thompson,

THE GREASE GUN

Known familiarly as the Grease Gun because of its resemblance to a mechanic's greasing tool, the M3 sub-machine gun entered service with US forces in the summer of 1943 as a cheap, easily mass-produced replacement for the much more sophisticated and costly Thompson gun.

In 1942, as the US Ordnance Department moved to a war footing, shortages of the Thompson forced military chiefs to search for a suitable alternative. More than 20 domestic and foreign weapons were evaluated, but it was the department's own M3 that was finally adopted on 24 December 1942.

Simplicity of manufacture was the gun's main advantage over its rivals. The M3's body, consisting of two tubular halves, was welded and all other components were either stamped or drawn.

In operation, the Grease Gun worked on the blowback principle with ammunition being fed into the chamber from a 30-round magazine located under the main body. Despite having a cyclical rate-of-fire of 400 rounds per minute, the muzzle did not 'kick' when fired, giving the weapon a fair degree of accuracy.

Initially, many frontline troops were unhappy with the M3, possibly because of a few teething troubles during its first months in service and their preference for the tried and trusted M1 carbine. However, most of the criticisms were unjustified and, after a few minor modifications had been made to the basic design, the M3 formed an invaluable part of the Marine Corps' inventory.

The Grease Gun remained in US service until the late 1950s.

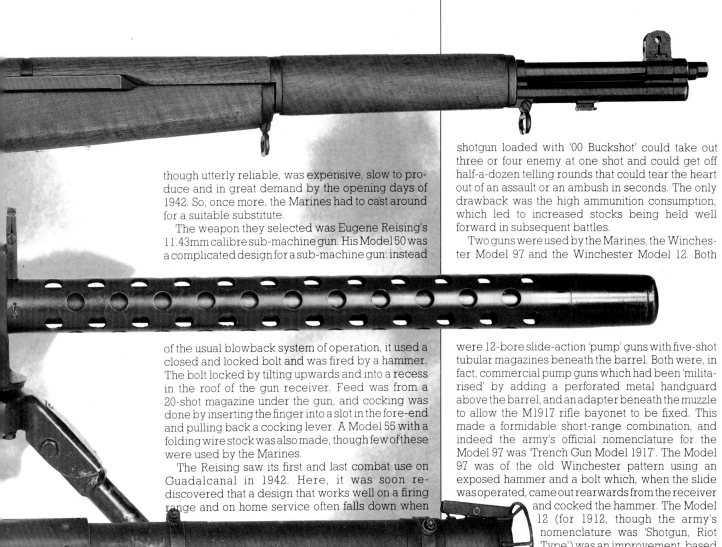

though utterly reliable, was expensive, slow to produce and in great demand by the opening days of 1942. So, once more, the Marines had to cast around for a suitable substitute.

The weapon they selected was Eugene Reising's 11.43mm calibre sub-machine gun. His Model 50 was a complicated design for a sub-machine gun: instead of the usual blowback system of operation, it used a closed and locked bolt and was fired by a hammer. The bolt locked by tilting upwards and into a recess in the roof of the gun receiver. Feed was from a 20-shot magazine under the gun, and cocking was done by inserting the finger into a slot in the fore-end and pulling back a cocking lever. A Model 55 with a folding wire stock was also made, though few of these were used by the Marines.

The Reising saw its first and last combat use on Guadalcanal in 1942. Here, it was soon rediscovered that a design that works well on a firing range and on home service often falls down when exposed to the rigours of actual combat. The basic defect of the Reising was that, although capable of unleashing up to 550 rounds per minute, dirt and sand would accumulate in the body recess, preventing the bolt from rising up to lock. Once this happened, the hammer would not release and the gun would not fire; and it required complete stripping to clean out the recess before it could be made to operate. It is said that most of the Guadalcanal weapons finished up in the waters of the Lunga river, their erstwhile owners arming themselves with anything else they could find. The after-action reports were blistering, and the Reising was withdrawn forthwith. Issued to guards, security details and police in the USA, where it received regular cleaning and attention, it was perfectly satisfactory and continued in use until the end of the war.

Another weapon which was used by the Marines on Guadalcanal was the shotgun. The US Marines have always favoured the shotgun as a close-quarters weapon, using it to some effect in France in 1918 and in China during the inter-war period. In the Pacific, they discovered that it was an ideal weapon for stopping Japanese *banzai* charges: a repeating shotgun loaded with '00 Buckshot' could take out three or four enemy at one shot and could get off half-a-dozen telling rounds that could tear the heart out of an assault or an ambush in seconds. The only drawback was the high ammunition consumption, which led to increased stocks being held well forward in subsequent battles.

Two guns were used by the Marines, the Winchester Model 97 and the Winchester Model 12. Both were 12-bore slide-action 'pump' guns with five-shot tubular magazines beneath the barrel. Both were, in fact, commercial pump guns which had been 'militarised' by adding a perforated metal handguard above the barrel, and an adapter beneath the muzzle to allow the M1917 rifle bayonet to be fixed. This made a formidable short-range combination, and indeed the army's official nomenclature for the Model 97 was 'Trench Gun Model 1917'. The Model 97 was of the old Winchester pattern using an exposed hammer and a bolt which, when the slide was operated, came out rearwards from the receiver and cocked the hammer. The Model 12 (for 1912, though the army's nomenclature was 'Shotgun, Riot Type') was an improvement, based on a newer patent in which the hammer was concealed and the bolt moved inside the receiver. Apart from that, there was little to choose between the two.

As noted above, the basic ammunition was the 00 Buckshot loading, comprising nine lead balls, weighing 286 to the kilogramme. This has a muzzle velocity of over 330m a second, and the shot pattern guaranteed three balls inside a 76cm circle at 40m range. The principal drawback that confronted the Marines in the Pacific was the abnormal humidity in the jungle, which caused the paper cartridge cases – they were conventional sporting cartridge cases – to swell, so that either they would not load, or would jam the gun. This the Marines had seen before, in the wet trenches of France in 1918, and they knew the answer – brass cases. After some sharp words from the USMC Commandant, the procurement people carried out some tests and settled on a Remington all-brass cartridge as the Marine standard. It was eventually accepted by the army as well, and became the 'Shell, Shotgun, All-brass M19'.

By the close of the war in the Pacific, the USMC was armed with a formidable array of weapons and equipment that had been proved in battle against the Japanese. Without the invaluable help of the LVTs and the firepower provided by their smallarms, whether standard issue or tailor-made for the job, the Marines might never have won such resounding and decisive victories as Tarawa and Okinawa.

Above, top: The clip-loaded M1 Garand rifle. **Above, centre:** The M1919A4 Browning machine gun, capable of unleashing up to 600 rounds per minute. **Above:** The 60mm rocket launcher. Better known as the bazooka, it had a maximum range of 215m and was deployed to deal with bunkers or armoured vehicles. **Left:** Tired leathernecks, armed with a variety of weapons including a Browning automatic rifle, an M1 carbine and a Thompson sub-machine gun.

THE AUTHOR Ian Hogg is an authority on smallarms, modern weapons systems and equipment, and the technology of warfare.

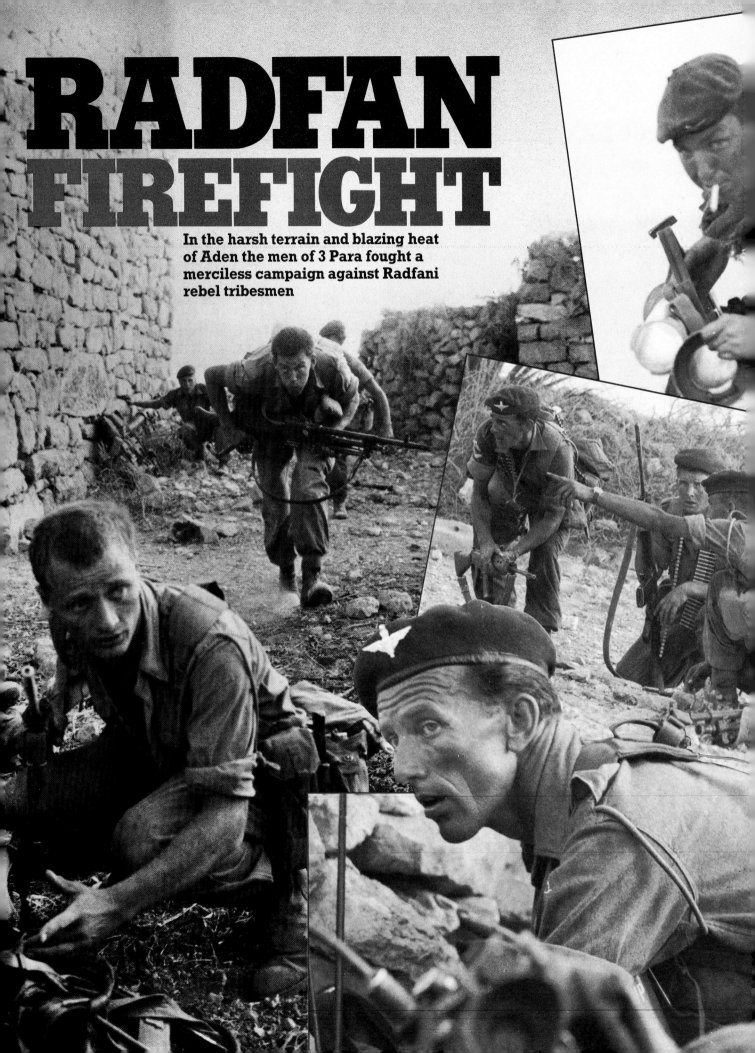

RADFAN FIREFIGHT

In the harsh terrain and blazing heat of Aden the men of 3 Para fought a merciless campaign against Radfani rebel tribesmen

IN LATE APRIL 1964, British Army trucks were rumbling up the Dhala road towards the village of Thumier, situated in the foothills of the Radfan mountains north of Aden. By the end of the month the strike force was assembled. The men of 45 Commando, Royal Marines, already based in Aden under the command of Lieutenant-Colonel Paddy Stevens, had established a camp just east of the road, and on the eve of the operation they were joined by the paras of B Company, 3rd Battalion, The Parachute Regiment (3 Para). Four rifle platoons with a section of 3in mortars, all under Major Peter Walter, were also brought up in support.

The operational plan formulated by Brigadier Louis Hargroves, overall commander of the force, had called for a parachute drop on the night of 30 April. The paras were to drop onto a key feature codenamed Cap Badge, occupying it until 45 Commando completed a sweep towards it from Wadi Boran. Unfortunately, the troop from 22 SAS which was detailed to mark the drop zone in the boulder-strewn landscape became embroiled in a fight for survival and was forced to withdraw. Also, the intensity of fire attracted by low-flying British aircraft in the area showed that the paras would be embattled immediately upon landing. The drop was therefore cancelled; instead, it was decided to undertake the operation entirely by night march.

On the night of 30 April, the marines and paras set out into the darkness. All were heavily laden, principally with ammunition and water. It was one of those marches which demand much of the infantryman.

For the officers navigating, there was the problem of maintaining direction across steep and

The campaign in the Radfan mountains was marked by a lot of foot-slogging under a blazing sun, and it proved a severe test of the paras' physical endurance. Support weapons such as the GPMG (below) and the rocket launcher (left) had to be carried long distances into battle, and GPMG ammunition was shared out amongst those armed with lighter weapons (below left). The principal threat to the paras was the Radfanis' highly accurate sniper fire (far left) and, as all these photographs show, the paras soon developed a healthy respect for the tribesmen's marksmanship. Bottom left: In the baking heat of the Radfan, the water-bottle constituted a vital piece of equipment.

THE RADFAN CAMPAIGN

The British Army, brought in by the Aden Federal government in April 1964 to curb tribal insurrection in the Radfan, was to see action in the region until the end of August.

The military campaign proceeded in three distinct stages, each marked by a new commander. The first British force, known as Radforce, was led by Brigadier Hargroves and comprised 45 Commando Royal Marines, B Company of 3 Para, two regiments of the Federal Regular Army, the 1st Battalion, of the East Anglian Brigade, an SAS troop and support units. Operations began on 29 April, Radforce gaining control of the northern sector of the Radfan by 5 May, but it was clear that a larger force was needed to tackle the tribes in the massif to the south.

On 18 May Brigadier Blacker, who succeeded Hargroves, led a much larger force, including seven infantry battalions, armoured cars, Centurion tanks, artillery and air support, against the Bakri ridge and into the Wadi Misrah, the stronghold of the predominant Quteibi tribe. Fighting in searing heat over hard terrain, Blacker's force finally defeated the Quteibis while taking the Jebel Huriyah on 10 June. On 14 June Brigadier Blair took over from Blacker and proceeded to consolidate the British victory. His troops were much in demand elsewhere in Aden, however, and by 24 August most of the force had been withdrawn. The Radfani tribesmen were never completely brought to account, therefore, and they continued to plague the British until their final withdrawal from Aden in 1967.

broken country. For every hundred yards of advance they were forced to climb or descend three hundred. Bearings were lost in the darkness and had to be rediscovered. If one of the heavily laden men fell, there was a constant fear that he had broken a limb, raising the question of whether he should be carried, which would entail abandoning important loads, or be left behind, perhaps to be found by a band of merciless tribesmen. They knew that they were marching against the clock, and that daylight would expose them to fire from all around.

As the sun rose, Major Walter saw that they were still far from their objective. Skirting crests and resting in shadows, he avoided an encounter on the line of march and at last he saw the village and the stone watch-towers which were his target. He had hoped to surprise the towers' garrisons by night, but now he had to close on them in daylight. Still half-a-mile distant, Radfani riflemen began firing, and as bullets ricocheted among the rocks the paratroopers were forced down.

Under cover, the men were neither safe nor pursuing their objective, so Major Walter led a dash with the majority of the leading platoon to clear the positions surrounding the central watch-towers. Two other platoons were deployed to clear the village. No sooner had the leading parties moved off than a group of tribesmen, believing them to be the entire force, came in to attack them from behind. The fourth platoon with supporting elements had yet to close up and its commander, Captain Barry Jewkes, saw what was happening. He quickly laid an ambush and the Radfani were killed.

The noise of this action, combined with that of

Below: The RAF Bristol Belvedere short-range tactical transport helicopter was of great value in the Radfan. However, the paras mostly relied on the smaller Scout helicopter as the Belvederes were frequently unavailable.

Left: A typical 3 Para combat section, armed with rifles and a GPMG, and linked by radio to a senior officer at their headquarters (below left). Below: A para returns Radfani fire as a radio operator reports back to base.

REBELLION IN THE RADFAN

The Radfan is a wild, mountainous region, scored by deep ravines, situated some 70 miles by road from the town of Aden. It is inhabited by the Quteibi, Ibdali and Bakri tribes, fierce and hardy people who have traditionally supplemented their meagre income with raids on travellers on the Dhala road, which connects Aden with the Yemen.

In the early 1960s, Aden and the small independent states surrounding it were becoming increasingly influenced by Arab nationalist movements. The Radfan peoples, already incensed by the establishment of a customs authority which was denying them their income from the highway, eagerly accepted arms from Yemeni sympathisers and began to mine the Dhala road and snipe at passers-by. In addition, they mounted a nightly fusillade on the Federal Guard fort at Thumier.

In January 1964 a limited punitive action was ordered by the Federal government of Aden. Codenamed Operation Nutcracker, an assault on the Radfan was carried out by the Federal Regular Army (FRA) of Aden, supported by RAF aircraft and a British artillery unit. Although it succeeded as a show of strength, capturing several known agitators, the withdrawal of the force was immediately followed by renewed tribal activity. Moreover, the tribesmen were now receiving assistance from trained members of the Aden National Liberation Front (NLF) which was determined to gain complete independence for Aden.

By April the government had lost control in the Radfan, and with the FRA now under pressure from rebels throughout the Federation, it saw no option but to call in the British Army to restore law in the mountains.

clearing the watch-towers and the village, drew the entire weight of the local forces down on the paratroopers. A prolonged struggle ensued for possession of the battleground. The British force had the valuable support of two mortars, but ammunition for these weapons was limited. Although the artillery at Thumier was out of range, the radio was used to bring RAF Hawker Hunters in to strike at Radfanis positioned in caves and sangars in the rocks. The aircraft were also able to suppress the fire from snipers spread out on the overhanging heights.

Late in the afternoon the paras were relieved to see the marines of 45 Commando driving the Radfani snipers from the heights. Soon 3 Para's padre appeared in a Belvedere helicopter, and the wounded were airlifted to the military hospital in Aden. The area was then secured by an infantry battalion and the marines and paratroopers withdrew to Aden.

The anti-tank platoon armed with rifles and machine guns, advanced to the deserted village of Shab Tem

Still, no-one in Aden believed that a day of warm skirmishing had conquered the Radfani, and a brigade headquarters was brought from Northern Ireland to continue the campaign of pacification. It was commanded by Brigadier C.H. Blacker. The rest of 3 Para, commanded by Lieutenant-Colonel A.H. Farrar-Hockley, was brought to Aden from the Persian Gulf to lend its strength to the campaign, leaving only the regimental band at their station to show the flag, the men taking up rifles in place of their musical instruments. Major Walter's B Company returned to the Gulf to support them.

The group which assembled in the Wadi Rabwa close to Thumier comprised 3 Para less B Company, I Parachute Light Battery, Royal Horse Artillery, with its four 105mm guns, 3 Para Engineer Troop, transport and medical elements, and a rifle platoon formed by the Royal Army Ordnance Corps detachment which normally looked after the platforms on which the paras dropped their heavy equipment. This force was to clear the ridge on which the Bakri villages lay. None of the big Belvedere helicopters of the RAF was available to carry heavy loads forward; at best there would be two Scout helicopters of 653 Squadron, Army Air Corps, to carry a few light loads and make reconnaissance flights. There was just a chance that Land Rovers might be able to crawl up the track leading out of the Wadi Rabwa. Otherwise,

PARA ARTILLERY

The guns deployed by I Parachute Light Battery in support of 3 Para in the Radfan mountains were 105mm Model 56 pack howitzers, known to the British as the 105mm L5. This field gun had been developed on behalf of the Italian Army, by OTO Melara at La Spezia in northern Italy, to replace their British 25-pounders and US 105mm howitzers, and it entered production in 1957. The weapon was well received worldwide, and the British Army imported considerable numbers to replace its own 25-pounders. Eventually, the 105mm Model 56 could be found in virtually all Royal Artillery batteries other than those based in West Germany.

At 1290kg it was a lightweight artillery piece, an important factor in hard country where equipment has to be manhandled. Its weight made it ideal for airborne units (a Belvedere could carry it in one load) and it was widely distributed among mountain units which were able to dismantle it into 11 components for pack transport by animal (hence the term 'pack howitzer').

Since the weight specification determined a short barrel, the range of the gun, using standard US 105mm M1-series ammunition, was only 10,575m. The three-section trail could be folded, and when weight was crucial one section could be removed, along with the shield. One attraction of the Model 56 was its great versatility. The gun could be set high for use as a howitzer, or cranked into a low-profile anti-tank position which also served to improve its stability when fired.

everything had to be backpacked from the start. The 105s had to remain in the wadi, considerably shortening any cover they might be able to offer forward.

On the night of 16/17 May, Farrar-Hockley advanced the anti-tank platoon, armed with rifles and machine guns, to the deserted village of Shab Tem, and from this outpost he took forward three patrols in bright moonlight to seek routes up to the far ridge. They discovered only one, and even this involved crossing several ravines with steep sides. Next day it became evident that the track out of the Wadi Rabwa was so poor that it could not be used by laden vehicles moving up to Shab Tem. The quartermaster and the mechanical transport officers, therefore, sent several empty vehicles across the worst break in the track and organised the manhandling of loads over to them: ammunition, water and food. If there should be a severe battle, these would be their sole source of replenishment.

On the night of 17/18 May, with the stocking up of supplies still in process, the column set off. A Company led, supported by the machine-gun and mortar platoons. C Company and the Royal Engineers were deployed as fighting porters, each officer and soldier carrying about 180lb and a personal weapon for self-defence. It was very hot, and progress was slow, only about half-a-mile an hour, up and down the precipitous slopes. Just before dawn, Farrar-Hockley halted on a knoll surmounted by two deserted houses. The porters shed their loads and returned to Shab Tem. As the remainder made camp, there was a brief flurry of fire from a flank, sending bullets

whistling over them. Two of the battalion's mortars fired a random response onto the flashes and, as the moon came up, all fell quiet.

Next day, the Army Air Corps Scout helicopters flew a series of loads forward from Shab Tem, while the paras watched the silent and apparently deserted landscape from five concealed observation posts. At nightfall, C Company reappeared to take on the role of an advanced guard, while A Company and the engineers humped the loads. A fighting patrol was despatched, and then the column set off, wending its way through the deep ravines, and finally securing its objective on the top of Hajib escarpment as dawn approached.

The Bakri fighting bands were uncertain as to what to do next. They did not like operating at night, preferring to use darkness to regroup and rest. All of them crack marksmen, they preferred to wage guerrilla war by day among the rocks and caverns with which they were familiar, sniping and closing in when any British position looked vulnerable. They had now lost a good deal of territory. Moreover, less than two miles from 3 Para's position was the Wadi Dhubsan, an area never previously penetrated by government forces, in which lay the Radfanis' principal grain stores. When the battalion group began to expand their positions, at first on the flank and then towards the height overlooking the Wadi Dhubsan, the Radfani resistance hardened.

When A Company began to advance towards this height, its left protected by the anti-tank platoon, groups of tribesmen opened fire from two villages ahead. C Company was drawn in, and the British artillery, firing at extreme range, dropped shells onto the Radfanis as the two companies advanced.

Beyond the villages and a little to one side lay a saddle of ground, beyond which stood stone watch-towers. They were beyond the guns' range, and too robustly constructed to be destroyed by mortars. The RAF Hunters were called down, and they ran in on the structures with bombs and 30mm Aden guns. The watch-towers fell silent: when the paras checked them later on, they found a 12ft bloodstain in one room.

The British force now looked down into the Wadi Dhubsan. This area, hitherto a safe base for Radfani operations, was to be entered as a demonstration of power, and the grain stocks held there were to be destroyed. Brigadier Blacker told Lieutenant-Colonel Farrar-Hockley, 'The aim is not to slaughter tribesmen, but to teach them that we will come

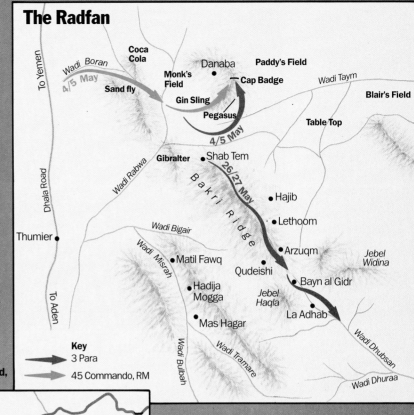

The Radfan

Cap Badge and Bakri Ridge
3 Para, May 1964

The mountains of the Radfan, in the north of the Federation of South Arabia, were the scene of a Yemen-backed revolt in the early 1960s. In January 1964 a joint British/Federal Government operation was launched in the Radfan to restore order, and late in the following April a force of marines and paras moved into the Radfan and commenced operations in the Bakri Ridge area. On 5 May, the Cap Badge feature was seized, and on 26 May 3 Para began their sweep along the Bakri Ridge.

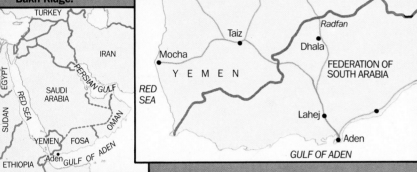

Left: Sheltered from sniper bullets, a machine-gun team enjoys a smoke while awaiting the order to advance. Right: A radio operator, his Sterling SMG beside him, acts as the eyes of para HQ. Below: Though sometimes marooned by lack of helicopter transport, British artillery provided effective support, even at extreme ranges.

wherever we need to if they misbehave.' In the event, the final assault was delayed by rainstorms. Stores remaining in the Wadi Rabwa were forwarded to a new dump on the Hajib escarpment, and the engineers worked round the clock to extend the track from Shab Tem in order to bring forward the guns of I Parachute Light Battery.

There were two tracks into the Wadi Dhubsan, one fair and one poor, which wound 3200ft down the mountain into the valley. Reckoning that there would be ambushes laid on both tracks, Farrar-Hockley decided to make a direct descent from the heights. Reconnoitring, he found a route which led down a 30ft rock face, along a boulder-strewn stream bed, and ended up directly in the rear of the village of Bayn Al Gidr. On the night of 25 May, while C Company picqueted the Jebel Haqla to the right, the main column used ropes to abseil down the rock face and it descended in the darkness, to the village. Sentries posted by the tribesmen around the village rapidly woke the garrison and it promptly fled. By 0600 hours, the upper wadi had been cleared without a shot being fired.

The cliffs on either side were milling with turbanned tribesmen, firing their rifles

X Company of 45 Commando, under Farrar-Hockley's command for this operation, was now advanced down the right side of the wadi, while A Company of 3 Para pushed along the heights to the left. Very quickly, small groups of tribesmen were seen hurrying into positions ahead. They were coming from an ambush position on the better of the two approaches in the upper slopes. Fire opened between the forces, the shots echoing along the sides of the wadi. Meanwhile, Farrar-Hockley, who was talking to Brigadier Blacker, himself just arrived in Bayn Al Gidr, was given map co-ordinates of the marines' position, and he elected to take a Scout to check their progress.

Taking off, Farrar-Hockley's Scout flew towards the map reference given him on the radio. Major Jackson, the pilot, sought the shelter of the cliffs as they skimmed the Wadi Dhubsan, over the battalion headquarters and support elements on the valley floor. They crossed a deserted tract and, suddenly, approaching the map reference point, the ground and cliffs on either side were milling with turbanned tribesmen, shaking their fists and firing their rifles. The noise of the engine obscured the sound of their shots, but then the men in the Scout heard a sound like the opening of beer cans. Fuel began to spray over the forward observation perspex.

'Can you keep flying?' asked Farrar-Hockley. 'This is the last place to put her down.' 'I've got power,' said Major Jackson. Coolly, he turned the Scout towards the head of the wadi, but then the engine or the rotors started making a clattering noise. As they swept forward, the advanced element of battalion headquarters on the valley floor swung into sight. 'Down there,' said Farrar-Hockley. They landed safely and Major Jackson switched off the power. Around them a firefight was in progress; a further 50 tribesmen had moved into position and more waited behind them, no doubt those seen by the Scout earlier on. There were now some casualties to be evacuated, including Lieutenant Ian McLeod who had been shot through the wrist in the Scout. The regimental

Left: With blasted Radfani watch-towers behind him, a para edges forward in the parched terrain. Above: Paras comb the hillsides, taking with them a Radfani with his unconventional flag of surrender. Below left: The paras became adept at the tribesmen's technique of sniping from hidden positions in the rocks.

sergeant-major led a party from the main element of the headquarters to the damaged helicopter, but was wounded on the way. The Bakri riflemen were shooting with accuracy at 800 yds range. Even as the padre helped carry the wounded back, the heels of his boots were clipped by bullets.

It was a tiresome morning and afternoon. In the end, the difficulty of breaching the tribesmens' well-concealed defences was overcome by C Company. Ordered to outflank them by marching round from the Jebel Haqla, they did so rapidly, surprising the Radfanis' left flank and forcing them to abandon their positions. The battalion then formed a defensive perimeter for the night, within which lay the crippled Scout. By torchlight, two aircraft technicians from the Royal Electrical and Mechanical Engineers worked through the hours of darkness, trying to repair the helicopter before dawn.

Next morning, as the Radfani grain stores were set alight, Major Jackson climbed into the Scout and tried the starter motor. The engine fired, the rotors turned, and when the helicopter lifted, hovered and then rose rapidly into the air, there was a hearty cheer. Major Jackson disappeared through the smoke billowing up from the grain stores and 3 Para, with the marines, began the long climb out of the wadi to the heights. From there, they were airlifted by Wessex helicopters of the Royal Navy to the heart of Aden and the delight of a cold beer.

THE AUTHOR General Sir Anthony Farrar-Hockley was, as a lieutenant-colonel, Commanding Officer of the 3rd Battalion, The Parachute Regiment, during the British operations against guerrilla tribesmen in the Radfan mountains of Aden in 1964. He retired in 1983 and is now a defence consultant.

When the Germans
launched Operation
Barbarossa in June 1941, the
Soviet Air Force, although
having a frontline strength
of over 10,500 aircraft, was
ill-prepared to meet the
onslaught of the 2770
aircraft fielded by the
Luftwaffe. By any standard,
most of the Soviet designs
were obsolete and, despite
a process of modernisation,
pilots were unable to meet
the Luftwaffe on anything
like equal terms. Less than
half the Soviet combat
strength in the west
consisted of modern types;
the rest were clearly out-
dated.
The brunt of the Luftwaffe's
attacks were borne by units
of the Leningrad, Baltic,
Kiev, Odessa and Western
Special Districts. Each
consisted of between 600
and 1400 aircraft of all types;
by 23 June, their
commanders were
admitting to the loss of some
1200 planes. The Western
Special Military District,
with its headquarters in
Minsk, received the
greatest mauling. One of its
units, the 9th Composite
Division, lost all but 63 of its
409 aircraft.
After three months of bitter
fighting, Hitler ordered the
Wehrmacht to capture
Moscow. Over 1200 of the
Luftwaffe's aircraft were
moved into the area to
support the operation, code-
named 'Typhoon'. Scraping
the bottom of the barrel to
oppose this thrust, the
Soviets were able to field
less than 400 aircraft.
Despite initial successes,
Typhoon ground to a halt,
the German forces crippled
by the Russian winter.
Remarkably, the Red Army
went over to the counter-
attack on 5 December,
supported by some 350
aircraft. Despite appalling
weather, the pilots flew over
50,000 sorties in defence of
Moscow, with 1254 men
winning awards. The
Luftwaffe's loss of 1400
aircraft marked a turning
point in the air war.
Above: The Soviet Army
Aviator's badge.

Locked in a deadly air war with the Luftwaffe, the pilots of the Soviet 16th Guards Fighter Regiment lived up to their creed to fight to the last

ON 22 JUNE 1941, the German armed forces unleashed a devastating Blitzkrieg on Russia. During the opening phase of the operation, codenamed Barbarossa, wave after wave of the Luftwaffe's bombers, dive-bombers, and fighters pulverised targets along a front stretching from the Baltic to the Black Sea. Caught unprepared, the Voenno-vozdushnye Sily (Soviet Air Force) suffered appalling losses.

By the evening of the first day's fighting, the Luftwaffe's victory claims stood at 1811 enemy aircraft destroyed for the loss of only 35 of their own. Moreover, although the greater number of these aircraft had been destroyed on the ground, when Soviet fighter pilots did give battle in the air, their obsolescent aircraft and poor tactics were no match for the Luftwaffe's battle-hardened fighter forces.

Yet this view of the combat capabilities of the Soviet fighter pilot took no account of the very real handicaps of poor equipment, inadequate training, and a command structure paralysed by fear and suspicion in the aftermath of Stalin's purges. Under such conditions, it was remarkable that in the dark days of 1941-42 there were individual Soviet fighter pilots and a select number of fighter regiments that distinguished themselves in action.

One unit that was held in especially high regard was the 55th Fighter Regiment, commanded by Lieutenant-Colonel N.V. Isayev. Later to gain greater fame as the 16th Guards Fighter Regiment, it was flying MiG-3 interceptors in the Odessa Military District at the outbreak of the war, and was, as stated by the official history of the Soviet Air Force in the Great Patriotic War, 'rightly considered to be one of the finest air regiments'. However, the MiG-3, although a more modern design than the Polikarpov I-153s and I-16s which equipped the majority of the

FORWARD TO
VICTORY

Soviet fighter units, was not a particularly successful aircraft. It was difficult to fly, poorly armed and, because it had been intended for the high-altitude bomber interception role, did not perform well at the low and medium levels where most air combats took place.

Therefore the 55th Fighter Regiment had to rely on the courage and tenacity of its pilots in combat, rather than any advantages gained from the qualities of its aircraft. Three of the unit's airmen particularly distinguished themselves in the early air battles. The high quality of leadership displayed by Isayev was recognised by the award of the Hero of the Soviet Union, the highest Russian military decoration, and one of his squadron commanders, Captain Anatoly

Sokolov was a combat veteran of air battles over Manchuria with the Japanese Army Air Force in 1939. Sokolov was remembered by Senior-Lieutenant Alexander Ivanovich Pokryshkin, the most promising member of his squadron, as 'a splendid pilot' and 'a calm, cool-headed fellow, both on the ground and what is more important in the air'.

The Soviet fighter regiments each comprised some 40 aircraft during the early months of the war, although experience soon showed this to be rather too cumbersome to

Main picture: Soviet fighters take off from a rudimentary grass airstrip to do battle with the Luftwaffe. Clockwise from top: Heroes of the Soviet Union. Kankeshev Ahmet Haptal, credited with six victories in nine days; Alexander Pokryshkin, winner of the award on three occasions; N.V. Isayev, Commander of the 55th Fighter Regiment; and Grigory Rechkalov, a former miner, who scored 22 kills.

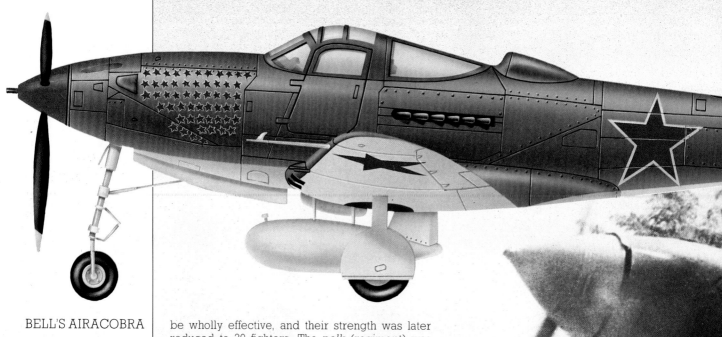

BELL'S AIRACOBRA

In 1935, after viewing an impressive display of the American Armament Corporation's T9 37mm gun, senior members of the Bell aircraft company asked their designers to come up with the blueprints for a fighter that could carry the cannon, fired through the propeller, and two 12.7mm machine guns synchronised to fire through the blades. The decision to house the T9 in the forward fuselage forced the designers to place the aircraft's engine to the rear of the cockpit, and the subsequent problems of balance meant that a tricycle-type landing gear had to be fitted to the front of the aircraft.

Given the go-ahead by the US Army Air Corps, Bell produced a series of successful prototypes and full-scale manufacture of the fighter, known as the P-39 Airacobra, began in August 1939, with the first large batch of fighters being delivered in early 1941. Although more than a dozen versions of the Airacobra were produced, the basic design remained remarkably unaltered. The P-39M, typical of the series, had a maximum speed of 621km/h and a range of over 1000km. Armament comprised the T9 cannon, two 12.7mm machine guns in the front fuselage and four 7.62mm machine guns mounted in the wings. The final production versions, the P-39N and P-39Q, were mainly supplied to the Russians.

be wholly effective, and their strength was later reduced to 30 fighters. The *polk* (regiment) was made up of three *eskadrilya* (squadrons), which were sub-divided into *zvena* (flights) of three, or later four aircraft. The strength of a regiment was some 200 officers and men – 34 of whom were pilots, 130 mechanics, and the remainder administrative and support troops.

Pokryshkin's first combat on 22 June 1941 provided an ironic illustration of the Soviet High Command's lack of preparedness for war. Encountering a formation of unfamiliar light bombers over Moldavia, Pokryshkin dived into the attack. His first burst of fire was accurate, but on breaking away he saw to his consternation that his victim was marked with red stars. In fact, he had attacked a formation of Soviet Sukhoi Su-2s, that was based at Kotovsk, near his own airfield at Mayaki. As he later bitterly commented, 'any peasant women on their way to market could have seen them there', but the Su-2s' existence had been kept secret from the pilots of the 55th.

However, on the following day there was no mistake. In the vicinity of the German airfield at Jassy, Pokryshkin surprised a formation of Messerschmitt Bf 109Es and succeeded in shooting one down before he was himself attacked from behind: 'White ribbons of his tracers shot by and then my plane shuddered – its port wing had been torn by bullets. I dived to zero feet and hedge-hopped all the way home.' On 20 July Pokryshkin was less fortunate: his MiG-3 was hit by flak during a reconnaissance mission over the Beltsy area and he had to come down behind enemy lines. Joining up with Soviet troops cut off by the German advance, he fought his way through to Soviet territory and was able to rejoin his regiment a week later.

On 7 March 1942 the combat record of the 55th Fighter Regiment was recognised by the award of the coveted 'Guards' title and the unit became the 16th Guards Fighter Regiment. This honour had been first instituted in the Soviet Air Force during December 1941, to coincide with the Red Army's counter-offensive in the Moscow area. In an elaborate ceremony, the retitled unit was presented with new colours and all members took the following oath:

'In the terrible years of the Great Patriotic War, I swear to you my country and to you my party to fight to the last drop of blood and my last breath –

and to conquer. Such is the Guards' creed. Forward to victory! Glory to the party of Lenin!'

The Guards aviation units were a true elite; each member's uniform was distinguished by a special badge and this emblem was often painted on their aircraft. They were also given priority in the supply of replacement aircraft and in re-equipping with new types as they became available. Yet these distinctions were not lightly earned, as the regiments were expected to spearhead Soviet air operations and to set an example to other units by their courage and tactical skill in fighting the Luftwaffe.

After participating in the defensive air battles over the Caucasus in 1942, the 16th Guards Fighter

Above left: Pokryshkin's Airacobra with his victories marked on the fuselage. Above: Chocks away! – a Soviet fighter begins a sortie. Right: Armourers check over machine-gun belts and bombs before a mission.

Regiment's first chance of offensive action came in the spring of 1943, during the fierce combats for air superiority over the German Kuban bridgehead. The loss of Kuban would threaten German forces in the Crimea, and provide the Soviets with bases within range of the Romanian oilfields. By this time, the unit's unsatisfactory MiG-3s had been replaced by Bell P-39 Airacobras. These American aircraft had been supplied under the Lend-Lease programme and ferried from Iran to the Caucasus front by their Soviet pilots. Nicknamed the *britchik* (little shaver), the P-39 was popular in Soviet service and pilots particularly valued its nose-mounted 37mm cannon. However, the fighter had its faults, recovery from a flat spin being especially difficult.

When the fighting over Kuban began, the 16th Guards Fighter Regiment was commanded by Lieutenant-Colonel I.M. Dzusov and Pokryshkin was one of his squadron commanders. The latter was by then, in the words of the Soviet official history, 'an

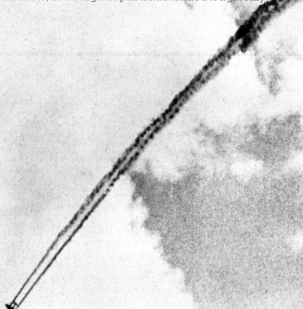

experienced, mature commander and a remarkable fighter pilot, who had completed more than 350 sorties and shot down nearly 20 enemy aircraft.'

Pokryshkin's influence on Soviet fighter tactics was to be far-reaching, for as he wrote:

'the offensive spirit was now the keynote of our activity. It was over Kuban that the pilots of our regiment arrived at the formula for aggressive air combat. It consisted of four elements: altitude, speed, manoeuvre, fire.'

Hitherto, Soviet fighter pilots had tended to fight only in the horizontal plane, flying in inflexible three-aircraft formations and forming defensive circles as soon as they were attacked. Their new-found confidence and willingness to seize the initiative was shown by the adoption of the Luftwaffe's two-aircraft element of leader and wingman, known in Russian as the *para*. This enabled more fluid combat tactics, with manoeuvre in both the horizontal and vertical planes. Superior altitude and speed, Pokryshkin stressed, gave Soviet pilots the initiative and freedom of manoeuvre. Once an advantageous position had been gained behind an enemy aircraft, the fighter pilot would close to minimum range in order that his fire would have the maximum effect.

The Kuban battles were a severe test of individual endurance as the Soviet fighter pilots flew from dawn to dusk, sometimes carrying out as many as seven sorties in a day. Massive air battles involving up to 100 aircraft were commonplace, and 16th Guards Fighter Regiment pilot Grigory Golubev, who often flew as Pokryshkin's wingman, has described the confusion of such fights, 'the flash of tracer, the rattle of machine-gun fire, flak bursts and the wild intermingling of aircraft at various altitudes.' Yet, whenever possible, the Soviet fighters were controlled by the air division or regimental commander from his ground control post. For example, on 29 April General A. V. Borman, the 216th Fighter Division's commander, directed Pokryshkin's P-39s to intercept a formation of 12 Luftwaffe fighters over the battlefield. Borman's instructions enabled the Soviet fighters to surprise the enemy formation and eight of them were claimed as destroyed. Pokryshkin himself recalls.

'As far as I was concerned the Kuban battle began one spring morning when I led a flight of aircraft to the patrol area. We were flying fast machines and in this sortie we had the opportunity of putting into practice all the elements of our air combat formula: altitude, speed, manoeuvre and fire.

'We approached the front line at high altitude and great speed. I espied three Soviet LaGG-3s below us desperately keeping at bay 10 Messerschmitts. The LaGGs were having a hard time of it. They were maintaining a circling defence. Our patrol already had the advantage over the Germans of altitude and speed. It now remained to bring the third element of our formula into play: manoeuvre. I ordered the patrol to attack.

'We swooped down upon the swarm of Messerschmitts. It was a "falcon's strike" accompanied by accurate fire from short range. The pilot I attacked reacted with the delay of a split second, but this was enough to undo him. A single burst, fired point-blank, set his aircraft on fire.'

Pokryshkin's achievements were recognised by the award of the Hero of the Soviet Union

The record of air victories gained by the pilots of the 16th Guards Fighter Regiment over the Kuban bears eloquent testimony to the rejuvenation of the Soviet fighter force. Pokryshkin himself was credited with 20 victories during the campaign and his achievements were recognised by the award of the Hero of the Soviet Union on 24 May 1943. Senior-Lieutenant Grigory A. Rechkalov received the same decoration at that time in recognition of his 11 victories. He ended the war as the fourth highest-scoring Soviet air ace, with a total of 56 victories gained in 609 combat missions. Fifteen of N. Ye Lavitskiy's 26 victories were gained with the 16th Guards Fighter Regiment over the Kuban and he too received the highest Soviet award on 24 August 1943. One of the most promising of Pokryshkin's pilots was A.F. Klubov, in whom his commander saw 'the true seed of the born fighter – the ability to impose one's will upon one's adversary.' This confidence was fully justified, for at the time of his death in a flying accident in November 1944, Captain Klubov had gained a total of 50 air victories.

Fine leadership and careful training had brought the pilots of the 16th Guards Fighter Regiment to a peak of efficiency. Pokryshkin had realised that courage alone was no substitute for skilled tactics, and the performance of his regiment showed the way forward for the rest of the Soviet fighter force, in the finest traditions of the Guards units. Pokryshkin continued to serve with the Soviet Air Force after the war, but his finest achievement was without doubt during the spring of 1943 when he did so much to give substance to the Soviet fighter pilot's motto: 'Seek out Your Enemy'.

Above: Its wings riddled with machine-gun bullets, a German fighter trails smoke as it dives to destruction. With mounting confidence in their own deadly skills, the hard-pressed pilots of the Soviet Air Force were gradually able to wrest control of the skies away from the Luftwaffe. Losses on both sides were very high, but the Russians, with help from their British and US allies were more able to supply their frontline units with much-needed replacements.

THE AUTHOR Anthony Robinson was formerly on the staff of the RAF Museum, Hendon and is now a freelance military aviation writer. He has edited the books *Aerial Warfare* and the *Dictionary of Aviation*.

In September 1943 the dashing German special forces commander, Otto Skorzeny, led a daring commando raid to rescue Mussolini.

THROUGHOUT HIS lunch, Captain Otto Skorzeny, chief of Germany's special forces, had had a nagging feeling that something was wrong. Leaving his coffee, he placed a call to his headquarters at Friedenthal. His nagging thoughts were answered: all of Berlin was trying to find him. He had orders to be at Tempelhof airfield by 1700 hours, ready to fly to Hitler's wartime headquarters, the 'Wolf's Lair'.

A Ju 52 was waiting to deliver Skorzeny in isolated splendour and his second-in-command, Lieutenant Karl Radl, had his dress uniform ready for him. The only light that Skorzeny could throw on this sudden call to visit Hitler was that the Italian government had fallen and that Mussolini was missing.

The aircraft touched down at Lotzen in East Prussia, where a Mercedes staff car was waiting. The car took Skorzeny to the HQ, stopping many times for his papers to be examined. At last, after waiting in an ante-room, he was summoned into Hitler's presence. The Führer informed Skorzeny that Mussolini had been arrested and that it would be up to him to rescue

GRAN SASSO RESCUE

Il Duce. He carried on, telling the young captain that it was to be a secret mission, only a small group of people would know of it, and that he would be nominally under the command of General Kurt Student, chief of airborne troops.

Skorzeny then spent several hours itemising the men and equipment that he might need in Italy, and had the requirements sent to his own HQ. He requested 50 men and included a shopping list that ranged from machine guns to priests' robes. The following morning, he flew with General Student to Rome. Three days later the rest of his team arrived and the search for Mussolini moved into top gear. For several weeks, rumours abounded and were followed up, only to disappear as quickly as they had surfaced. Then, finally, the whereabouts of Mussolini was pinned down.

In Rome, Skorzeny and his staff had toured the bars and cafes hoping to overhear any information that might give them a new clue. It was an intercepted, coded message, 'Security measures around the Gran Sasso completed', from a General Cueli to the Italian Ministry of the Interior, that put them on the

Above left: Mussolini is led to safety by German paras on 12 February 1943. In a daring swoop on his hotel prison (left), commandos, under Otto Skorzeny, freed the dictator without firing a shot in anger.

TRACKING THE QUARRY

After three fruitless weeks in Rome discounting rumours, Skorzeny was presented with the first hard facts: Mussolini (below) had been moved from Rome on 27 July and taken to the naval base at Gaeta, some 120km south of the capital. From there, he had been transferred onto a corvette, the *Persefone*, which sailed for the island of Ponza on the 28th. However, before Skorzeny could prepare any rescue plans, other intelligence sources indicated that Mussolini had been moved again, to La Maddalena, an island off the northeast coast of Sardinia. On 18 August, Skorzeny carried out a reconnaissance flight over the island to gather detailed photographic evidence. On the 20th, Skorzeny began his preparations for the rescue mission, scheduled to take place on 27 August. In readiness for the raid, the commandos moved to the port of Anzio and Skorzeny ordered a more detailed look at the villa. Reaching the island on the 26th, Skorzeny and a fellow officer, Lieutenant Warger, tricked one of the Italian guards into revealing that Mussolini had been moved by seaplane to the Italian mainland. After landing at Braccianno, a lake in the mountains east of Rome, he had been placed under house arrest at Albergo-Rifugia, a hotel situated 6500ft above the valley.

scent. This was the break that they had been after – it was known that Cueli was in charge of Mussolini.

It soon became obvious that the Hotel Albergo-Rifugio on the Gran Sasso, a mountainous ridge northeast of Rome, had been turned into a military camp, with the only approach being by cable-car. Several of Skorzeny's men were sent into the area around the mountain hotel, but they could not get through the cordon of Italian troops. Skorzeny decided to fly over the area in an He 111 to see the hotel for himself. He was accompanied by Radl and the corps intelligence officer. The plan was to photograph the whole of the area, but when they tried the main camera, they found that it was jammed. The

only way they could take any pictures was to hang out of the rear turret and use a hand camera. This method was not to be recommended when dressed in light tropical uniform. On the first run, Skorzeny was dangled out, with Radl holding his legs. When he was hauled back into the aircraft, half frozen, he discovered Radl roaring with laughter. Pulling rank, he soon got rid of Radl's hilarity by ordering another run, this time dangling Radl out of the back.

On the return trip, Skorzeny must have thought that the Allied air force had a personal vendetta against him. His aircraft was forced to hug the ground as

American bombers and fighters attacked the German headquarters and the commando barracks at Frascati. The place was a wreck and the photo lab had been destroyed, as had a lot of the men's kit. It was 8 September 1943, Italy had surrendered and on the 9th the Allies landed at Salerno.

The pictures were developed and printed, confirming what Skorzeny and Radl had seen from the air. The squat hotel was situated on a small plateau, a small triangle of clear ground with the top station of the cable-car on one side. Final confirmation of their intelligence came when it was reported that the local trade union was complaining that the hotel staff had been evicted, 'Simply to accommodate that Fascist, Mussolini.' He was there.

General Student would supply 90 men for the landing and the commandos the rest. A second group of commandos and paras would, at the same time as the main assault, take control of the lower end of the cable-car. A third team would free Il Duce's wife and family from house arrest at their country residence near Rocca della Cominata. Student ordered 12 DFS 230 gliders and their tugs to carry the commandos, but it would take at least three days to get them from the south of France. D-day was fixed for dawn on 12 September. Skorzeny and Radl fleshed out the bare bones of the operation: each

Below, far left: Smiling paras check over their weapons and equipment prior to boarding their DFS 230 assault gliders for the short flight to Gran Sasso. Once at the target (bottom), they fanned out for the dash to the hotel where Mussolini was confined.
Below left: After the action, paras stand around one of their DFS 230s waiting for the order to withdraw.

glider could take a section of 10 men plus the pilot. The para intelligence officer would fly in the first glider and act as pathfinder. Skorzeny would travel in the third glider and Radl in the fourth.

The launch had to be put back several hours because the gliders had been delayed. It was also decided, at the last minute, that it would be a good idea to take an Italian officer, General Soletti, along to help with the guards. When he arrived, Student, through an interpreter, told the general that, at Hitler's own request, he was to go on the raid and help reduce the possibility of bloodshed. Soletti was very impressed and agreed to go along. As the morning progressed, the tugs and gliders arrived

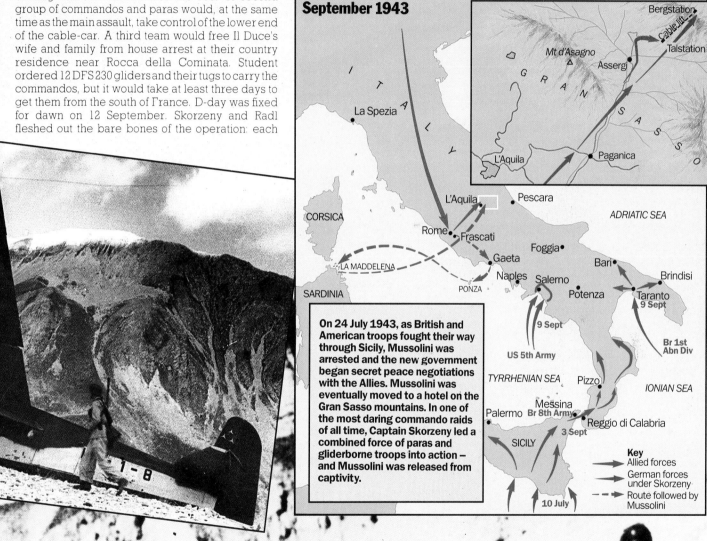

Rescuing Mussolini
September 1943

On 24 July 1943, as British and American troops fought their way through Sicily, Mussolini was arrested and the new government began secret peace negotiations with the Allies. Mussolini was eventually moved to a hotel on the Gran Sasso mountains. In one of the most daring commando raids of all time, Captain Skorzeny led a combined force of paras and gliderborne troops into action – and Mussolini was released from captivity.

Key
→ Allied forces
→ German forces under Skorzeny
--→ Route followed by Mussolini

Bottom left: Mussolini is escorted to the waiting Storch. Left: Paras, including Second Lieutenant Schwerdt (far right), salute Skorzeny before take-off. Bottom right: Second Lieutenant Berlepsch, (right) greets the leader of the valley assault force, Major Mors (left). Below: Hitler welcomes Mussolini to Germany.

and were at once refuelled. Final briefings were held, and Student told the glider pilots that under no circumstances were they to crash-land.

At 1230 hours the air-raid sirens went off, and everyone dashed for shelter. By 1300, the raid was over – the assault aircraft had been missed, but the runway had several holes along its length. The order was given for an immediate take-off. Skorzeny and Soletti shared a seat in a cramped glider. With a ceiling of 9000ft, the armada was ordered to assemble above the clouds.

Skorzeny's pilot reported that the first two gliders had not made the rendezvous. Disaster had struck. Both of them never left the ground, running into craters on the runway. Skorzeny freed his knife and hacked away at the flimsy canvas that clad the glider. Through this small hole, he was able to get his bearings and shout the route to the glider pilot, who then passed it on to the tug. As the hotel came into view he ordered the glider to release the towing line.

The Italian guards just stood in amazement as the gliders landed. No-one fired a shot.

As the glider banked to the right, it became obvious to both the pilot, Lieutenant Meyer, and Skorzeny that the landing site was not flat, but a steep slope. Meyer looked at Skorzeny for help. All that he could do was to order the pilot to bring the glider down. Disobeying General Student's express order, the young pilot crash-landed within 30ft of the hotel. Never one for half measures, Skorzeny thrust himself through the canvas and wood of the glider, and raced for the hotel. The Italian guards just stood in amazement as the gliders landed. No-one fired a shot.

Dashing through an open door, Skorzeny found a signaller frantically trying to transmit a warning. A well-aimed boot sent the man flying and the butt of Skorzeny's machine pistol neatly fixed the transmitter. Discovering that the room was a dead end, the commandos retraced their steps. Rounding the corner of the hotel, they were faced with a nine-foot wall. Using Corporal Himmel's back, Skorzeny was quickly over, followed by the rest of his squad. Total chaos reigned as the Germans pushed their way through

the front door, while the Carabinieri tried to escape in the opposite direction. Later on, Skorzeny was to be amazed that not a single shot was fired during the first, crucial moments of the raid.

The commandos rushed up the main stairs and, opening the first door on the right, found Mussolini and two officers. Second Lieutenant Schwerdt escorted the two officers out of the room, leaving his boss and Mussolini alone. They were not to remain by themselves for long: the heads of two commandos, who had climbed up a lightning conductor, appeared at the window.

Watching the remaining gliders coming in to land, Skorzeny was horrified to see the eighth glider, caught by a warm thermal, picked up like a paper plane and then sent crashing into the mountain side. Sickened by the sight and hearing distant gunfire, he shouted for the senior Italian officer. A colonel was produced, and the surrender of the garrison demanded. The man asked for time to consider. Skorzeny allowed him exactly one minute. The colonel left the room and quickly returned with a glass of wine, which he offered to Skorzeny, and formally surrendered. A white bedspread was hung out of the window. The guards placed their weapons in the dining room; the officers were allowed to keep their pistols. As the first Germans reached the hotel by the cable-car, a message was sent to General Student, informing him that the raid was a success.

It had been planned that a Fieseler Storch should land in the valley, with Skorzeny and Mussolini flying out from there. Unfortunately, the Storch damaged its undercarriage when it landed and would take some time to repair. This meant the only other possibility was for Captain Gerlach, who had been acting as a spotter, to land his Storch near the hotel itself.

A short landing strip was prepared by rolling the larger boulders to one side. The aircraft landed safely enough, but the captain was not amused by the idea of cramming in both Mussolini and Skorzeny. He was finally convinced by the use of the Führer's name. Once the aircraft had taken off, the rest of the troops would descend to the valley by cable-car. To guard against any trouble, two Italian officers would go with each load.

Mussolini sat in the rear seat, with Skorzeny squeezed in the luggage space behind. Commandos held onto the aircraft as the pilot built up the revs. Suddenly, the aircraft raced forward and tried to rise. It bounced down on its left landing wheel, then shot over the edge of the cliff. The pilot fought with the aircraft and got it under control barely 100ft from the valley floor. At Rome, the Storch had to make a two-point landing because of the damaged wheel.

Skorzeny and Mussolini, after receiving a formal greeting from senior staff, boarded an He 111 and flew straight to Vienna. It was here that the celebrations and phone calls started. Just before midnight, there was a knock at Skorzeny's door; it was the chief-of-staff of the Viennese garrison. Entering the room, he congratulated Skorzeny on the success of the mission. Removing the Knight's Cross from his own neck, he presented it to Skorzeny. By order of Hitler, he was the first man to be presented with the Knight's Cross on the day he had won it.

THE AUTHOR Mike Roberts runs a major picture library that deals with military subjects and has worked in defence research for television.

THE MOST DANGEROUS MAN IN EUROPE

Born in Austria in 1908, Otto Skorzeny (above) was an early member of the Nazi Party and, with the Waffen-SS, fought in France, Yugoslavia and Russia. In 1943 he transferred to Hitler's Security Office where he began working in an undercover capacity.

Skorzeny first rose to prominence in the following September when he led the small group that freed the Italian dictator, Benito Mussolini from his hotel prison at Gran Sasso in Italy. Much admired by Hitler for his daring exploits, Skorzeny was empowered to raise No.502 Special Services Battalion and, later, a number of Jagdverbände – anti-partisan units.

In late 1944, Skorzeny and his men were responsible for ensuring the continued loyalty of the Hungarian government to the Nazi cause by the simple expedient of capturing the buildings on Castle Hill in Budapest that housed the offices of the wavering ministers.

Skorzeny also organised and led the forces involved in Operation Greif in the winter of 1944. Disguised as US Army personnel, his troops worked in advance of the German forces involved in the Battle of the Bulge to sow confusion behind enemy lines. In the event, the mission was only a very limited success.

UNCOMMON VALOUR

On Iwo Jima, in the shadow of Mount Suribachi, the leathernecks of the US 28th Marines fought one of the toughest battles of the Pacific War

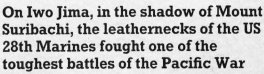

Bottom: Storming Iwo Jima – assault waves head for the beaches under the menacing bulk of Mount Suribachi. Far left: An early casualty, Corporal Rudolph Engstrom, lies wounded in a shell crater, examining the piece of shrapnel that did the damage. Left: A heavily laden leatherneck moves inland to take on the Japanese defenders.

IT WAS the easiest landing I ever made; I didn't even get my feet wet. It was the only thing about Iwo Jima that was easy. D-day, 19 February 1945, was bright and clear with a blue sky and moderate sea. Much too beautiful a day to be killed, I thought, although a lot of us would be.

We left the hard-packed beach, flung ourselves against the terraced, black-sand escarpment and stalled. Trying to run in that loose sand was like running on the spot or, as someone said later, like trying to climb a waterfall. I looked around to see where I was. Glowering down at me personally on my left was the 556ft Mount Suribachi. On my right, also glowering, was six-foot four-inch Colonel Harry B. 'Harry the Horse' Liversedge, commander of the 28th Marine Regiment, whose job it was to take Suribachi away from the Japanese.

According to the plan, we were to take Suribachi in 12 hours. It took us four days and cost 904 casualties, including 212 dead. But Suribachi was only the beginning: the 28th took nearly three times that many casualties after we joined the fighting for the northern half of the island. But we didn't know about all that when we landed – thank God.

Liversedge looked at me as if he expected me to do something, but I wasn't about to do anything until he did. 'We can't just sit here,' Liversedge growled to his operations officer, Major Oscar Peatross. We stood up and waded perhaps 50yds more inland through the shifting sand. H-hour, the beginning of the landings, was 0900 hours. Within the next half hour, all the assault forces were ashore. It seemed extraordinarily quiet, and I remembered something a rose-cheeked naval gunnery officer had said back aboard ship during the thunder of the pre-landing bombardment, 'There won't be a live Jap left on that island.' I said something rude because I was at Tarawa, where the admirals learnt, or should have learnt, at the expense of Marine lives that naval gunfire had certain limitations.

Except for a few mortar rounds and some sniper fire, we were getting very little resistance. 'There's something screwy,' said Cor-

ASSAULT FORCES

The build-up to the US assault on Iwo Jima began long before the first waves of assault troops hit the beaches on 19 February 1945. On 15 June 1944 carrier aircraft raided the island for the first time, and the bombing continued for the rest of the year.

Nearer D-day, a 72-hour naval bombardment from six battleships and their escorts pulverised the known enemy positions. With unremitting fury, some 1950 rounds of 16in shell, 1500 rounds of 14in, 400 of 12in, 1700 of 8in, 2000 of 6in, and 31,000 of 5in turned the island into an apparently lifeless moonscape. Overhead, flight after flight of aircraft bombed, napalmed and rocketed the Japanese as they hid in their tunnels and caves.

The invasion fleet earmarked for Iwo Jima comprised some 800 ships of all types: on board the transports were the 60,000 assault troops of Major-General H. Schmidt's V Amphibious Corps. The first wave to hit the beaches consisted of the 4th and 5th Marine Divisions under the command of Major-Generals Clifton B. Cates, a veteran of Guadalcanal, and Keller E. Rockey, a marine who had fought in World War I. Both divisions were to land a little way north of Mount Suribachi and then be transported to their objective by nearly 500 amphibious vehicles. The 3rd Marine Division, commanded by Major-General Graves B. Erskine, was the corps reserve. At 47, Erskine was one of the youngest serving generals in the US Marine Corps. His men were expected to come ashore three days after the initial landings. Above: The shoulder insignia of the 5th Marine Division.

After the fall of the Mariana Islands in July 1944 and the capture of most of the Philippines in early 1945, the war in the Pacific moved into its final phase. Both the Japanese and the US High Commands were quick to spot the strategic importance of the islands of Iwo Jima and Okinawa. Both were roughly equidistant from Japan and the American bases in the Marianas and the Philippines, and both formed part of the inner ring of defences around Japan. For the Japanese, Iwo Jima, with its two airfields and a third under construction, was an unsinkable 'aircraft carrier' from where fighters could strike at US bombers on their way to the mainland, or launch spoiling raids against the enemy forces on Saipan, Tinian and Guam. Less than two-hours flying time from Japan, Iwo Jima also proved an invaluable early-warning station from which to monitor US attacks on the home islands.

At the emotional level, Iwo Jima, administratively part of the Prefecture of Tokyo, was seen as part of Japan proper and its loss would have a profound effect on civilian morale at home. Capture of the island would also confer some potentially decisive advantages on the Americans in the final stages of the war. Using the island's airfields, short-range escort fighters would be able to fly top cover for US bomber forces and the airstrips could also be used by damaged bombers as an emergency stopping point. After the fall of Iwo Jima, the Americans exploited its advantages: after the landing strips had been repaired, fighters started arriving on 6 May. Although Japanese airpower had been virtually eliminated by the summer of 1945, over 1900 fighter sorties and 3000 strikes against targets in Japan were flown from the island. Over 2500 bombers, damaged over the mainland, made emergency landings on the airstrips before the Japanese surrender.

Leonce 'Frenchy' Olivier, a Louisiana Cajun. He had been one of the first men ashore at Tarawa and commanded respect. Then, as if responding to a gigantic electric prod, Iwo Jima leaped into life. More than 20,000 Japanese defenders, all of them underground, came out shooting. Suribachi, far more deadly now than when it was a live volcano, spewed fire on the Marines from 1000 caves, block-houses, pillboxes, trenches and spider traps. The jagged hills and ridges to the north, where the main defence lines lay, exploded simultaneously. As if on cue, somebody was heard to say, 'Oh Christ, the honeymoon is over.'

Things were proceeding exactly as Lieutenant-General Tadamichi Kuribayashi, the Japanese commander, had planned. A good family man, a fifth generation samurai and a very smart general, he had made his key decision months before. Against the bitter opposition of dissident officers, especially members of the navy, Kuribayashi had decided that he would not fight for Iwo on the beaches. The Japanese had not been able to stop the Americans on the beaches at Tarawa, Guam, Saipan or Tinian, Kuribayashi argued. Nor had the Germans been able to stop the Allies in Normandy. Why have his forces blown away by naval gunfire on the beaches?

Instead, Kuribayashi decreed, his men would hold their fire until after the Americans had landed and started moving inland. Then, as we struggled through the loose black sand towards the narrow neck of desolate earth that linked Suribachi to the main body of the island, we would be naked and exposed. Then, he could slaughter us. And he did.

Kuribayashi knew that Iwo Jima was doomed; that, indeed, Japan was doomed. On 3 February, he wrote to his wife, 'Please stop hoping that I can return alive, that you will ever see me again.' Hence, his whole effort was geared to take as many of us with him as possible. There would, for example, be no banzai charges. 'Do not go and get them,' Kuribayashi ordered. 'Stay in your holes and make them come and get you.'

Johnson turned to his troops and yelled, 'Okay, you bastards, let's get the hell off this beach.'

Late on D-day, aboard his command ship offshore, Lieutenant-General Holland M. 'Howlin' Mad' Smith, the terrible-tempered overall commander of the Marine forces, told war correspondents, 'I don't know who he (Kuribayashi) is, but the Jap general running the show is one smart bastard.' Just how smart none of us would know until the battle ended five weeks later. Iwo Jima was the only battle of the Pacific War in which the Americans suffered more casualties, although not more dead, than the Japanese.

The 28th's plan of attack was simple: cut across the island at its 750yd-wide isthmus, then wheel to the left and drive towards Suribachi. Second Lieutenant Frank J. Wright had two of his men still with him when they reached the opposite beach 90 minutes after landing.

They blew up some pillboxes, by-passed others, knocked out a 20mm gun emplacement and shot their way through a Japanese command post because they had no choice. In retrospect, that was the easy part.

Marines on the eastern slope of Suribachi were temporarily paralysed by the intensity of the enemy fire. Somebody had to get up. One who did was

Second Lieutenant Norman D. Brueggman. 'If you want to win this war, you'd better get the hell up here,' he shouted. A moment later, he was a dead hero. A short, fat man had better luck. He was Lieutenant-Colonel Chandler W. Johnson, whose 2nd Battalion, 28th Marines, was destined to plant the flag atop Suribachi. Casually contemptuous of enemy fire, Johnson turned on his cringing troops and yelled, 'Okay, you bastards, let's get the hell off this beach.' And they did. They would follow Johnson anywhere. His luck ran out weeks later at the northern end of the island. He literally vanished after a direct hit by a high-explosive shell. Afterwards, all they found was a shoe.

An awed private, his face pressed against the sand, turned to his sergeant and asked, 'Was Tarawa anything like this?' 'No,' was the reply, 'Nothing was ever like this.' The private felt better right away, although the dead and dying lay all around him. Now, he knew how to react.

The first of the walking wounded came into the aid station by himself. The flesh of his jaw hung by a piece. A navy doctor pushed the sagging mass of flesh and bone back into place and wrapped a bandage around his head. A couple of hospital corpsmen stood up to take him down to the beach for evacuation. He waved them aside and tried to talk, but only a strange mumble came from what was left of his mouth. A big, powerful man with hair cut so close you could see his sunburned scalp, he tried to write in the loose volcanic sand. But as fast as he wrote, the sand filled in what he had written. Disgusted, he gave the sand an indignant brush and stood up. He was ready to go now.

To its immense regret, the 28th had to leave its regimental mascot, a young lion named Roscoe, in Hawaii. But on D-day we discovered that we had a four-footed companion: a feisty brown-and-white fox terrier named George. The dog gambolled through the carnage as if the whole battle was some new kind of game, often stopping to lick the hand of a nervous marine. He survived the battle; his master did not.

Captain Dwayne E. 'Bobo' Mears, who charged across the island attacking enemy positions with a pistol, was stopped by a bullet in the neck and collapsed from loss of blood. A hospital corpsman crawled to Mears' side and began covering the big man with sand to make him less of a target to Japanese marksmen. 'Get the hell out of here and get going,' Mears snapped. 'I'm all right.' He died the next morning aboard ship after being evacuated.

Then there was Tony Stein, at 24 a veteran of three campaigns in the Solomon Islands. A toolmaker back in Ohio, Stein had designed his own special weapon for Iwo. It was a hand-held machine gun made from the wing gun of a wrecked navy fighter. Stein called it his 'stinger'. Working with two other marines, one of them a demolitions man, Stein knocked out one pillbox after another. During his first hour on the island, he killed at least 20 Japanese. Then he took off his helmet and shoes and ran for the beach to get more ammunition. According to one historian, Stein made a total of eight trips to the beach that day and twice his stinger was shot from his hands. But at the end of the day, he was still going. As his Yugoslavian mother always said, 'He's a tough one, that Tony'.

By the end of D-day there were 30,000 Marines ashore, but the 28th was only interested in its private

Right: The savage beaches of Iwo Jima. Pinned down by Japanese machine-gun fire from Mount Suribachi, men of the 28th Marines await the order to advance.

Iwo Jima
3rd, 4th and 5th Marine Divisions, Feb-Mar 1945

As the American central Pacific offensive entered its final phase, three US Marine divisions launched their assault on the island of Iwo Jima. The battle for the island raged for nearly a month before the invading forces could declare it secure — and by then, nearly 6000 marines had lost their lives.

JAPAN
Iwo Jima
PACIFIC
AUSTRALIA

Key
Allied Pacific offensives, Aug 1942 — Feb 1945
Japanese defensive lines
Japanese artillery positions
1/27 US Marine units (battalion/regiment)
US landing beaches
US Marines

Kitano Point
• Kita
Airfield
Motoyama Plateau
Airfield
Tachiwa Point
Airfield
1/25
3/25
Mt Suribachi
2/23
1/23
Blue 2
Blue 1
Yellow 2
Yellow 1
1/27
2/27
Red 2
Red 1
Tobiishi Pt
2/28
1/28
Green

Iwo Jima: defences and landing beaches

The Battle for Iwo Jima, Feb-Mar 1945

Kitano Pt
Hill 362B
Airfield
Hill 362A
Motoyama
Airfield
Hill 382
3rd Marine Division
Airfield
Tachiwa Pt
4th Marine Div
Mt Suribachi
5th Marine Div

Taking Suribachi
22 Feb After four days of fighting, the 28th Marines completely encircle Suribachi and prepare for the final assault.
23 Feb The 2nd Battalion, 28th Marines claw their way up to the peak of Suribachi.

②

Mt Suribachi
28th Marines
27th Marines

Mount Suribachi
28th Marines, Feb 1945

①

Onto the beaches
19 Feb 0900 The first marines hit the beaches of Iwo Jima. Little resistance is encountered at the outset. Struggling through the sand, the 28th Marines cross the neck of Iwo Jima and wheel left towards Mount Suribachi.
1030 As the men of the 27th Marines push northwards. and B Coy, 28th Marines, reaches the west shore of Iwo Jima, the bulk of the 28th Marines begins the hard fight for Suribachi. By the end of the day, Japanese resistance has stiffened considerably.

After a massive preliminary bombardment, the assault on Iwo Jima went in at 0900 on 19 February 1945, with the 4th Marine Division on the right flank and the 5th Marine Division on the left. As the leading elements reached positions some 200 yards inland, the marines came under a withering crossfire from the defending Japanese forces — and from that moment onwards the fight for Iwo Jima became a grim and bloody contest.

While the 5th Division struggled to secure the southwest end of the island — with the 28th Marines assaulting Mount Suribachi — the 4th Division pushed north and east. On 24 February, with Suribachi secure, the two divisions, now reinforced in the centre by the reserve 3rd Marine Division, advanced slowly through Iwo Jima's central plateau. After five days of bitter fighting the assault on the complex of tunnels and bunkers on Hills 382 and 362A began. Hill 382 fell on 1 March and Hill 362A was taken the following day after a night attack. The pocket at Kitano Point was cleared by 16 March.

Below: As an M4 Sherman tank is consumed by fire after taking a direct hit from a hidden anti-tank gun, a carbine-armed leatherneck blazes away at Japanese positions around Nishi. This village in the northwest of the island formed part of the enemy's last line of defence and was held with fanatical determination. Below right: Exhausted by the bitter fighting, a group of marines takes shelter in an abandoned pillbox. Right: 'Devil's breath on Hell island' – two marines use their flame-throwers to clear out a Japanese bunker at the foot of Mount Suribachi.

war for Suribachi. Harry the Horse Liversedge moved his command post about 200yds closer to the front. It was, in fact, well ahead of his three battalion command posts. When Lieutenant-Colonel Robert H. Williams, the executive officer, was asked if this wasn't a bit unusual, he grinned and said, 'It isn't exactly SOP [standard operating procedure] but it's a hell of a good way to make your battalions move faster.'

The importance of Suribachi was that it was the island's dominant terrain feature. So long as the Japanese held it, they could observe every move we made. But it also had great psychological importance to the Americans. Said one report:

'Suribachi seemed to take on a life of its own, to be watching these men, looming over them, pressing down upon them... In the end it is probable that the mountain represented to these marines a thing more evil than the Japanese.'

Liversedge was under relentless pressure from higher headquarters to get the job done. But, despite heavy casualties during the first 24 hours, his request for relief forces was flatly rejected.

Suribachi itself was formidable enough. But the desolate wasteland of stone and scrub that covered the approach to the mountain was, if anything, worse. When the 28th reported a pillbox every 10ft, it was

DEFENDING IWO JIMA

The Japanese commander on Iwo Jima, Lieutenant-General Kuribayashi, was well aware of the position's importance, saying, 'this island is the gateway to Japan'. Knowing that he could not expect any help, he turned the island into a deathtrap, to be held to the last.

Kuribayashi's men had worked hard to improve Iwo Jima's natural defences. Although covering an area of less than 10 square miles, the island bristled with some 800 pillboxes, three miles of tunnels, as well as extensive minefields and trenches. Gun emplacements were sited to cover the beaches and a succession of inland defensive lines.

Kuribayashi had charge of a large, fanatical garrison. Aside from the 13,586 men of the 109th Division, he also had some 7347 Navy troops to hold Iwo Jima. Artillery support was lavish: 361 guns over 75mm calibre, 300 anti-aircraft guns, 20,000 light guns, 130 howitzers, 12 heavy mortars, 60 anti-tank guns and 70 rocket-launchers. Over 20 tanks were placed in hull-down positions.

When the 4th and 5th Marine Divisions hit Iwo Jima on 19 February, they faced the most extensive defence system seen in the Pacific theatre in World War II.

only a slight exaggeration. So many men were fighting in such a small place that as one marine observed, 'You don't dare sit down on this goddam rock for fear of getting a bayonet up your ass.' Enemy fortifications were so dense that one company inadvertently set up its command post on a bunker still full of Japanese.

Fighting was often hand-to-hand. Private First Class Leo Jez was moving towards a pillbox when a Japanese officer charged him swinging a sword. Jez caught the blow with his hands, wrenched the sword away from the officer and chopped off his head with it. Jez turned up later at the aid station with a nearly severed thumb, a gash on the back of his hand – and the sword.

The 22nd was a miserable day with a cold, hard rain and strong winds. Weapons clogged. There was no air support. Artillery support was negligible. A mortar fell on the 28th's command post, killing, among others, the regimental surgeon. But, by the end of the day, Marine patrols had encircled Suribachi. More men would die for that ugly little pile of real estate, but for all practical purposes the mountain was ours. A sergeant, who had scrambled part way up the north face of the mountain and met no resistance, paused to ask if he should continue. Liversedge decided it was too late in the day for the final ascent. That would come the next day. Thus the stage was set for the greatest picture of World War II: the flag-raising atop Mount Suribachi.

With Suribachi secured, members of the 28th were allowed a few days of rest. Many wrote letters home saying that now that they had taken Suribachi, their job was done and they would be leaving the island. What they didn't know was that the worst was

It would have been hard to find two more dissimilar men than Colonel Harry B. 'Harry the Horse' Liversedge, the commander of the 28th Marine Regiment, and his executive officer, Lieutenant-Colonel Robert H. 'English Bob' Williams.

Whereas Liversedge was tall and awkward looking, Williams was slim and elegant. Whereas Liversedge was shy and taciturn, Williams was sophisticated and articulate. Whereas Liversedge was as American as apple pie, Williams cultivated the airs of a British officer and gentleman. If Liversedge slouched, Williams was ramrod straight. If Liversedge cared little about his personal appearance, Williams was always immaculate. As an unshaven Liversedge gave orders for the assault on Mount Suribachi, Williams shaved – with an old-fashioned straight razor and a steady hand. They made a formidable fighting pair. Both had collected Navy Crosses in the Solomon Islands, where Williams also collected a bullet in his left lung.

An early 1920s Olympic track and college football star, Liversedge was six-feet four-inches tall with a long, loping stride that made his nickname inevitable. 'Hell, he even looked like a horse,' said a fellow marine. Given the task of capturing an extinct volcano, Liversedge was, in fact, born in Volcano, California.

More than anyone else, Liversedge and Williams personified the 28th Marines. 'Liversedge taught me compassion,' one officer said, recalling an incident where he had recommended stiff punishment for an erring enlisted man only to have Liversedge dismiss the man with a fatherly talk. Williams was well-versed in the military technology of his day. Liversedge was more at home leading a patrol through the jungles of Nicaragua. One day he confessed to an aide, during training, that he didn't really understand how to operate a radio. He was taken out into the boondocks for some private lessons, but he was never really comfortable with the radio.

A man who liked his drink, Liversedge was addicted to slot machines. At Camp Pendleton, California, a 50-cent machine was installed in the officers' club for the colonel's special use. When Liversedge hit a winning combination and the machine refused to pay out, he picked it up and hurled it through a window into a gulch 15ft below. It made an enormously satisfying crash, according to witnesses.

HARRY THE HORSE AND ENGLISH BOB

Below: The two masterminds of the capture of Mount Suribachi, Colonel Harry 'Harry the Horse' Liversedge (left), commander of the 28th Marines, and his executive officer, Lieutenant-Colonel Robert 'English Bob' Williams (right), confer on their next move. Independent, strong-willed characters, they nevertheless formed a formidable fighting team, and their calmness under pressure inspired the 28th Marines to battle on despite taking heavy losses. Both men had long, distinguished careers with the Marine Corps, seeing action in many of the island-hopping operations of the Pacific campaign.

The son of a Wisconsin clergyman, Williams liked gracious living. Some of his happiest days were as a member of the famed 4th Marines in pre-war Shanghai, where he was a member of the polo team. The duty hours were short, eight to noon, and the nights were long. As a dashing young lieutenant in the late 1930s, Williams served a hitch as a White House aide under President Roosevelt. He loved the social whirl. His British mannerisms alternately amused, angered or outraged his fellow officers. In addition to his nickname, 'English Bob,' he was also known as 'The Stick', for the swagger stick he carried.

Upon returning to Camp Pendleton one night in a carnival mood, he lost his stick through a hole in the floorboard of the rusty old car he was driving. Next day, according to a possibly exaggerated account, he had a whole battalion out looking for it.

Williams became famous for his carefully laid out officers' mess, with crisp white linen, and special mess nights in the British style. In Hawaii, he insisted on being served pheasant under glass. One officer thought this was going too far and said so. 'Look at it this way, Fred,' Williams said, 'Think of all the time we've spent in chow lines. We've earned it.'

In 1947 Williams got himself assigned to The Staff College in England. He couldn't have been more pleased. He had a batman to shine his leather and press his uniforms. He managed to stretch his six-month tour to two more years.

Williams divided his later years between Washington DC and Wisconsin. When he learned that he had terminal cancer, he returned to the family home in Wisconsin. He died there in 1983 at the age of 75.

Right: Two marines bring up extra machine-gun ammunition during the fight for Hill 362. The position was finally taken by the 28th Marines. Centre right: Two gunners turn a captured Hotchkiss machine gun on the enemy. Bottom right: Jubilant marines display the trophies of their victory; some 23,000 of their comrades were killed or wounded.

yet to come. Having fought and won their own private war against Suribachi, the 28th Marines now joined the main battle in the north.

After taking Suribachi, the 28th Marines and the rest of the 5th Division began moving up the west coast of the island, heading for the enemy's main defensive line along the Motoyama plateau. In a cruel sea of jumbled rock and stinking sulphur pits, the regiment took 240 casualties daily for three straight days. Advances were measured in tens rather than hundreds of yards. On 28 February, five days after the fall of Suribachi, the division faced the Japanese defenders holding Hill 362A. The first attack by the 27th Marines was thrown back after bitter hand-to-hand fighting.

It took three days of savage fighting to neutralise the enemy defences on Nishi ridge

On the following day, the 28th Marines took over. A Company went round the right side of the position in a flanking attack. Corporal Tony Stein, back in action after receiving a shrapnel wound in his shoulder on the 21st, led 20 men into the fray. Only seven returned; Stein was one of the dead. Three of the men who raised the two flags on Suribachi, Sergeant Hanson, Sergeant Strank and Corporal Block, were also killed. By nightfall, however, the hill was in American hands. Harry the Horse Liversedge won his second Navy Cross.

Pushing north along the coast, the regiment hit Nishi ridge, a jagged volcanic outcrop running from the plateau to the sea. It took three days of savage fighting to neutralise the defences. On the day of the ridge's capture, 3 March, Sergeant William G. Harrell, a tough Texan, won the Medal of Honor. Losing his left hand to a grenade during a night attack, he fought on. Undaunted, he continued to battle until his other hand was torn off by a second grenade.

By 9 March, the division was in sight of the sea on the northern coast of the island. The remnants of the Japanese defenders were holed up along a ridge overlooking Kitano gorge. It took over a week of hard fighting, using flame-throwers and satchel charges, to clear out the warren of caves and pillboxes that covered the area. Iwo Jima was declared secure on 16 March, but the mopping-up operations continued until the end of April.

The capture of the island had cost the lives of 5931 marines and a further 17,372 were wounded. Fewer than 250 of the garrison were taken alive. The 28th Marines had suffered appalling losses: of the 3900 men who had landed on 19 February, only 600 remained fit for action by the end. Commenting on their outstanding contribution to victory, Admiral Chester W. Nimitz paid them the ultimate tribute: 'Among the Americans who served on Iwo Jima, uncommon valour was a common virtue.'

THE AUTHOR Keyes Beech served with the 28th Marines as a sergeant combat correspondent during the landings on Iwo Jima. After the war, he was a correspondent for the *Chicago Daily News* and won the Pulitzer Prize for his coverage of the Korean War.

It was probably the hottest flag raising in history. Without doubt it produced the most famous photograph of World War II or, perhaps of any war. This was Joe Rosenthal's picture of the raising of the American flag on Mount Suribachi taken on 23 February 1945. Forty years after the event, that picture is still

STARS AND STRIPES OVER SURIBACHI

The true story behind the raising of the American flag over Iwo Jima by Keyes Beech.

Johnson, the rough, tough commander of the 2nd Battalion, 28th Marines, told First Lieutenant Harold G. Schrier to take a patrol to the top of Suribachi, now subdued and strangely silent after four days of bitter fighting. 'And put this up on the hill,' Johnson told him, handing him a flag. As Schrier, a lean-hipped ex-raider, and his 40-man patrol climbed the north face of Suribachi, they were easy targets for Japanese marksmen. But nothing happened. When they reached the top at about 1015 hours, somebody found a length of pipe and the marines proceeded to plant the flag. Sergeant Louis R. Lowery, a *Leatherneck* magazine photographer, started clicking away.

A short, sharp firefight followed as a few Japanese defenders came out of their holes. One Japanese threw a grenade and ran towards the flag, waving his sword. A marine shot him dead. Another Japanese threw a grenade in Lowery's direction. Lowery threw himself over the rim of the crater, rolling down the mountain side 50ft or more before coming to a stop. His camera was smashed. But the film was safe inside. As Richard F. Newcomb wrote later; 'This was the flag raising on Iwo Jima that thrilled the troops. The one that thrilled the world was still to come, nearly two hours later.'

Joe Rosenthal, who wore thick glasses and was so myopic that he had been rejected by all the services, reached the summit just as the marines were preparing to raise the second flag. It was much bigger and could be better seen elsewhere on the island and offshore. Rosenthal looked around for a good shooting spot.

Rosenthal shot 18 pictures that day, some of which were posed. The film pack was sent back to the photo pool on Guam for processing. When he received a query from his photo editor asking if 'the' picture was posed, Rosenthal, who had seen neither the negative nor the prints, said yes. He thought the editor was talking about the last pictures he had taken, which were posed.

the subject of controversy.

Some people say there were two, not just one, flag ceremonies. That is correct. Some people say that because Rosenthal was too late for the first flag raising and 'shot' the second, that his picture was posed, a fake, a re-enactment. Not true. As Rosenthal himself has often said, 'If I had posed that picture I would be a great photographer. As it happened, all I did was click the shutter at the right time.'

Here's what happened that day. Lieutenant-Colonel Chandler W.

Below: Signal victory. Triumphant leathernecks raise the Stars and Stripes over Mount Suribachi after days of hard fighting. Taken by Joe Rosenthal, this picture remains one of the 'classic' war shots of all time.

In 1962 Captain Jeremy Moore led the men of L Company, 42 Commando in an up-river operation from Brunei to free hostages held at Limbang in Sarawak.

IT WAS A beautifully clear, tropical day. At 0600 hours, 11 December 1962, as the early morning sun rose over Brunei airport, Brigadier 'Pat' Patterson greeted Captain Jeremy Moore, the newly arrived commander of L Company, 42 Commando, Royal Marines. Moore was a veteran of the campaigns in the Malayan jungle 10 years before, and had been awarded the Military Cross. Perched on the bonnet of his Land Rover, Brigadier Patterson, commander of 99 Gurkha Infantry Brigade and now head of operations against the North Kalimantan National

Below left: By a stroke of extraordinary good fortune, the Royal Marines located two Z Craft on the harbourside at Brunei Town. These front-loading lighters were to make excellent amphibious assault craft for the raid on Limbang. Below right: Brigadier 'Pat' Patterson (seated on left at rear) travels up the Limbang river on the afternoon of the raid. Bottom: The harbour at Brunei, with a lighter alongside the outer jetty.

Army (TNKU) in Brunei, made his directive quite plain: 'Your company will rescue the hostages in Limbang.'

Situated just across the border in the 5th Division of Sarawak, Limbang was a small community 12 miles up river from Brunei Town. On 8 December, pursuing a well co-ordinated plan, the TNKU had moved into Limbang, Seria, Miri, and other towns to seize pro-British hostages. The terrorists held about a dozen of them in Limbang, including the British Resident of the 5th Division, Dick Morris, and his wife Dorothy, another woman, and Fritz Klattenhof, a US Peace Corps officer.

As Captain Moore, his second-in-command Lieutenant Paddy Davis, and his company sergeant-major, QMS Scoins, took stock of the situation, the marines prepared themselves for the task ahead. Only 56 men of L Company had reached Brunei, together with a section of medium machine guns. Three hours after Moore's landing in Brunei, the commanding officer of 42 Commando, Lieutenant-Colonel Robin Bridges, and his intelligence officer,

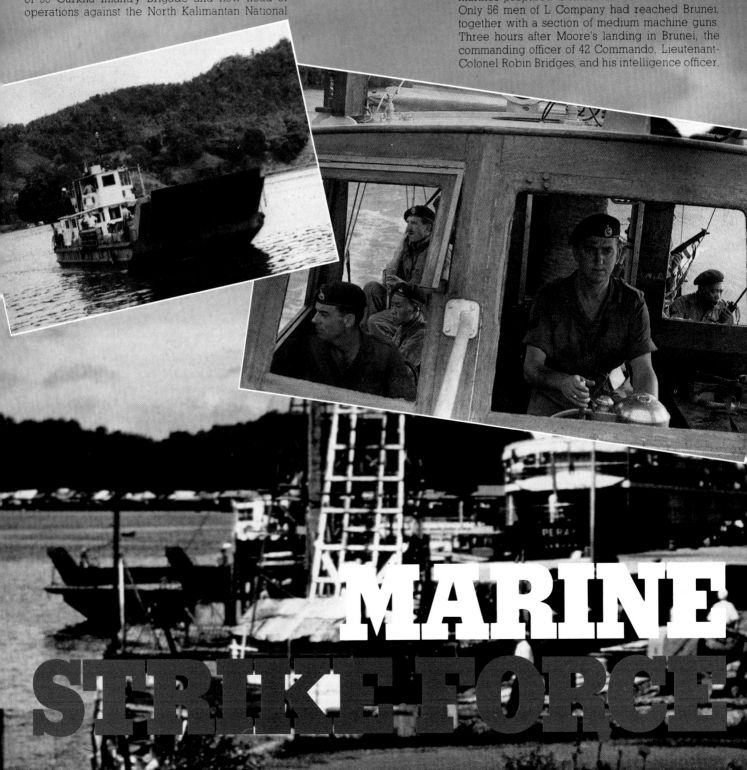

MARINE
STRIKE FORCE

REBELLION IN BRUNEI

On 8 December 1962, the 4000-strong North Kalimantan National Army (TNKU) rose up to wrest power from the Sultan of Brunei. There was no immediate reaction from the British, other than placing units on full alert, as it appeared that the Brunei police had the situation in hand. However, it soon became clear that the revolt was far more widespread than previously thought, and two companies of the 2nd

Gurkhas were ordered from Singapore to Brunei Town. They deployed in support of the police and attempted to relieve the oil complex at Seria, but were beaten back. Meanwhile the security forces in Brunei Town were coming under heavy fire and further reinforcements were requested. They included another company of the 2nd Gurkhas and elements of the Queen's Own Highlanders. On 11 December Seria was taken and the hostages held there were released. The TNKU were holding hostages all over Brunei, and additional units were summoned to confront their captors. At the time, 42 Commando was awaiting Christmas in Singapore after an extremely busy year of exercises, and on 8 December the commandos were put on short notice to move to Brunei. Two days later they were on their way, with Commando Headquarters and L Company flying via Labuan to Brunei Town, where the Gurkhas had restored order. They were given the task of ousting the rebels from the town of Limbang, situated on a river in the area of Sarawak which separates the two enclaves of Brunei protectorate.

Royal Marine, 42 Commando, Brunei 1962

This marine has the standard jungle-green uniform issued to men serving in the Far East. He is wearing the green Royal Marine beret and 1958-pattern web equipment. Woollen puttees are worn over leather boots with rubber soles. His armament is the British 7.62mm L1A1 rifle with a curved 30-round magazine, and the bayonet is worn on his left side.

Lieutenant Bengie Walden, arrived to take over the difficult task of obtaining information and intelligence for the coming operation. It was clear in everyone's mind that speed and surprise were essential, and the decision was soon made that the raid would have to take place at dawn the following morning.

Of prime importance was the need to find some river craft in which to mount the operation. Paddy Davis and I set about this task by inspecting the myriad of small boats along the Brunei waterfront. There were hundreds of them, but none particularly suitable for transporting the men up river for 12 miles and then carrying out a frontal assault. Just as we reached the north end of the extensive waterfront, we came across two old lighters, known as Z Craft, which belonged to the Brunei government and appeared to be in working order.

Just after midday, two coastal minesweepers HMS *Fiskerton* and HMS *Chawton*, sailed into the harbour. Paddy and I had wondered who was going to man and drive the Z Craft on the operation, but a quick trip on board as soon as they came alongside sorted that one out. The Royal Navy immediately took charge of the situation, providing the minesweeper first lieutenants to command the craft, and engine room staff to ensure that they were both in working order.

The minesweeper captains, Lieutenant Harry Mucklow and Lieutenant Jeremy Black, came ashore and helped Captain Moore with the detailed planning. This was the first meeting between Moore and Black, and 20 years later they were to find

Above right: Equipment is loaded aboard one of the pair of lighters moored on the waterfront of Brunei Town. The craft used on the operation received an urgent overhaul by engineers from the Royal Navy to make them fit for their task. Below: Marines of 42 Commando ready themselves for battle.

themselves in action together again in the South Atlantic, when Moore was the land-force commander and Black the captain of HMS *Invincible*.

By late afternoon, both craft were mechanically ready and were being given protective 'armour' as far as possible, with large packs acting as sandbags. Meanwhile, Moore was collecting as much intelligence as he could, with no more than small-scale maps and an out-of-date air photograph to help him. He had been told that a small police launch which had approached Limbang town two days earlier had been driven off by heavy smallarms fire. Information on the strength of the enemy and his dispositions was virtually non-existent; estimates varied from 30 men to over 100, but it was known for certain that the rebels were there in some numbers and possessed captured police weapons in addition to their own. Even so, Moore assessed that their firepower would be fairly ineffective at over 100yds range, and at close quarters the firepower of the two sides would be about equal. He knew, therefore, that his highly trained marines would be more than a match for a poorly led enemy.

He anticipated that he might be able to bluff the rebels into surrendering by a show of force, but if that

Limbang raid
L Company, 42 Commando, RM
13 December 1962

In 1962 the North Kalimantan National Army launched a revolt in Brunei aimed at seizing power from the Sultan and scotching the proposed accession of Brunei to a Federation of Malaysia. The rebels moved on key positions in Brunei and in parts of Sarawak and North Borneo. In Limbang and Seria the insurgents seized British hostages. Seria was retaken on 10 December – and the stage was set for L Company's daring raid on Limbang.

Key
Marines →

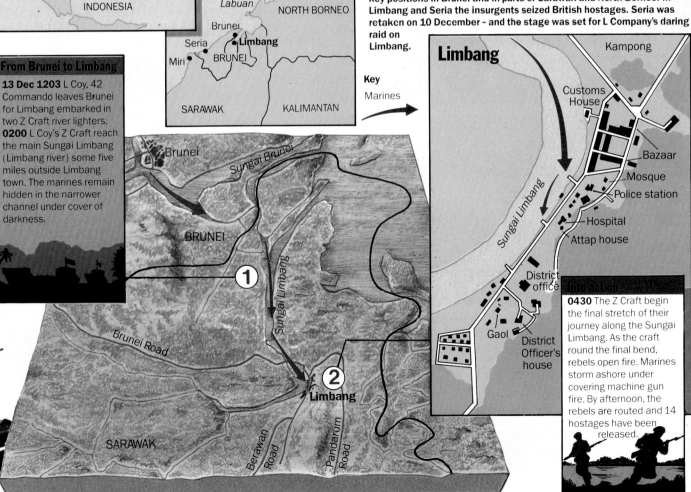

From Brunei to Limbang

13 Dec 1203 L Coy, 42 Commando leaves Brunei for Limbang embarked in two Z Craft river lighters.
0200 L Coy's Z Craft reach the main Sungai Limbang (Limbang river) some five miles outside Limbang town. The marines remain hidden in the narrower channel under cover of darkness.

Limbang

Kampong
Customs House
Bazaar
Mosque
Police station
Hospital
Attap house
District office
Gaol
District Officer's house

Into action

0430 The Z Craft begin the final stretch of their journey along the Sungai Limbang. As the craft round the final bend, rebels open fire. Marines storm ashore under covering machine gun fire. By afternoon, the rebels are routed and 14 hostages have been released.

SOUTH CHINA SEA
BRUNEI
MALAYSIA
Kuala Lumpur
SARAWAK
NORTH BORNEO
Kuching
SINGAPORE
KALIMANTAN
Pontianak
INDONESIA

SOUTH CHINA SEA
Kuala Belait
Kota Kinabalu
Labuan
NORTH BORNEO
Brunei
Seria
Limbang
Miri
BRUNEI
SARAWAK
KALIMANTAN

Brunei
Sungai Brunei
BRUNEI
Sungai Limbang
Brunei Road
SARAWAK
Berawan Road
Pandarum Road
Limbang

L2A3 Sterling SMG

fore sight assembly — chambered round (fired) — magazine release — cocking handle — sear — bolt

barrel casing — barrel

magazine housing

34-round box magazine —

trigger —

guard

trigger mechanism

THE STERLING

The precursor of the modern Sterling sub-machine gun appeared in 1942 as a proposed replacement for the Sten gun. Designed by a Mr George Patchett and known as the Patchett machine carbine, the weapon underwent numerous trials and modifications and was finally introduced into service as the L2A1 in 1951. Manufactured by the Sterling Engineering Company, the gun soon became known as the Sterling. A modified version, the L2A2, arrived in 1953, but it was only with the introduction of the L2A3 in 1954 that the British Army deemed the Sterling a worthy replacement of the trusty Sten.
Since it has minimal recoil, the Sterling can be fired either from the shoulder with the stock extended, or from a crouching position with the folded stock resting in the pit of the stomach. Fired from below, the gun is aimed by 'walking' the rounds up to the target. The weapon uses low-powered 9mm ammunition and is generally preferred only for close-quarters fighting over a range of 30yds, beyond which it has uncertain stopping power. It functions well in poor conditions, due to the inclusion of a ribbed bolt which clears the gun while it fires and forces accumulated carbon out of the receiver.

failed, or if the operation was prolonged, they would probably either shoot the hostages out of hand or threaten to do so in order to make him withdraw. His prime concern was the safety of the hostages, but he did not know where they were being held. Several possible locations presented themselves: the police station, the hospital, the administrative offices and the British Residency, all separated by at least 300yds. He decided that the police station was the most likely place for the rebels to have set up their headquarters, and he planned to knock this out before they had a chance to harm their hostages. His simple plan was to go straight for the enemy and overwhelm their headquarters as fast as possible, each marine holding his fire until the rebels opened up. He intended to call on the enemy to surrender in the hope that, by a brave show, he could bluff his way in.

Under Lieutenant Paddy Davis, the other two subalterns and the troop NCOs, the depleted company prepared for action. Ammunition and equipment were checked, the medium machine guns were mounted forward on the Z Craft (where they would be most effective), and food and rest were hastily taken during what was left of the day.

In order to arrive off Limbang at dawn, it was decided to sail at about midnight, guided by the Brunei Director of Marine, Captain Muton, who had earlier brought the minesweepers up-river. Lieutenant David Willis, *Chawton's* first lieutenant, cast off the leading craft at three minutes past midnight. He was aided considerably by a clear night and a nearly full moon. His route lay in a series of complicated, winding channels varying from 30 to 100yds wide and flanked by the hideous Nipa swamp. The 100 marines on board, including members of L Company who had arrived just before nightfall, snatched whatever catnaps they could.

The two craft, keeping just within sight of each other, crept slowly down the narrow channels, keeping as silent as they could. No lights or noise emanated from their decks, and only the grinding engines might have announced their presence to a waiting guerrilla ambush. After half an hour the leading craft slewed across the river; one of her engines had decided that enough was enough and it had to be revived. Occasionally the craft bumped perilously against mangrove roots protruding into the narrower passages. By 0200 hours, both craft had reached the main Limbang river, and until 0430 they laid up,

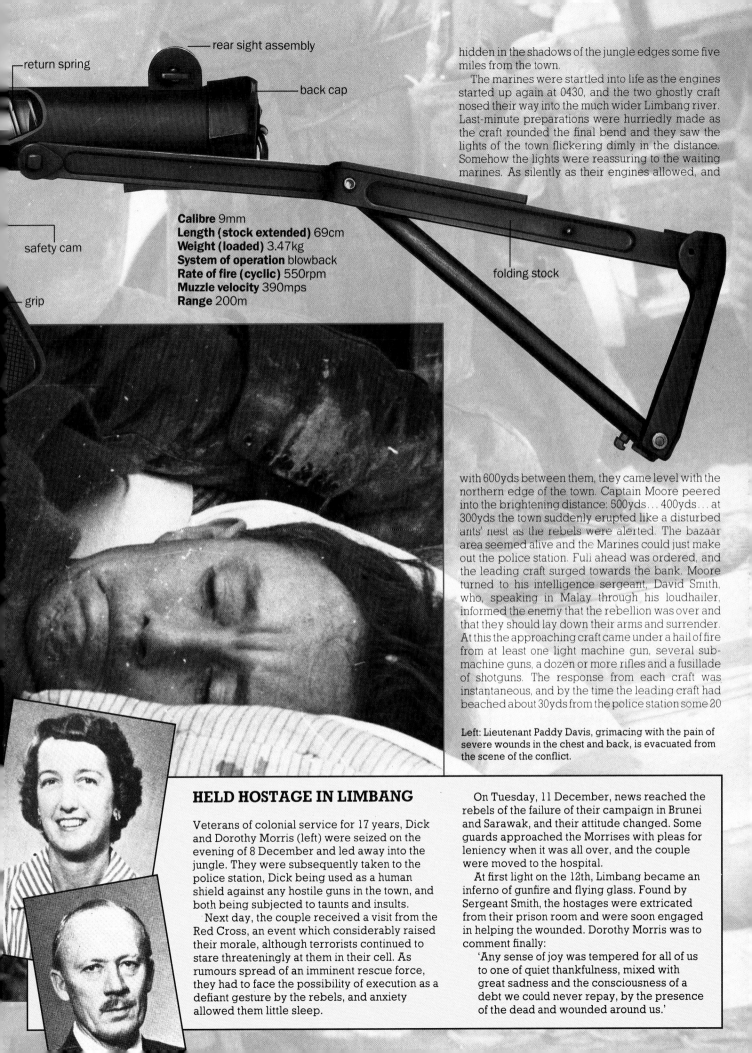

return spring

rear sight assembly

back cap

safety cam

Calibre 9mm
Length (stock extended) 69cm
Weight (loaded) 3.47kg
System of operation blowback
Rate of fire (cyclic) 550rpm
Muzzle velocity 390mps
Range 200m

folding stock

grip

hidden in the shadows of the jungle edges some five miles from the town.

The marines were startled into life as the engines started up again at 0430, and the two ghostly craft nosed their way into the much wider Limbang river. Last-minute preparations were hurriedly made as the craft rounded the final bend and they saw the lights of the town flickering dimly in the distance. Somehow the lights were reassuring to the waiting marines. As silently as their engines allowed, and with 600yds between them, they came level with the northern edge of the town. Captain Moore peered into the brightening distance: 500yds... 400yds... at 300yds the town suddenly erupted like a disturbed ants' nest as the rebels were alerted. The bazaar area seemed alive and the Marines could just make out the police station. Full ahead was ordered, and the leading craft surged towards the bank. Moore turned to his intelligence sergeant, David Smith, who, speaking in Malay through his loudhailer, informed the enemy that the rebellion was over and that they should lay down their arms and surrender. At this the approaching craft came under a hail of fire from at least one light machine gun, several sub-machine guns, a dozen or more rifles and a fusillade of shotguns. The response from each craft was instantaneous, and by the time the leading craft had beached about 30yds from the police station some 20

Left: Lieutenant Paddy Davis, grimacing with the pain of severe wounds in the chest and back, is evacuated from the scene of the conflict.

HELD HOSTAGE IN LIMBANG

Veterans of colonial service for 17 years, Dick and Dorothy Morris (left) were seized on the evening of 8 December and led away into the jungle. They were subsequently taken to the police station, Dick being used as a human shield against any hostile guns in the town, and both being subjected to taunts and insults.

Next day, the couple received a visit from the Red Cross, an event which considerably raised their morale, although terrorists continued to stare threateningly at them in their cell. As rumours spread of an imminent rescue force, they had to face the possibility of execution as a defiant gesture by the rebels, and anxiety allowed them little sleep.

On Tuesday, 11 December, news reached the rebels of the failure of their campaign in Brunei and Sarawak, and their attitude changed. Some guards approached the Morrises with pleas for leniency when it was all over, and the couple were moved to the hospital.

At first light on the 12th, Limbang became an inferno of gunfire and flying glass. Found by Sergeant Smith, the hostages were extricated from their prison room and were soon engaged in helping the wounded. Dorothy Morris was to comment finally:

'Any sense of joy was tempered for all of us to one of quiet thankfulness, mixed with great sadness and the consciousness of a debt we could never repay, by the presence of the dead and wounded around us.'

seconds later, it was clear that L Company had the fire advantage, thanks largely to the heavy weight of lead pouring from their Vickers medium machine guns.

Two marines of the leading troop were killed even before they got to the bank, and Lieutenant Peter Waters was hit in the leg as he jumped ashore. The coxswain of the leading craft was also hit, as were Lieutenant Paddy Davis and a seaman in the second craft, which was still standing off and giving covering fire. No.5 Troop stormed ashore, clearing the police station in its stride, with Corporal Bill Lester taking his section across the road, mopping up and providing a cut-off to the rear. Sergeant Johnny Bickford, a corps footballer and physical training instructor, with his section commander, Corporal Bob Rawlinson, pressed home the attack though Rawlinson was soon wounded in the back.

Meanwhile, with its coxswain wounded, the leading craft had drifted off the bank. Lieutenant David Willis immediately took the wheel and drove it back into the bank again, although now the unwieldy craft was beached halfway between the residency and the hospital, some 150yds from the initial landing.

Captain Moore now re-assessed the situation and ordered his troop sergeant, Sergeant Wally MacFarlane, ashore with the reserve section. Sergeant Smith, having decided that his loudhailer was no longer an adequate weapon, accompanied them. By this time there was only spasmodic fire, and Sergeant MacFarlane moved stealthily north, clearing the enemy from their hiding places in the jungle fringe. They reached the hospital without incident, and Sergeant MacFarlane decided to press on to join up with the force near the police station.

Suddenly, all hell was let loose as a group of determined rebels opened fire, killing the troop sergeant and two marines. The marines fought back, eliminating all the guerrillas in the area other than those who had fled into the jungle. Then, through the sounds of battle, Sergeant Smith heard some unharmonious singing from within the hospital. Recognising the tune as a version of *Coming round the mountain*, he called out to them in English and discovered Dick and Dorothy Morris, along with several other hostages, unharmed but severely shocked. Their guards had fled. Captain Moore, his main task of freeing the hostages now achieved, checked with Dick Morris that no-one was being held elsewhere.

During the whole of this time, the second craft had been manoeuvring in the fast-flowing river to give the best supporting fire possible. The company sergeant-major had taken command of the situation when Lieutenant Davis had been severely wounded. At this juncture the reserve sections on the second craft came ashore, the craft itself once again taking up a position in mid-stream to cover any eventuality with its medium machine guns.

A number of rebels were soon routed by 5 Troop in the area of the Attap House, whilst 6 Troop cleared the police station and 4 Troop moved north, past the

mosque to the back of the bazaar. There, one of the rebels engaged them from a room full of women and children, but he was soon dislodged with no further casualties. From this time on most of the enemy resistance collapsed, although a number of rebels held out in the town and the jungle, and there was considerable movement and sniping for the next 24 hours.

As soon as the second craft beached, Terry Clark, the Royal Naval sick berth attendant, made his way to the hospital and set up a dressing station, treating the casualties while the released hostages helped him to prepare dressings. Four of his six cases of gunshot wounds were in the legs. Sergeant Smith set about interrogating the hostages and other ex-prisoners, and discovered that more were being held in the gaol and in the southern area of the town. By late afternoon this area had been systematically cleared and a total of 14 hostages had been rescued.

Later in the morning, the Z Craft returned to Brunei, this time quickly and triumphantly, bringing the hostages and the casualties with them. L Company had lost five dead and five wounded, plus one sailor, and the wounded were quickly flown to Labuan and thence to Singapore. When L Company consolidated the next day, 15 rebel bodies were found and about 50 prisoners were taken. It was learned subsequently that many others died of wounds in the jungle. It transpired that initially nearly 350 rebels had held Limbang, many later discarding their uniforms and melting anonymously into the bazaar areas of the town.

Much later, Captain Jeremy Moore made the following observations:

'It is perhaps interesting to note that, though my assessment of where the enemy headquarters might be was right, I was quite wrong about the hostages. Furthermore, it was chance that the second beaching happened where it did, that resulted in us taking the hospital from the direction we did. It could be that this saved us heavier casualties, though I assess the most important factor in the success of the operation was first class leadership by junior NCOs. Their section battlecraft was a joy to watch, and the credit for this belongs to the troop and section commanders.'

This action, along with others by the Queen's Own Highlanders at Seria, and by the Gurkhas at Tutong, crushed the revolt within five days of its breaking out. For the action at Limbang, Captain Jeremy Moore was awarded a bar to his Military Cross, and Corporals R.C. Rawlinson and W.J. Lester received the Military Medal. Lieutenant David Willis was awarded the Distinguished Service Cross, and Petty Officer D.J.D. Kirwin the Distinguished Service Medal. Marine Barry Underwood was mentioned in despatches.

Top: Lieutenant Peter Waters, who was shot in the leg as he reached the shore at Limbang, tells the story of the assault as he awaits evacuation from Brunei. Above: Captain Jeremy Moore, MC, commanding officer of L Company on the Limbang raid. Twenty years later, Moore commanded the British land forces in the Falklands campaign of 1982.

THE AUTHOR Captain Derek Oakley, Royal Marines, was a staff officer of 3rd Commando Brigade, Royal Marines, in 1962. He was liaison officer to 99 Gurkha Infantry Brigade during the revolt in Brunei.

The two Lynx helicopters aboard HMS *Brilliant* were to play a major role in neutralising the threat of the Argentinian submarine *Santa Fé* during the 1982 Falklands campaign

ACTION LYNX!

EIGHT SLEEK, sharp-prowed ships knifed their way through the sunny waters, heading south for the dreary wastes of the South Atlantic. The day before, 2 April 1982, a signal had been received directing the FOF1 (Flag Officer First Flotilla) to race south from the North Atlantic – Argentina had invaded the Falkland Islands. The spearhead group comprised HMS *Glamorgan*, the flagship, and five other destroyers, HMS *Antrim*, *Glasgow*, *Coventry*, *Sheffield* and *Plymouth*, with the Type 22 frigate HMS *Brilliant* and the Type 21 frigate HMS *Arrow*. Altogether they made a fast, hard-hitting, Exocet-armed task force.

The final stages of Exercise Springtrain, based on Gibraltar, had been abandoned, and the spearhead group paired up with ships returning to Britain in order to swap stores. Positioned alongside her sister ship HMS *Battleaxe*, *Brilliant* began the first of the 'vertreps' (vertical replenishments by helicopter) which were eventually to become commonplace during Operation Corporate. For 12 hectic hours she took aboard, via jackstay, boat and vertrep, *Battleaxe's* stores of Sea Wolf missiles, torpedoes, machine guns, internal security gear, ammunition, and all manner of naval and victualling items, steadily sinking into the water as *Battleaxe* rose. Both her Lynx helicopters (commonly abbreviated to 'helos') flew continually in support of *Brilliant* and the other ships, landing cross-deck with underslung loads.

The helicopters acted as the eyes of the task force, beyond the range of its radar

Then, in high frequency (HF) radio and radar silence, sailing between 25 and 50 miles apart, they headed at up to 25 knots through 'absolutely gin clear' air towards Ascension Island. As the Anglo-Argentinian diplomatic efforts continued to founder, the speeding ships practised operational techniques, honing themselves for battle should hostilities actually arise. The main Argentinian threat was seen as a surface one, and emphasis was laid on surface reporting and OTHT (over the horizon targeting), in which the helicopters acted as the eyes of the task force, beyond the range of its radar. In the absence of an aircraft carrier, however, air defence exercises could not be conducted at task-force level: that was to come later when HMS *Hermes* and *Invincible* arrived on the scene. During the voyage, the aircraft and the Royal Marines practised attacks against Sheffield-class Type 42 destroyers (similar to those deployed by the Argentinians). Pacific Seariders (inflatable assault boats) were successfully mounted with Carl Gustav anti-tank weapons, and the all-purpose Lynxes made dummy sorties using the limited weapons available to them.

Although their potential role as gunships was appreciated, neither of *Brilliant's* helos had been fitted with the standard mounting for the GPMG (7.62mm General Purpose Machine Gun), and the first of many clever improvisations was devised. The metal section of a typist's swivel chair was upturned and bolted to the deck, and a brass mounting constructed to carry the GPMG. It was then operated by two Royal Marine gunners to great effect, and an oil drum was sunk first time on a practice shoot.

Although the men were prepared for the worst, the atmosphere aboard *Brilliant* was one of excitement, almost a holiday spirit, and there was no appreciation of threat. As one crew member put it, they were off to 'shake a gunboat at those dagoes'. This feeling transmitted itself to the helo aircrews. The flight commander, Lieutenant Commander Barry Bryant, and his pilot, Lieutenant Nick Butler, with the crew of the second Lynx, Lieutenant Commander Clark and Lieutenant McKay, threw themselves into the exercises with great determination.

Practising surface actions and other OTHT procedures, the spearhead group arrived at Ascension, where *Antrim*, *Plymouth* and *Tidespring*, a fleet tanker, were diverted to South Georgia. There, in Operation Paraquet, they were to land some 60 men, drawn from the 22nd Special Air Service Regiment, the Special Boat Squadron, and the Royal Marines, to retake the island from the Argentinians. The remainder of the force kept out of sight of Ascension Island for security reasons, and the helicopters plied between them, replenishing vital stores. *Brilliant* also exchanged her basic type of Lynx for a more advanced model that was capable of firing Sea Skua missiles. This helicopter had been dismantled, and it arrived in bits at Ascension after a 12-hour flight in a Hercules. It was assembled in less

ANTI-SUBMARINE OPERATIONS

The Type 22 Broadsword-class frigates were the first vessels of the Royal Navy to exchange primary gun armament for extensive anti-submarine warfare (ASW) weaponry, in addition to their Exocet anti-ship missiles and Seawolf point-air-defence system. The two Lynx helicopters carried by each frigate perform a vital role in ASW operations. Their initial task is submarine detection, for which they use sonar, which is dipped in the water ('dunking sonar'), search radar and a passive radar receiver, and MAD (magnetic anomaly detectors), which locate an underwater metal hull by identifying the disturbance it creates in the earth's magnetic field.

Following contact with the submarine, the Lynx will often act as the frigate's primary weapon delivery system, although it may carry out mid-course correction of surface-to-surface missiles from the parent ship by employing its radar. The Lynx's own armament comprises two Mk 44, Mk 46 or Stingray torpedoes, or two Mk 11 depth-charges, or four Sea Skua semi-active homing anti-ship missiles. The Sea Skua is designed to be guided by target reflections of signals from the Lynx's Ferranti Seaspray radar.

Page 1081: The Westland Lynx, armed with Sea Skua missiles, and the Type 22 frigate *Brilliant*, with its badge.
Above: A Lynx circles over *Sheffield*. Left: The ships set sail. Right: One of *Brilliant's* Lynxes supplies smallarms ammunition to *Hermes*. Bottom: Nicknamed 'Humphrey', *Antrim's* Wessex Mk3 helicopter was to play a vital role in Operation Paraquet.

ROYAL NAVY
XP 142

THE LYNX HAS.MK2

In 1967, Westland Helicopters and Aérospatiale in France agreed to co-produce three helicopter types. The French assumed design responsibility for two, the Puma and the Gazelle, while a British project, begun by Fairey in the 1950s and then known as the WG.13, went ahead to become the versatile Lynx.

In all, 13 prototypes were built, each intended for a specialised role, and the first flew on 21 March 1971. The Royal Navy prototype, tailored for anti-submarine work and known as the Lynx HAS.Mk2, first flew on 25 May 1972 and entered service with No.702 Squadron for aircrew training in 1977.

The Lynx incorporates several important design innovations, including a new kind of gearwheel, the Wiktor/Novikov conformal gear, and a one-piece rotor hub forged in titanium which has enabled rotor diameter to be cut down to only 42ft.

The Lynx HAS.MK2 is

powered by two 900shp Rolls-Royce Gem 2 turboshafts, while the uprated Lynx HAS.Mk3 has 1120shp Gem 41-1s. The former aircraft has a cruising speed of 144mph at maximum weight, and its range is 369 miles.

The Lynx normally has a crew of two, or a pilot (whose Naval Air Arm wings are shown above) and up to 10 troops. Torpedoes

or depth-charges fired from the pylons can be replenished from the cabin.

than 24 hours in primitive conditions under a canvas awning.

At 1635 hours on 14 April, *Brilliant's* commander, Captain John Coward, was ordered to lead a group of ships far into the South Atlantic towards the Falklands, in an attempt to escape the attention of Argentinian aircraft and 'become lost'. Led by *Brilliant*, the ships *Arrow*, *Coventry*, *Glasgow* and *Sheffield* headed south at 25 knots. A freight tanker, *Appleleaf*, and an afloat support ship, *Fort Austin*, were to follow and rendezvous.

Brilliant's Lynxes continued to vertrep stores even as the ships headed south, the last trip being made from Ascension in pitch darkness. Around midnight, Nick Butler brought his helo in with just 12 minutes of fuel left, well below the acceptable safety margin. The deck was pitching wildly and the flightdeck crew was 'invited' to unload very quickly indeed. The pilot had identified the ship by her 'red head', a flashing red light at the top of her mast. As he brought the aircraft in, hovering at 25ft to lower the load, his only guide a horizontal bar of light, two men made their way over a deck 'goffered' with spume, harnessed the load and unhooked it in 30 seconds flat. As the Lynx came in to touch down, the ship lurched, and one of the aircraft's main wheels struck Air Engineer and Mechanic House a glancing blow on the head, sending him sprawling on the deck. More shaken than hurt, he was able to stagger to the comparative shelter of the open hangar.

'Wolf! Wolf!' came clearly over the radio, and the Wessex went into a depth-charge attack

On 22 April, *Brilliant* detached from the group at maximum speed to offer support to *Antrim's* group off South Georgia. This group had had only three Wessex helicopters at its disposal, and two of them had crashed on a glacier, forcing on *Brilliant's* two Lynxes a vital role in implementing the landings. Smashing through mountainous seas in the teeth of a howling gale, her stern rising and falling 30ft, *Bril-*

liant joined *Antrim* and *Plymouth* 150 miles north of South Georgia. The invasion of South Georgia had been scheduled for 25 April, but an additional complication had arisen: the Argentinian submarine *Santa Fé* had been spotted off Grytviken. *Antrim*, now acting as flagship, decided that the landing must be deferred until the submarine was eliminated. At 0855 hours on 25 April, *Antrim's* surviving Wessex 3 sighted her coming out of the harbour. She had landed troops and was preparing to dive to clear the area. 'Wolf! Wolf!' – the signal for submarine on the surface – came clearly over the radio, and the Wessex went into a depth-charge attack.

Aboard *Brilliant*, Lynx 341, at alert five, was directed to join in the attack. (Alert 45 meant a helo at 45 minutes' readiness; alert 15 at 15 minutes' readiness, and alert five, at five minutes' readiness for immediate take-off. Usually take-off took only three and a half minutes.) Lynx 341's pilot and observer were aboard, and an MK 46 torpedo had been loaded. As the Lynx strained at her 'harpoon' decklock system, four members of the flightdeck crew undid the aircraft lashings, under the watchful eye of the SMR (Senior Maintenance Rating) Chief Petty Officer O'Hara. Spray, driven by a fierce wind off the glaciers, lashed across the violently pitching deck as the order came from the ops room: 'Action Lynx!' Nick Butler pressed the starter button, both engines roared into life, the rotors were engaged, and Barry Bryant punched in the computer sequence. Lieutenant Commander Morris, the FDO (flight deck officer), cleared the flightdeck. 'Launch!' came over the intercom. The pilot released the harpoon and the Lynx lifted off, making for the *Santa Fé*.

Ahead, the Wessex hovered, having dropped two depth-charges, waiting for Lynx 341 to arrive before returning to *Antrim* to re-arm. The Argentinian submarine was heading for Cumberland Bay and Grytviken harbour, and the Lynx crew could see that her fin was damaged and she was weeping oil from the stern. They made a classic visual torpedo attack, but the submarine captain, seeing the Mk 46 on its parachute landing in the water alongside him,

Above: For maximum stability on pitching decks, the landing gear of the naval Lynx can be angled away from the fuselage. Left: A Lynx receives its anti-submarine missile armament.

decided to remain on the surface. He was fully aware that the MK 46 was strictly an underwater weapon, only able to operate at a minimum depth of 30ft. There he was, resting on the surface, with enough high explosive circling beneath him to blow the *Santa Fé* out of the water.

The Lynx was determined to keep him on the surface, and after the observer had scrambled into the back to man the GPMG, the pilot took the helo in, making a low pass 'to sharpen him up', gun chattering. The submarine crew scattered on the conning tower, and it was not until the third pass that they replied with their own GPMG. A 7.62mm bullet would have little effect on a submarine's fin, but it could smash a periscope or radar antenna and it certainly kept the crew on their toes. The helo swept in again and again to strafe the fin at 100yds range and at a height of 30ft.

The Lynx had joined the Wessex at 0905 hours, 50 or 60 miles from *Brilliant*, too far for low frequency transmission, so they used HF radio, on the frequency common to the whole of the task force. Over 300 miles away, the pilots of *Hermes* and *Invincible* sat in their aircraft on the flightdecks, listening incredulously over their radios to Nick Butler's blow by blow commentary on the machine-gun action with the *Santa Fé*. They could hardly believe that he was being fired at by an enemy. Over the radio came, 'Do not strafe survivors with GPMG,' much to the chagrin of the aircrew, who had not the slightest intention of doing so. They hung about 'causing vexation', using their height advantage to fire on the *Santa Fé*, hoping for a hit on either the periscope or the radar.

Suddenly, at 0930 hours, the trail of an AS. 12 wire-guided missile, fired from a Wasp, flashed beneath the Lynx, now flying at 800ft, to crash into the fin of the submarine, causing more oil to weep. A second AS. 12 went up in the water ahead of the *Santa Fé*. *Brilliant's* other Lynx, 342, arrived on the scene, supplementing the machine-gun attack. Another Wasp came in to fire more AS. 12s at the damaged submarine, which was still limping towards Grytviken, leaking even more oil and streaming smoke. As the *Santa Fé* reached King Edward Point in Grytviken itself, groundfire from machine guns ashore caused the aerial attack to break off. The decision was then taken to send in the ground troops.

The three close-flying helos went straight into the bay, very fast and very low, 15ft above the water

Lynx 341 refuelled and searched the indented north coast of South Georgia on the look-out for lurking Argentinian FPBs (fast patrol boats), even though there was not much likelihood of them having reached the island in the time available. As bad weather closed in, and in that latitude it could happen in a very few minutes, visibility was reduced to a quarter of a mile and flying became very hazardous. The Lynx, 'flogging around' the hostile cliffs, was surrounded by 'millions of enormous sea birds', mainly albatross. Not being used to aircraft, the birds constituted one of the biggest menaces the crew encountered at South Georgia, and at Bird Island the number of birds increased to the point of becoming positively lethal.

Following its patrol, Lynx 341, after refuelling and food, launched from *Brilliant* at 1430 to begin landing the SAS. Foiled by the increasing deterioration in the weather from going into Cumberland Bay via a devious route, the three close-flying helos went straight into the bay, very fast and very low, 15ft above the water, to take the enemy by surprise. At 1715, the Argentinians surrendered and a white flag appeared. The SAS landings were halted, despite the troops 'bickering and wingeing' in their anxiety to get ashore. About 10 minutes later, the commander of the *Santa Fé* handed Barry Bryant and Nick Butler a certificate, announcing that a Lynx helicopter of the British Navy had attacked and captured his submarine, and signed 'the submarine captain'. He thought depth-charging was fair enough, but machine gunning was just 'not cricket'!

Next day, the commander of *Brilliant*, Captain John Coward, himself an ex-submariner, flew into Gryt-

viken to inspect the *Santa Fé*, now at the jetty and slowly sinking. She was listing to port and down by the head, her fin and casing riddled by bullet holes and part of her bridge area blown away by the AS. 12 missile attack. Most of the AS. 12s had punched straight through before exploding. Apart from surface damage and innumerable bullet holes, there was little evidence that the submarine had suffered harm. Inside, it was another story. *Santa Fé* was a total shambles, she was slowly taking water into the bilges and probably also into the battery tanks, the tankside valves were passing almost as much air shut as open, and there was only emergency lighting.

After attempts to restore full buoyancy had failed, it was decided to move the submarine away from the jetty. Rather than sink her in deep water, she was to be towed alongside a shallow berth at the old whaling station where she could settle on the bottom. A small number of the Argentinian crew were to man the switchboard in the control room, under the supervision of a British officer and guarded by Royal Marines; the commander of the *Santa Fé* would be on the bridge with Captain Coward. Blowing tanks throughout, the submarine was limping slowly towards its new berth when suddenly it listed and showed signs of losing buoyancy. The Argentinian commander issued a stream of orders in Spanish, trying to get the crew to blow all ballast, but the men

Top left: The South Georgia task group possessed three Westland HAS. Mk 1 Wasps, two on *Endurance* and one on *Plymouth*. Attacking in support of the Wessex and Lynxes, they fired AS.12 missiles which shot through the submarine's glass-reinforced plastic conning tower without exploding.

SOUTH ATLANTIC

South Georgia
April 1982

Ice fjord

Leith

Stromness bay

Fortuna glacier

Cumberland bay

King Haarkon bay

Hestesletten tussock

Esmark glacier

Grytviken

Mt Sugartop

Brown Mt

Annenkov Island

Christopherson glacier

Ross glacier

On 25 April 1982 HMS *Brilliant*'s Sea Lynx helicopter was ordered into action following the sighting of an enemy submarine. At 1445 the same afternoon, Operation Paraquet — the retaking of South Georgia — was under way.

ARGENTINA

SOUTH ATLANTIC

FALKLAND ISLANDS

SOUTH GEORGIA

CHILE

SANDWICH ISLANDS

Top right: Captain Coward (right) and Lieutenant-Commander Bocain inspect the damage on *Santa Fé*. Background: The Argentinian submarine, listing heavily to port, in the shelter of Grytviken. Above: The shattered conning tower, showing the holes made by the AS.12 missiles.

in the control room panicked, thinking the boat was going down. A petty officer, presumably rushing to carry out his orders, was shot dead in the belief that he intended to scuttle the submarine. Despite this tragic incident, the *Santa Fé* was finally berthed.

Experiencing surface attack and hazardous night flights, dicing with icebergs, Lynx 341 and her crew flew a total of 56 hours in support of Operation Paraquet. They were deployed from 25 to 28 April, in

often appalling conditions, without missing a single sortie or take-off, and no man who was present would deny the enormous contribution they made to the successful action in South Georgia.

THE AUTHOR Bernard Brett left the Royal Navy at the end of World War II, and has since written several books on ships, sea power and naval warfare. He is currently preparing a history of modern sea power.

GIGN

In the early 1970s, officers of France's Gendarmerie Nationale, a militarised police force with a strength of over 60,000 men, were studying the possibility of creating a specialist anti-terrorist unit. The terrorist atrocities at the Munich Olympics in 1972 and the siege of the Saudi Arabian embassy in Paris during 1973 added impetus to their activities, and on 3 November 1973 GIGN (Groupement D'Intervention de la Gendarmerie Nationale) was formed. Originally, GIGN was divided into two commands: GIGN 1, based at Maisons-Alfort near Paris, was responsible for northern France; GIGN 2, based at Mont-de-Marsan, was assigned to watch over the south of the country. In the beginning, only 15 men, working in three five-man teams, were assigned to GIGN; overall command lay with Lieutenant Prouteau. In 1976, the northern and southern commands were merged, and the unit's strength was increased. Three years later, GIGN comprised two officers and 40 NCOs organised into three strike teams, each consisting of two five-man intervention forces, a team commander and a dog handler. Normally, one of the two officers or the senior NCO would take charge of a mission. Under normal circumstances, each of the strike forces is on full alert, ready for deployment at a moment's notice, for one week in three. GIGN's primary role is to act as France's premier hostage rescue unit, both at home and abroad. However, the squad is also used to deal with prison unrest, to provide protection for VIPs and to transfer dangerous prisoners between jails. Above: GIGN's badge.

DAY OF THE SNIPER

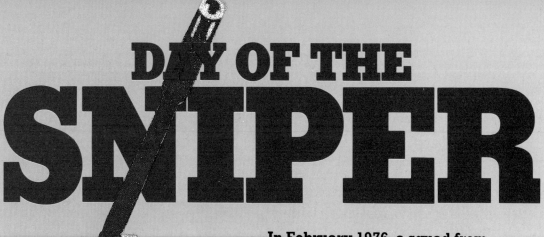

In February 1976, a squad from GIGN, France's crack anti-terrorist force, gave an awesome display of precision shooting to secure the release of 30 children held hostage in Djibouti

SHORTLY BEFORE 0800 hours on the morning of 3 February 1976, four members of the FLCS (Front de Liberation de la Côte des Somalis – Somali Coast Liberation Front) hijacked a party of French children as they made their way from the airbase in Djibouti to their school in the town's port area. As the coach carrying the children turned onto the main coast road, the terrorists flagged it down and, once on board, ordered the driver to head south towards the village of Loyada, near the border with Somalia.

After passing through Loyada, the driver was forced to halt the coach some 180m from a Somali border post. Another terrorist then crossed the frontier in a pre-arranged move, and joined his comrades on the bus. Using the 30 children, aged between six and 12 years, and the driver as their pawns, the five hijackers then issued their demands: the immediate independence of the French territory of Afars and Issas, of which Djibouti was the capital. If their demands were not met, the children would have their throats cut.

Negotiations between the commanding officer of the 6000 French troops stationed in the colony and the hijackers began around midday. Conditions on the coach, stationed in the open under the merciless sun, quickly deteriorated, and although the terrorists allowed food and water to be served, the health of the children began to cause great concern.

As the local French negotiators sought a swift, peaceful end to the crisis, the High Commissioner of the Republic of Djibouti, Christian Dablanc, contacted senior members of the French government to discuss possible military solutions to the situation. After considering the available options, ministers decided to send a nine-man team of the Groupement d'Intervention de la Gendarmerie Nationale (GIGN), a crack anti-terrorist unit, under Lieutenant Prouteau, to the scene. Leaving Roissy airport in the greatest secrecy, the squad flew to Djibouti on board a specially converted DC-8.

On the journey from Djibouti to the Somali border, Prouteau considered the likelihood of success. His men were untried, yet they had undergone one of the toughest and most stringent selection and training programmes in the world. Then, like now, few men made the grade.

All candidates for GIGN are volunteers drawn from the Gendarmerie Nationale, France's para-military police force. Each man who successfully makes it through the preliminary screening process then receives a personal interview with GIGN's commander. During this critical interview, the candidate is evaluated in relation to his responses to specific questions and to an explanation of the hardships he will face while serving with the force.

Those candidates who make it through the initial stages go on to join about 100 others for the physical portion of the induction process. Endurance, agility, and marksmanship tests make up this part of the selection course. Among the physical tests are a run over eight kilometres with full combat pack, to be completed in under 40 minutes, a 50m swim in under 35 seconds, a seven-metre rope climb in under seven seconds, and various tests of rappelling ability. Candidates are also expected to be able to swim well under water. Tests of courage and skill include being pitted in hand-to-hand combat against a fully-fledged member of GIGN, all of whom are highly trained in the martial arts, or against an attack-trained dog. As excellent marksmanship is also a

Left: A GIGN marksman lines up his FR-FI sniper's rifle during an exercise. Below: Sharpshooters practise their rapid-firing drill with Manurhin handguns. Top: GIGN men pose for the camera before a SCUBA lesson. Above: Lieutenant Prouteau, the youthful and energetic commander of GIGN, in light-hearted mood.

vital anti-terrorist skill, the minimum shooting score for admission is 70 out of a possible 100 at 25m with the revolver, and 75 out of 100 at 200m with the rifle.

However, training does not end with admission to GIGN's ranks: both recent recruits and veterans are constantly and rigorously put through their paces. This diversified programme is designed to keep all members of the unit at a high state of readiness and to give them the skills and adaptability to deal with any crisis that might arise.

Because of the high pitch of physical readiness required of members of GIGN, training never stops. Both long distance steeplechase-style running and sprints are included, along with calisthenics and weight-training, to keep France's anti-terrorist team at peak efficiency. Additional training includes cross-country and downhill skiing at Barèges. Ski practice for GIGN is not only designed for physical fitness, but also to add an extra dimension to the methods by which the GIGN commandos can be inserted into an area. Along with skiing, other mountaineering skills are also taught.

As one can gather from the selec-tion procedure, swimming also

plays an important part in GIGN training. In addition to being able to swim 50m rapidly, every member of GIGN is expected to be able to swim for long distances without rest, even while pulling a 75kg dummy representing someone being rescued. Up to four hours per week are spent on underwater swimming, including both free-diving and SCUBA. One hair-raising GIGN training technique which is used to develop confidence requires unit members to dive into the Seine and lie on the bottom of the river, while huge barges pass only a few metres overhead. This exercise not only develops patience and confidence underwater, as the diver must avoid disorientation, panic and claustrophobia, but it also prepares the diver for underwater infiltration under difficult circumstances.

One of GIGN's free-diving exercises requires the swimmer to dive to the bottom of a deep ditch, read a question on a tablet, write the answer on a second tablet with a waterproof pen, and then return to the surface – all without breathing apparatus. Endurance and the ability to think quickly are developed by this exercise. GIGN men also train in 'locking in' and 'locking out' of submerged submarines as part of their SCUBA training. The various aquatic techniques are designed to prepare the commando for silent approaches to a hijacked ocean liner or other vessel. To avoid detection in such operations, GIGN has 'closed circuit' suits available which do not give off bubbles that might betray the infiltrator's presence.

All members of GIGN are parachute qualified, having attended the French jump school at Pau, and many are commando qualified as well. Since they must always be ready to carry out a parachute infiltration, each member of GIGN makes at least five training jumps per year. These exercises will normally include at least one 'wet jump' into the water, followed by a SCUBA infiltration.

A GIGN man is expected to be able to hit a moving target at ranges out to 25m

Scaling and rappelling techniques are considered of prime importance for gaining entry into terrorist-controlled buildings and, as a result, are regularly practised by GIGN. Team members are especially adept at rappelling into position, holding the rope with one hand and shooting accurately with a revolver held in the other hand.

However, all these methods of getting to the point where a terrorist incident is in progress, are only a means of putting the GIGN commander in position to do his main job: the neutralisation of his target. Since GIGN's philosophy is one of avoiding lethal force unless absolutely necessary, each member of the unit is an expert in hand-to-hand combat. Both karate and judo are studied, along with related disciplines. Quite a few members of GIGN, including Prouteau himself, have, in fact, been black belts. When GIGN men are taught karate, they normally use full contact to enhance the training benefits. Disarming and rapid neutralisation techniques are emphasised.

When more lethal force is called for, the GIGN commando has to be able to stop a terrorist or criminal immediately. GIGN firearms training is intended not only to build expertise, but also to give each unit member such confidence in handling his weapons that any 'cowboy' attitude has been eliminated. Exact shot placement is considered to be of extreme importance since any hostage-taker must be dealt with before he can harm a hostage.

With the revolver, the GIGN man is expected, as a minimum, to be able to hit a moving target at ranges out to 25m within two seconds. Additionally, each man must also be able to engage up to six targets at the same distance within five seconds. With the rifle, at a range of 200m, the GIGN sharpshooter must achieve a minimum score of 93 hits out of 100 shots. Most GIGN members can score much better, 98 with or without telescopic sights being the norm at 200m.

Below: After abseiling down the side of a building, GIGN members smash their way into a room. Right, from top to bottom: Learning the art of helicopter insertion, recruits prepare to rappel to the ground; quick-draw practice; a recruit uses a knife to hack the ice of a frozen lake.

Standard rifle drill includes firing at ranges out to 300m, though exercises may be set up that require even longer shots. Each member of GIGN averages at least two hours per day on the range, and normally fires more than 9000 rounds through his revolver and 3000 rounds through his rifle each year.

Additional range time will also be spent in practising with the sub-machine gun and fighting shotgun as well as familiarisation sessions with other weapons, including a highly sophisticated slingshot using steel balls for silent head shots! Other specialised exercises involve shooting within mock-ups of aircraft cabins and at moving vehicles. Combined with CS gas, pyrotechnics, and other such aids, these exercises train the GIGN man to score hits in the most unfavourable conditions.

GIGN members were originally armed with 9mm automatic pistols as their basic handgun, but their primary weapon is now the Manurhin 73 .357 Magnum revolver. Highly reliable, this weapon entered service in 1974. As the Manurhin remains each GIGN member's constant companion, it must be considered his basic weapon. However, each GIGN operative is also issued with his own FR-F1 sniper's rifle. The FR-F1, really a modified MAS 36, used by GIGN is in 7.62mm calibre. This bolt-action rifle has a free-floating barrel to enhance its accuracy and is fitted with butt spacers, a bipod, and a flash suppressor. Magazine capacity is 10 rounds.

The Djibouti crisis, in early 1976, was the unit's first taste of counter-terrorist work

When a sub-machine gun is needed, GIGN normally uses the Heckler and Koch MP5 in one of its many versions. The MP5A3, MP5SD, and MP5K are all used in special situations, the latter primarily in VIP protection or other covert opertions. Riot guns and various sound-suppressed weapons are also available for special operations.

As with any modern counter-terrorist unit, GIGN is also equipped with a wealth of surveillance and detection hardware. Specialist equipment includes parabolic directional microphones for listening to conversations of terrorists or other hostage-takers at a distance; thermal imagers for locating targets within a building; endoscopes (a device for obtaining 120 degree vision into a room through a tiny hole); starlight or other night-vision optics; and various other high-tech communication, detection, and surveillance devices. Pyrotechnics and explosives, including stun grenades, door openers and other frame charges, are all part of the GIGN arsenal.

GIGN's training and hardware, though impressive, are designed with one purpose: to allow GIGN to carry out its assigned missions without the loss of the hostages involved. Operationally, GIGN's record is excellent. Since its formation, the unit has rescued well over 250 hostages. These successes stem from the fact that GIGN not only functions as France's primary anti-terrorist unit, but also as a national SWAT (Special Weapons and Tactics) team called upon whenever a major crisis arises. Many crack anti-terrorist units have to wait years for employment, but GIGN sees action much more frequently. The Djibouti crisis, in early 1976, however, was the unit's first taste of counter-terrorist work. Although Prouteau's team was to carry out the actual rescue of the children, it was backed up by members of the French Foreign Legion, since there were Somali border guards close by who might try to intervene

ised that it was important to get the children out of any possible line of sight, as their presence made it difficult to align on the terrorists. Towards achieving this end, at 1400 hours on 4 February, a meal containing tranquilisers was allowed through to the children. The hope was that the children would fall asleep after eating the food, thus removing their silhouettes from the bus windows. This was precisely what happened, and at 1547 hours, all four terrorists known to be aboard the bus were visible in the snipers' sights at the same time. After patiently waiting for 10 hours for just such a moment, the GIGN snipers were given the 'shoot' order, resulting in all the terrorists being taken out simultaneously. A fifth terrorist was hit outside the bus.

A group of Somali border guards opened fire on the GIGN men almost immediately, pinning them down, but the Foreign Legionnaires gave covering fire and Prouteau with two other men rushed towards the bus to free the children. Another terrorist had boarded the bus under the covering fire from the Somalis, and he managed to kill one little girl before being cut down by the GIGN assault force. The girl was quickly avenged, however, as the Legionnaires and GIGN containment force poured withering fire into the border post and its garrison. It was reported that the leader and planner of the terrorist attack was killed during this engagement.

The Djibouti operation was a classic hostage rescue mission: the men of GIGN had to travel to another continent with little notice, quickly gather intelligence in a hostile environment, plan an attack, wait patiently for the proper moment to strike, and make every shot count when the order to fire was finally given. Though one hostage was lost, the operation was a success in that 29 other children were saved. By their prompt action, GIGN had sent out a clear signal to

against any rescue attempt. After carrying out a reconnaissance of the area, Prouteau established his command post in a palm grove close to the hijacked bus and placed his nine marksmen, all armed with the FR-F1 sniper's rifle, at advantageous sites around the target.

GIGN tactical doctrine in such a situation called for Prouteau to be in constant radio contact, using throat microphones, with the marksmen. Before moving into position, each shooter had been assigned to watch over a particular portion of the bus and, to ease the flow of information, each terrorist had also been given a recognition number. Using this system, each of the marksmen could instantly let the commander know when he had his particular terrorist in his sights just by giving the target's number. Since all the terrorists had to be eliminated at the exact same time to avoid a general massacre of the children, Prouteau decided that he would only give the 'shoot' order when all of his sharpshooters had a clear view of the hijackers.

When planning the rescue attempt, Prouteau real-

GIGN first shot to prominence in February 1976, when members of the Somali Coast Liberation Front hijacked a coachload of children in Djibouti. Flown out at a moment's notice, Prouteau and nine of his men took up positions around the coach, and using FR-F1 rifles, dealt with the hijackers simultaneously. Above left: The scene on the coach after the release of the hostages. Although the children spent little more than a day on the bus, conditions on board deteriorated quickly, with many of them suffering from heat exhaustion and stomach cramps. Left: One of the lucky survivors of the crisis walks to freedom. Above right: Smiles all round as members of GIGN return to France.

those contemplating terrorist acts against France: they could respond to any outrage with lethal finality.

In the years since Djibouti, GIGN has been used on other well-known operations such as the attempted prison break at Clairvaux prison in January 1978, in which GIGN marksmen once again saved several hostages through precision shooting. As are the SAS and Germany's GSG9, GIGN is used overseas to foster France's diplomatic interests by training and assisting foreign anti-terrorist units and VIP protection groups. Perhaps the most famous instance of their deployment in this role occurred in 1979 when members of GIGN helped train the Saudi Arabian National Guard for the operation to retake the Great Mosque which had been occupied by fanatics. However, GIGN has trained many other units, especially those in France's former colonies.

GIGN's skills have remained sharp through exchange training with other Western anti-terrorist units and through employment on high-risk assignments within France. 'Gigene's' ready team, sitting at Maisons-Alfort waiting to move into action as these words are being written, remains one of the world's most formidable counters to chaos.

THE AUTHOR Leroy Thompson served in Vietnam as a commissioned officer in the USAF Combat Security Police.

Djibouti
GIGN, February 1976

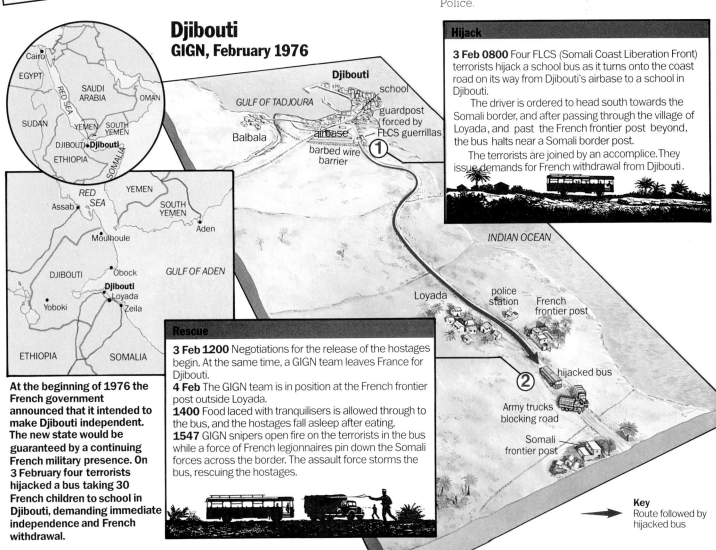

At the beginning of 1976 the French government announced that it intended to make Djibouti independent. The new state would be guaranteed by a continuing French military presence. On 3 February four terrorists hijacked a bus taking 30 French children to school in Djibouti, demanding immediate independence and French withdrawal.

Hijack

3 Feb 0800 Four FLCS (Somali Coast Liberation Front) terrorists hijack a school bus as it turns onto the coast road on its way from Djibouti's airbase to a school in Djibouti.

The driver is ordered to head south towards the Somali border, and after passing through the village of Loyada, and past the French frontier post beyond, the bus halts near a Somali border post.

The terrorists are joined by an accomplice. They issue demands for French withdrawal from Djibouti.

Rescue

3 Feb 1200 Negotiations for the release of the hostages begin. At the same time, a GIGN team leaves France for Djibouti.
4 Feb The GIGN team is in position at the French frontier post outside Loyada.
1400 Food laced with tranquilisers is allowed through to the bus, and the hostages fall asleep after eating.
1547 GIGN snipers open fire on the terrorists in the bus while a force of French legionnaires pin down the Somali forces across the border. The assault force storms the bus, rescuing the hostages.

Key
Route followed by hijacked bus

NO. 56 SQUADRON

On 8 June 1916 No.56 Squadron was formed around a nucleus supplied by No.28 (Reserve) Squadron at Gosport in Hampshire. In the following month it moved to London Colney in Hertfordshire and began a protracted period of preparation for service in France. In March 1917 it received its first SE5 fighters, becoming the first squadron to be equipped with the type, and in April it flew to France.

On 23 April Captain Albert Ball claimed the squadron's first victim while flying the unit's one Nieuport scout, only to bring down another the same day in an SE5. The other pilots soon followed his example, and they were involved in countless dogfights over the Western Front. Their aircraft were present at the Battle of Messines, the Third Battle of Ypres, and at the tank attack on Cambrai, strafing enemy positions in support of the Allied ground forces. In 1918, now equipped with SE5a scouts, the squadron used 20lb bombs to supplement their machine-gun attacks.

Following the Armistice, No.56 Squadron was disbanded. It was re-formed as a fighter squadron in 1922, and during World War II it operated the Hurricane, the Typhoon, the Spitfire IX and the Tempest. Its many roles included escorting convoys, ground attack, and countering the V1 flying-bomb offensive.

In 1946 No.124 Squadron was renamed No.56, the World War II unit becoming No.16 squadron. The postwar formation flew a succession of fighters in defence of the UK, and now operates Phantom Mark 2 interceptors.

Above: No.56 Squadron's current badge: the phoenix motif refers to the squadron's ability to survive all adversity and rise to fight another day.

PHOENIX SQUADRON

In April 1917, the young pilots of No.56 Squadron flew their SE5 scouts over the Channel to do battle over the Western Front

WHEN CAPTAIN JAMES McCudden, then serving as a flying instructor and destined to become one of the highest-scoring air aces of World War I, was sent to No.56 Squadron in the summer of 1917 for a refresher course in fighter tactics, he thought it the most impressive outfit he had ever seen. Equipped with what was then the latest British aircraft, the SE5a scout (fighter plane), the squadron included a remarkable and innovative team of mechanics, led by Lieutenant H.N. Charles, who, in addition to getting the best out of the machines in their charge, supplied several excellent musicians for the squadron's band, which had become a famous institution within the Royal Flying Corps (RFC). The men of No.56 shared an easy comradeship born of an established tradition of superb flying ability and success in combat. Several of the RFC's most distinguished pilots, in-

cluding the legendary Captain Albert Ball, had flown with the squadron, and McCudden became determined to join the unit at the first opportunity.

No.56 Squadron had first moved to France on 7 April 1917, when 13 SE5 scouts flew across the English Channel to an airfield at Vert Galant, south of Doullens. Their aircraft were to provide a welcome reinforcement for the hard-pressed British flying units on the Western Front, whose losses at that time were so severe that the period has become known in aviation history as 'Bloody April'. However, before the SE5s could begin operations, the squadron's mechanics needed to modify a number of unsatisfactory features of the design. Work was needed on the engine and armament, the unpopular 'greenhouse' semi-enclosed cockpit canopy was replaced by a conventional windscreen, and various other changes were made. The first patrol, therefore, was delayed until 22 April. Yet once the SE5's teething troubles had been overcome, it matured into a highly effective aircraft, and many pilots came to think it the finest British fighter of the war.

The commanding officer of No.56 Squadron at this time was Major R.G. Blomfield, and it was he who was

Above: The fine combat record of No.56 Squadron was built up by such aces as Keith Muspratt (top, with his SE5), James McCudden (left) and Albert Ball (right). Below: The aces' aircraft, hard-hitting SE5 biplanes. Inset below left: No.56 Squadron officers, with Major Blomfield (front, centre).

THE ROYAL FLYING CORPS AT WAR

British military aviation began in April 1911 with the formation of the Air Battalion, Royal Engineers. The Royal Flying Corps (RFC) was formed around that battalion in April 1912, and Military and Naval Wings were established. There was no shortage of volunteers, and they were picked from the best men in the army.

The British Army saw its aircraft solely in the role of reconnaissance platforms, reporting on troop dispositions and movements behind enemy lines, and four RFC squadrons flew to France in 1914 for that purpose. Though initially unchallenged by rival aircraft, the vital importance of intelligence gained from the air was soon realised, and duels were fought between Allied and German aircrews armed only with rifles, pistols and grenades.

The next development was the introduction of armed 'scouts', whose function was to protect the virtually defenceless recce planes. From then on the opposing forces evolved ever more efficient fighters to win control of the air. When No.56 Squadron arrived in France with its SE5s in April 1917, the machines, tactics and piloting skills of both sides had evolved out of all recognition. The chivalrous duels of 1914 had given way to a desperate, no-holds-barred struggle for air supremacy.

CAPTAIN ALBERT BALL

Albert Ball was born on 14 August 1896 at Nottingham, and on the outbreak of World War I he enlisted in the Sherwood Foresters as a private soldier. Later that year he was commissioned and transferred to the North Midland Divisional Cyclist Company. He then determined to become a pilot, and on completion of his flying training he was posted to No.13 Squadron in France, flying BE2c two-seaters.

In May 1916 Ball joined No.11 Squadron, which then operated a mixture of two-seater FE2bs and Bristol Scout and Nieuport single-seaters. It was the latter which especially appealed to the individualistic and aggressive Ball, and during the following two months he had many combats with German aircraft.

In August 1916 Ball was posted to No.60 Squadron, which flew Nieuport scouts, and in the following month he was appointed to command the squadron's 'A' Flight. He returned to Britain in October.

Ball was very much the lone wolf in the air and also tended to prefer his own company when not flying. Yet the combat tactics of this withdrawn and self-sufficient young man were bold to the point of foolhardiness. He would attack any enemy aircraft that he encountered and took no heed of the odds he faced. Ball returned to France with No. 56 Squadron in April 1917, and the following month he was killed in action. His final score was 32 German aircraft shot down, 21 forced to land and two sent down out of control. He was awarded the Victoria Cross posthumously.

to transform it into one of the top RFC scout units. Blomfield had joined the squadron in January 1917 and Lieutenant Cecil Lewis has described him: 'Efficiency was his watchword. In appearance he was shortish and slightly built. He wore leggings, and invariably carried a short, leather-covered cane, with which he directed everything, reminding one irresistibly of a dapper little ringmaster.'

Since squadron COs were forbidden to fly in combat, Blomfield's job was primarily that of an organiser. Tactical leadership of the squadron was exercised by his three flight commanders, whom Blomfield had carefully selected for their experience and skill.

Left: Captain Albert Ball, having downed 32 planes and been awarded the Military Cross, applied for leave in 1916 to rest his strained nerves. The RFC rewarded him with a spell as observer in an unarmed BE2C, which was perhaps the most terrifying task on the Front. Below: The von Richthofen brothers, Lothar and Manfred (right), two of Germany's most dangerous pilots.

Foremost amongst them was Captain Albert Ball, commanding 'A' Flight, who then had over 30 victories to his credit. 'B' Flight was led by Captain C.M. 'Billy' Crowe, and 'C' Flight by Captain H. Meintjes. Among the inexperienced squadron pilots fresh from training school were Lieutenants Arthur Rhys Davids, Gerald Constable Maxwell, Leonard Barlow and Keith Muspratt, all of whom were to gain great reputations as air fighters.

Accommodation at Vert Galant airfield was spartan. Most officers and all other ranks were living under canvas during a period of bitterly cold weather with frequent showers of snow and sleet. Yet morale was high and everyone was keen to get into action. The squadron's first success came on 23 April, when Ball shot down an Albatros over Cambrai. On that occasion he was flying a Nieuport 17 scout, which he used for solo patrols. Later the same day he gained his first victories with the SE5, an aircraft which at first he had disliked flying. By the end of the month the squadron had claimed a further five enemy aircraft destroyed and five sent down out of control.

Often, however, No. 56 Squadron found itself outnumbered by the German fighters. Lieutenant Cecil Lewis has described the confusion of a dogfight in which three or more different fighter formations became engaged, 'as if attracted by some mysterious power, as vultures will draw near to a corpse in the desert':

'A pilot, in the second between his own engagements, might see a Hun diving vertically, an SE5 on his tail, on the tail of the SE another Hun, and above him again another British scout. These four, plunging headlong at 200 miles an hour, guns crackling, tracers streaming, suddenly break up. The lowest Hun plunges flaming to his death, if death has not taken him already. His victor seems to stagger, suddenly pulls out in a great leap, as a trout leaps on the end of a line, and then, turning over on his belly, swoops and spins in a dizzy falling spiral with the earth to end it. The third German zooms veering, and the last of that meteoric quartet follows bursting… But such a glimpse, lasting perhaps 10 seconds, is broken by the sharp rattle of another attack.'

On the evening of 7 May, 11 of No. 56 Squadron's SE5s set out on patrol, despite poor weather conditions and a mass of cloud building up over the Western Front. The British formation soon broke up into small groups and became heavily engaged, at a serious disadvantage, with German fighters which were out in force. Only five of the SE5s returned to Vert Galant that evening and all three flight commanders were amongst the missing. Rhys Davids had force-landed behind British lines and Crowe had come down at another airfield. Both were unhurt. Lieutenant J.O. Leach and Meintjes were wounded, while Lieutenant R.W. Chaworth-Musters and Ball were missing. It was later discovered that they had been killed. Leutnant Lothar von Richthofen of Jagdstaffel 11, brother of the 'Red Baron', was credited with bringing down Ball, but it has been suggested that he was brought down by a machine gun mounted in the tower of a church. The news of his loss 'cast a gloom through the whole Flying Corps', recorded a staff officer at RFC Headquarters in France.

The loss of both his fellow flight commanders in a single combat threw a tremendous burden onto Captain Crowe, but he was equal to the challenge. During the weeks when Captain Philip Prothero and Captain G.H. 'Beery' Bowman, the new commanders of 'A' and 'C'

THE SE5

Designed by H.P. Folland, whose earlier SE4 aircraft had attained an unofficial world speed record, the first prototype of the SE5 single-seat scout made its maiden flight on 22 November 1916. Powered by a 150hp Hispano-Suiza V-8 engine, the biplane had staggered wings of equal span and featured the first use of tail-trimming gear and the first adjustable seat. The initial production batch of SE5s, manufactured by the Royal Aircraft Factory at Farnborough, began service in March 1917 with No. 56 Squadron. Armament consisted of a .303in Vickers gun firing through the propeller by means of Constantinesco CC synchronising gear, and a .303in Lewis gun on a Foster mounting on the upper wing, which the pilot could angle to fire forward or upward. (The SE5 shown left was that of Captain Albert Ball, who removed the Vickers in order to reduce the aircraft's weight.) The SE5 provided an exceptionally firm gun platform, substantially increasing the range of effective fire in combat.

The SE5 had been in production for only three months when the SE5a was introduced. The power plant was uprated to a 200hp Hispano-Suiza engine, later superseded by the Wolseley-made Viper, and by the time of the Armistice about 5000 SE5 and SE5a aircraft had been built.

A4850

Flights, were gaining experience after several months away from the Front, Crowe ran all three flights virtually single-handed. Rhys Davids, who was a member of Crowe's 'B' Flight, had a great regard for his abilities. 'He is not afraid of anything and goes after old Huns like a rocket, and yet he is extraordinarily prudent.' At a time when morale in the squadron was low, Crowe helped to restore the pilots' confidence in the SE5, which had come under suspicion as the cause of Ball's death. He also advocated new fighting tactics which made good use of the SE5's speed and steadiness as a gun platform in diving attacks, in preference to the turning fight which was more suited to such nimble scouts as the Nieuport 17 or Sopwith Pup.

At the end of May the squadron moved north to Estrée Blanche in preparation for the Battle of Messines. During its first five weeks in combat, it had been credited with 57 victories for the loss of 10 pilots. However, a welcome respite from the grinding daily routine of offensive patrols over the Front came on 21 June, when No.56 Squadron was withdrawn to Bekesbourne in Kent for two weeks. The move was intended to boost Britain's defences against the German Gotha bombers which had bombed London eight days earlier. 'We do absolutely nothing,' reported Arthur Rhys Davids, 'We spend the whole day playing cards or ragging about and some of us go out every evening on the bust.' On 4 July the Gothas raided the East Coast, but the following day the squadron flew back to France.

During the summer of 1917 the squadron's SE5s were replaced by the improved SE5a, which was fitted with a more powerful engine that gave it a higher rate of climb and increased speed. Yet, as with its predecessor, early problems with the aircraft's engine and armament had to be resolved by Lieutenant Charles and his mechanics before the SE5a performed entirely satisfactorily. On 21 July, Lieutenant V. P. Cronyn scored No.56 Squadron's one hundredth victory, but its considerable successes had not been gained without loss. Captain Prothero was shot down on 26 July, bringing the unit's casualties up to 23 pilots lost since April. Captain Crowe left the squadron in July, his health suffering from the intense strain of his command and frequent combat (he had gained six victories during his period as 'B' Flight commander). However, by that time Captain Bowman had settled into his stride and during the 10 months that he led 'C' Flight he was credited with 26 personal victories. Maxwell was promoted to captain and took command of 'A' Flight, while the 'B' Flight commander vacancy was filled by Captain James McCudden in mid-August. With three such able and experienced flight commanders, the squadron soon reached a peak of efficiency, especially since many of its other pilots were by then highly skilled air fighters. Lieutenant Richard Maybery was at that time credited with 9½ victories, and during one epic low-level bombing and strafing mission on 31 July, he attacked two enemy airfields, a column of marching troops, two trains and for good measure shot down a two-seater observation aircraft. Rhys Davids brought his score up to 15 victories on 5 September by accounting for three enemy aircraft in that single day. Barlow was credited with six victories and the Canadian Lieutnant R.T.C. Hoidge had no fewer than 13 to his credit.

McCudden's 'B' Flight was especially strong in talent, its pilots comprising Barlow, Rhys Davids, Muspratt, Lieutenant Maxwell Coote and Cronyn. They were 'as splendid a lot of fellows as ever set foot in France,' thought their flight commander. McCudden himself at that time had scored only five victories, but in the following months he was to increase this total more than tenfold. His first successful combat with the squadron came on the morning of 18 August, when he attacked an Albatros DIII over Houthem. 'I attacked it at 50yds range, firing both guns,' he reported. 'Fired about 20 shots from each gun and EA [enemy aircraft] at once went down in a vertical spiral, going down very fast. I last saw it at about 6000ft still going down out of control.'

I heard clack-clack-clack-clack, as his bullets passed close to me and through my wings

No.56 Squadron's most famous combat took place on the evening of 23 September, when 'B' Flight's six SE5a scouts engaged a Fokker FI triplane (a prototype for the Dr I series) west of Poelcappelle. Its pilot was the German ace Leutnant Werner Voss, Staffelführer of Jasta 10. In a fighting career which lasted barely ten months, Voss had accounted for some 50 Allied aircraft – an achievement second only to that of Manfred von Richthofen at the time. McCudden's flight dived down onto the triplane, but failed to damage it during the initial attack. McCudden recalled that:

'The German pilot saw us and turned in a most disconcertingly quick manner, not a climbing nor Immelmann turn, but a sort of flat half spin. By now the German triplane was in the middle of our formation and its handling was wonderful to behold. The pilot seemed to be firing at all of us simultaneously and although I got behind him a

Below: A German airman takes a bomb aboard. The first bombsights were mounted on the side of the fuselage: the bombardier would lean over, wait, then release the weapon by pulling a trigger.

Below: Lieutenant Arthur Rhys Davids, who downed the German ace Werner Voss, and (right) a page of one of his combat reports.

Combats in the Air.

Army Form W. 3348.

Squadron: NO. 56

Type and No. of Aeroplane: SE.5 No.B.525.

Armament: V and L.

Pilot: 2/Lt.A.P.F.Rhys Davids.M.C.

Observer: None.

Locality: West of Westroosibeke - Houthem.

Date: 23/9/17

Time: 5.45 - 6.35.

Duty: Offensive Patrol

Height: 8,000 - 1,000ft.

Sheet No.1

Remarks on Hostile machine :—Type, armament, speed, etc.

Worth Reading

Narrative.

Crossed lines with formation and flew over clouds for some time, ground was not visible and we returned and came down West of Ypres. Then patrolled over lines at 8,000ft. under clouds under very heavy and accurate A.A. fire. After some manoevering at 6pm. leader dived on an E.A.A.2-seater (D.F.W.) making E from West of Comines. Leader got very close and fired as E.A. turned N.E. Smoke came out of centre section and I dived very steeply and fired a short burst into E.A. which was diving N into a cloud. the ground about 1,000 yards S.N.E. of Houthem. Rejoined leader and climbed to 7,000ft. and patrolled area again. At 6.25pm. saw an SE.5 being attacked by an E.A. triplane and one red nosed Albatros Scout. Our second SE.5 formation now appeared and for 20 minutes, leader, myself, Lt.Hoidge and Lt.Maybery engaged the two E.A. and one other Scout West of Westroosibeke. About 11 other E.A. awaited us higher and further East, but did not come down & these were six SPADS & four Camels protecting us very well. The other E.A. scout now vanished but the red nosed Albatross and the triplane fought magnificiantly. I got in several good bursts at the triplane without apparent effect and twice placed a new Lewis drum on my gun. Eventually I got east & slightly above the triplane and made for it & got in a whole Lewis drum and a corresponding number of Vickers into him. He made no attempt to turn until I was so close to him I was certain we would collide. He passed my right hand wing by inches and went down, I zoomed. I saw him next with his engine apparently off, gliding West. I dived again and got one shot out of my Vickers, However I reloaded and kept in the dive, I got another good burst and the triplane did a slight right hand turn still going down. I had now overshot him (this was at 1,000ft) zoomed and never saw him again. Immediately afterwards I met the red nosed Scout who was a short way south east of me. I started firing at 100 yds., the E.A. turned and fired at me. At 30yards range I finished a Lewis drum & my Vickers stopped so I dived underneath him and zoomed.

A.Rhys Davids
56 RFC

The Western Front 1917–1918

NETHERLANDS

BELGIUM

Ostend
Ghent
Brussels
Calais
Poelcappelle
Ypres
Houthem
Messines
Boulogne
Lille
Estrée Blanche
Arras
Doullens
Cambrai
Vert Galant
Dieppe
Amiens
St Quentin
Lavieville
Rheims
Paris

ENGLISH CHANNEL
FRANCE

Key
* Major battles
— Front line, 9 April 1917
— Armistice line, 11 November 1918
+ Airfields

Formed in 1916, No. 56 Squadron, Royal Flying Corps, was deployed to the Western Front early in April 1917. The squadron flew SE5 and SE5a biplanes in the 'scout' or fighter role.No. 56 Squadron was involved in the Battle of Messines during the summer of 1917, and later, in the Third Battle of Ypres and the attack on Cambrai.

During the German offensives of March 1918 the squadron was heavily engaged, and by the end of the war the aces of No. 56 Squadron had accounted for a total of 401 enemy aircraft.

second time, I could hardly stay there for a second. His movements were so quick and uncertain that none of us could hold him in sight at all for any decisive time.

'I now got a good opportunity as he was coming towards me nose on and slightly underneath and had apparently not seen me. I dropped my nose, got him well in my sight and pressed both triggers. As soon as I fired, up came his nose at me and I heard clack-clack-clack-clack, as his bullets passed close to me and through my wings. I distinctly noticed the red-yellow flashes from his parallel Spandau guns. As he flashed by me I caught a glimpse of a black head in the triplane with no hat on at all.

'By this time a red-nosed Albatros scout had arrived and was apparently doing its best to guard the triplane's tail, and it was well handled too... The triplane was still circling round in the midst of six SEs, who were all firing at it as opportunity offered, and at one time I noted the triplane in the apex of a cone of tracer bullets from at least five machines simultaneously and each machine had two guns. By now the fighting was very low and the red-nosed Albatros had gone down and out, but the triplane still remained. I had temporarily lost sight of the triplane whilst changing a drum of my Lewis gun and when I next saw him he was very low, still being engaged by an SE marked I, the pilot being Rhys Davids. I noticed that the triplane's movements were very erratic and then I saw him go into a fairly steep dive and so I continued to watch and then saw the triplane hit the ground and disappear into a thousand fragments.'

On 30 September Maxwell gained the squadron's 200th victory, but the following month was a period of heavy casualties. Eight pilots were lost, including the young and brilliant Arthur Rhys Davids who was killed in action on 27 October. The squadron also lost Maxwell, who was posted to Home Establishment, and at the end of the month Major Blomfield was relieved as CO by Major R. Balcombe-Brown. In November, No.56 Squadron moved to Lavieville, near Amiens, in preparation for the Battle of Cambrai, during which it was heavily engaged despite periods of bad weather. Yet more experienced pilots were lost during the closing months of the year. Hoidge was posted to Home Establishment and Maybery (who had taken over from Maxwell as 'A' Flight's commander) was killed on 19 December.

December 1917 was chiefly remarkable for McCudden's outstanding fighting record, for of the 17 enemy aircraft brought down by the squadron during the month, 14 were his victories. His posting to Home Establishment in the following March marked the end of an era. During his period in command of 'B' Flight, No.56 Squadron had gained 175 victories, of which his flight had contributed 77 and he himself no fewer than 52. When Captain Duncan Grinnell-Milne was posted to No.56 Squadron in September 1918, he was told, 'You're in luck to be sent here. This is the most famous squadron in France.' With a final score of 401 victories, that fame had been hard earned.

THE AUTHOR Anthony Robinson was formerly on the staff of the RAF Museum, Hendon, and is now a freelance military aviation writer. He has edited the books *Aerial Warfare* and the *Dictionary of Aviation*.

Bottom: Riddled with holes, a German DFW CV lies crumpled in the mud. This type of plane, known as the 'C' class, was introduced by Germany in the spring of 1915 to fulfil general duties, and it was not until the advent of the first true single-seat fighter, the Fokker EI, that combat became a specialised role. The 'C' class aircraft were extremely vunerable to ground fire, though their chances of survival were later improved by the fitting of armour round the engine, the fuel tanks and the crew compartment.

Captain Albert Ball, No.56 Squadron, RFC France 1917

Captain Ball is holding the propeller and red-painted propeller spinner of the Nieuport 17 scout which he flew in preference to his squadron's SE5s. He is wearing the field service dress of a Royal Flying Corps officer, which included breeches and high boots. The badge of the RFC is on his cap and lapel, and the badges of his rank are on his sleeve. Above the left pocket are the RFC wings and the ribbons of his DFC and MC. The uniform is completed by the Sam Browne belt.

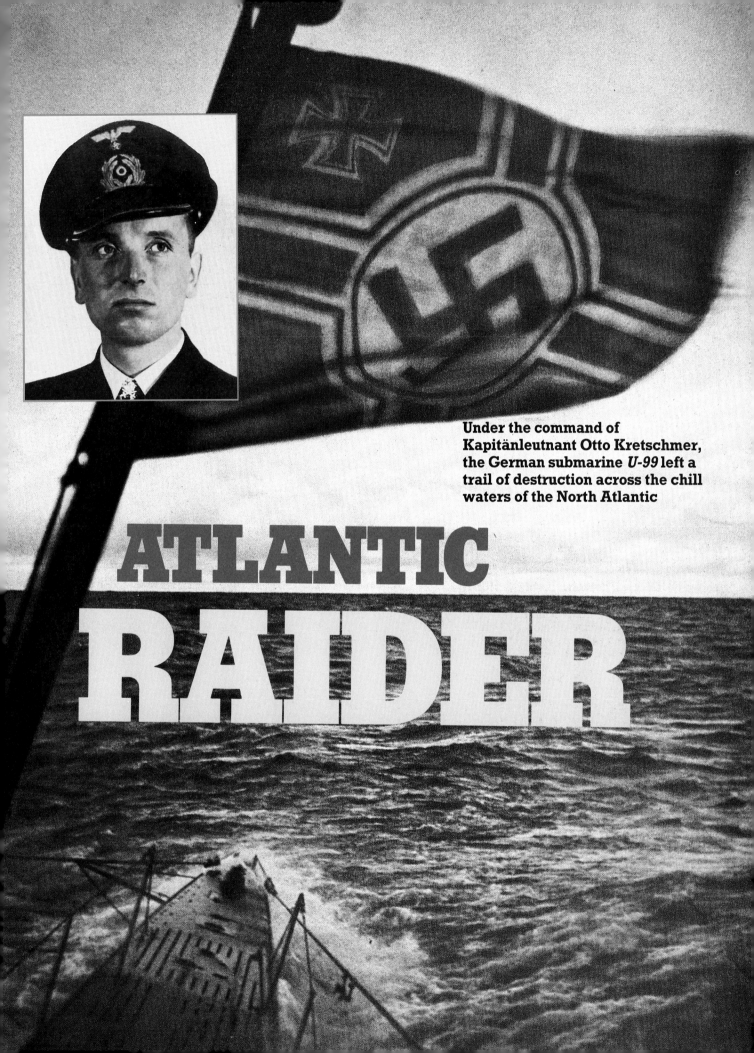

Under the command of
Kapitänleutnant Otto Kretschmer,
the German submarine *U-99* left a
trail of destruction across the chill
waters of the North Atlantic

ATLANTIC
RAIDER

OTTO KRETSCHMER

In 1936, at the age of 24, Otto Kretschmer, shown above with Hitler, volunteered for training in Germany's new expanding U-boat force. Cool, confident and dedicated to his chosen career, Kretschmer rose rapidly to the command of his own boat, the *U-23*, a 250-ton coastal attack craft. From the start of World War II, he was involved in operations in the North Sea and around the Orkneys and Shetlands, scoring some notable successes, particularly the sinking in February 1940 of the British destroyer *Daring*. On 30 April 1940 he assumed command of the newly commissioned ocean-going submarine *U-99*. His exploits in the Atlantic over the following year made him famous. Kretschmer did not affect the relaxed, somewhat indisciplined style adopted by some U-boat commanders, always maintaining his crew in strict military dress and behaviour whenever possible.

His only self-indulgence was a taste for cigars – he chain-smoked on the conning-tower throughout the course of surface operations. By the time his career was brought to an end by his capture in March 1941, he is reckoned to have sunk over 350,000 tons of British shipping, making him probably the greatest U-boat ace of the war.

As a prisoner of war, Kretschmer was promoted to full captain while in the camp and was finally released in 1947.

Page 1101: Its flag billowing in the wind, a Kriegsmarine raider heads for the atlantic in search of a convoy, and (inset) Otto Kretschmer, one of Germany's top U-boat aces. Left: Kretschmer's *U-99* returns to base on 10 November 1940 after a successful patrol. The flags commemorate a seven-hour tussle with two British escorts. Bottom: Officers and crew of *U-99* pose for the camera in Kiel during May 1940. Below: Life on a U-boat was cramped and uncomfortable.

AT 0806 HOURS on 8 July 1940, Kapitänleutnant Otto Kretschmer, commander of the German submarine *U-99*, then on its first marauding patrol in the North Atlantic, recorded in his war diary:

'Propeller noises heard approaching to starboard. I order depth to be trimmed at 100ft. I believe my crew are going to get their baptism of depth-charging this time. Escort approaching fast as though to attack.'

Minutes later, the U-boat shook violently as the first depth-charges exploded. It was the start of an ordeal that would last almost 20 hours. Completely at the mercy of their attackers, Kretschmer and his crew, their unshaven faces pale and drawn in the dim electric light, could only sit and sweat it out, cramped inside their narrow vessel. Chief Radio Operator Jupp Kassel, at the U-boat's hydrophone set, listened intently to the churning screws of the vessels above. Each time his cry of 'Attackers above, sir' rang out, the men braced themselves for the worst. Each time, the charges fell wide of their mark.

After two hours of depth-charging, the U-boat's oxygen supply failed. The crew donned their rubber oxygen masks – attached to air purifiers – and lay on their bunks to conserve what air remained. Gradually, the U-boat's electric batteries, which could only be recharged on the surface, were running down. As the U-boat lost power, it sank deeper, unable to maintain sufficient forward momentum to hold level. If the vessel sank below a critical depth, the weight of the ocean would split its hull plates, consigning the crew to certain death.

Kapitänleutnant Otto Kretschmer was the most gifted and innovative submariner of them all

Knowing that if he surfaced within sight of the British escort vessels, he would have no choice but to surrender, Kretschmer played a desperate waiting game, taking both his boat and the crew to the limits of their endurance. It was not until 0330 hours on 9 July that he finally felt safe to surface. The crew clambered stiffly out of the stinking interior of *U-99* on to the deck, gasping lungfuls of fresh sea air. Kretschmer wrote, 'We all felt like children at Christmas.' This experience of being the passive object of attack, the hunter hunted, was not one the commander would quickly forget.

Two days later, *U-99* was ordered to terminate its first patrol which, apart from the depth-charging incident, had been a great success: a total of seven merchant vessels had been sunk in a week. The U-boat was not to return to its original base at Kiel on the German Baltic coast, however. Admiral Karl Dönitz, mastermind of Germany's underwater war, had chosen a new headquarters, at Lorient in German-occupied France, from which to attack the Atlantic convoys. Dönitz was convinced that by operating from Lorient his U-boats could sink enough merchant shipping to bring Britain to its knees. As yet, his fleet was still short of submarines, but he depended on the outstanding fighting qualities of his officers and men to make up for any material deficiency. Foremost among his U-boat commanders were the three 'aces', the swashbuckling Joachim Schepke, commander of *U-100*, Günter Prien, a dedicated Nazi already famous for sinking the *Royal Oak* in Scapa Flow early in the war, and Kretschmer, the most gifted and innovative submariner of them all. On 24 July, *U-99* slipped out of Lorient on its

ATLANTIC HUNTERS

In an attempt to inflict even more crippling losses on the Allied merchantmen sailing the convoy routes of the North Atlantic, Admiral Karl Dönitz, Hitler's submarine chief, developed the concept of the 'wolf pack': the use of several U-boats to launch co-ordinated attacks on the convoys.

For the first few months of the war, the German Navy had too few submarines to make the technique worthwhile and the invasion of Norway in April 1940, precluded the use of wolf packs until the latter quarter of the year.

The fall of France gave Dönitz the opportunity to put his theory into practice. With the capture of France's Atlantic ports, his U-boats, previously based in the Baltic, would be able to reach the key convoy routes more readily and could remain on station for a much greater period.

By mid-September, the presence of the wolf packs was being felt by the British merchantmen. On the night of 21 September U-boats attacked a convoy, consigning 12 of its 41 ships to a watery grave. Losses mounted steadily: in two separate attacks on 18 and 19 October, two wolf packs stalked convoys *SC7* and *HX79*, sinking 32 out of 84 vessels.

During the following winter, atrocious weather reduced the impact of Dönitz's wolf packs, but in 1941, the U-boats returned to the fray.

second Atlantic voyage. Bizarrely, the crew were kitted out in British uniforms, captured during the German invasion of France in 1940. No suitable German uniforms had been available to replace their outfits that were hopelessly soiled on the first patrol.

At 1100 hours on 31 July, Kassel detected the sound of a convoy's propellers on his hydrophones. A deadly game of hide-and-seek began between the lone hunter and the pack of merchant vessels with its watchful escort. At 1400 hours *U-99* found itself right in the path of the convoy and was forced to submerge to about 300ft as the merchantmen passed overhead. When Kretschmer brought the boat back up to periscope depth, he could not resist picking off a slow-moving freighter, the *Jersey City*, which he found in his sights, and in return *U-99* was subjected to an hour-and-a-half's depth-charge attack by a destroyer. Having survived this onslaught, *U-99* then surfaced to put on speed and catch up with its quarry, only to be immediately forced to crash-dive as a Sunderland flying-boat swooped down on a bombing run. By 2100 hours, when Kretschmer could at last surface, all contact with the convoy had been lost.

But the crew of *U-99* had a masterly flair for tracking merchantmen in the wastes of the Atlantic. All night, Kretschmer made full speed on the surface in the convoy's estimated direction. Just at daybreak, he submerged momentarily to allow Kassel to take a hydrophone bearing on the enemy and then, back on the surface, set off once more in pursuit. Soon his look-outs, reputedly the best in the U-boat force, sighted smoke.

It took all of the remaining daylight hours for *U-99* to manoeuvre ahead of the convoy. When night fell, the boat was in perfect attacking position, but still Kretschmer held off. Then, at midnight, the escort vessels slipped away to protect another, supposedly more vulnerable, convoy. For Kretschmer, the ideal chance to experiment with new tactics had come. To the astonishment of his experienced crew, he ordered them to sail directly into the convoy on the surface. With the U-boat cutting across the bows of 20

The Battle of the Atlantic
1940–1941

GREENLAND

Denmark Strait

Arctic Circle

ICELAND

CANADA

Halifax

UNITED STATES

Pan-American neutrality zone

GREAT BRITAIN

Kiel

Lorient

GIBRALTER

MALTA

ATLANTIC

Unlike any other World War II battle, the Battle of the Atlantic lasted from the beginning of the war to the end. But it was during 1940 and 1941, when the United States was still neutral, air cover was limited, and many merchant ships had to cross the mid-Atlantic without even the benefit of surface escorts, that the German U-boat offensive came closest to defeating Britain.

Key
— U-boats
— Allied convoy routes
· Allied ships sunk, June 1940–March 1941
▨ Allied air cover up to March 1940
▨ Allied air cover after March 1940

Right: The calm before the storm: an engineer checks over machinery in a U-boat's diesel room. Above: Unaware of its impending fate, a heavily laden British freighter is framed by a submarine's periscope. Top: Great plumes of spray and acrid smoke signal the end of another merchantman. Despite their escorts, the ships remained vulnerable to torpedo attacks.

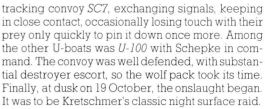

Above: The Submariner's War Badge was adopted in January 1918 and re-introduced in 1939 for U-boat crews who had either carried out two operational sorties or one particularly successful mission.

merchant vessels as they plunged forwards through the darkness, the chances of a collision seemed high. However, Kretschmer was determined to go in close to chosen targets and maximise the number of hits. As his first torpedo struck the stern of an oil tanker, the other ships began manoeuvring furiously to avoid attack. It was in vain. Within 30 minutes, two other tankers were sinking in flames, and another two ships had collided heavily in the general confusion. The approach of a British destroyer at high speed forced U-99 to withdraw, but Kretschmer considered his experiment a success.

When U-99 returned to Lorient on 8 August, each man received a hero's welcome. They had sunk a greater tonnage of shipping than any other U-boat had previously achieved in a single mission. Still wearing their British uniforms, they were inspected by the German Naval Commander-in-Chief, Admiral Raeder, who congratulated the men and decorated Kretschmer with the Knight's Cross.

U-99's record of success continued through September, and the crew were full of confidence when they set out for their fourth patrol on 14 October. By the 18th, nine U-boats were stealthily

tracking convoy SC7, exchanging signals, keeping in close contact, occasionally losing touch with their prey only quickly to pin it down once more. Among the other U-boats was U-100 with Schepke in command. The convoy was well defended, with substantial destroyer escort, so the wolf pack took its time. Finally, at dusk on 19 October, the onslaught began. It was to be Kretschmer's classic night surface raid.

While the other U-boats launched their torpedoes from outside the convoy, U-99 slid towards the British escort screen. Two British destroyers were clearly silhouetted against the moonlight, one at the head of the convoy and the other on its starboard beam. Kretschmer headed straight for the gap between them, praying that no sharp-eyed lookout would spot his U-boat's low profile. Within a matter of minutes U-99 was through and into the thick of the convoy. Kretschmer directed operations from the conning tower as merchant ships loomed out of the darkness all around him. First, Lieutenant Bargsten entered details of targets on the automatic aiming device. Then, as U-99 went into the attack, at full speed, merchant ships began to go under. The freighter Sedgepool, hit by a torpedo in the bows, dived straight down into the sea like a giant whale. Another ship, broken in two, sank almost immediately. A third vessel exploded spectacularly in a huge ball of smoke and flame. On several occasions, Bargsten's aiming mechanism apparently misfunctioned and targets were missed at close range. When Kretschmer chose to order a snap shot to be fired by guesswork, however, the success rate was virtually 100 per cent. At one point, Kretschmer shouted instructions to the helmsman for a sharp turn and, almost simultaneously, ordered the firing of one of the stern torpedoes. Some 300yds behind the U-boat, a freighter was hit amidships and began to sink.

Officers and look-outs had to be chained to the boat or risk being swept away by waves

The British escort vessels concentrated their attention on the other U-boats attacking from outside the convoy. The crew of U-99 could see the illuminating flares and hear the depth-charges exploding as the destroyers moved outwards to defend the convoy. Nothing had taught the Royal Navy to expect a raider within its protective screen. Kretschmer knew the enemy would eventually realise what was happening, however, and at around 0130 hours on 20 October he reduced speed, allowing the convoy to pull past him and disappear ahead – an elegant and simple means of disengaging from action. A small freighter which had dropped behind the convoy fell victim to U-99's last torpedo before the submarine set course back to port. Of 17 British vessels sunk that night U-99 had accounted for no less than nine.

By now, Kretschmer was famous. In November, after one more patrol in which U-99 sank two armed merchant cruisers, he was flown to Berlin to be decorated by Hitler himself. Back in Lorient, Prien, Schepke and Kretschmer celebrated their success in a restaurant, frivolously placing bets as to which would be first to sink 250,000 tons of shipping.

But as winter closed in over the North Atlantic, the mood darkened. On patrol once more from 27 November, U-99 struggled against awesome weather conditions. For days on end, officers and look-outs in the conning tower had to be chained to the boat or risk being swept away as waves broke over the deck. Surviving against the ocean almost took prece-

dence over the search for the enemy. However, despite the conditions, *U-99* still managed to sink almost 35,000 tons of shipping on this patrol, but not without coming close to disaster. On 8 December, the U-boat was surprised by British escort vessels and forced to crash-dive. The bad weather had put Kretschmer's main periscope out of action, so once underwater he was effectively blind. Hearing nothing on the hydrophones, after a short time he took the risk of surfacing again, only to find two of the British vessels waiting for him, less than a mile off with engines stopped. *U-99* dived again, but it had been spotted and was subjected to a depth-charge attack that it was extremely fortunate to survive.

Kretschmer picked out a tanker at the rear of the convoy and broke it in two with a hit amidships

Dönitz was well aware of the incredible strain imposed on U-boat crews and their commanders by constant patrolling in the Atlantic. When *U-99* arrived back in Lorient, the admiral tried to persuade Kretschmer to accept a shore posting. Kretschmer refused, but agreed that he and his men should take a spell of leave to shake off their war-weariness. It was a welcome break from combat, and when the crew reassembled at Lorient in late January 1941, they were visibly refreshed. Schepke and Prien were there to welcome Kretschmer back and to pay up – for Kretschmer had won the race to reach 250,000 tons sunk. Supplies of brandy and cigars were plentiful, and by the time they returned to action, *U-99*'s commander and crew were in high spirits. On 22 February the U-boat slid out of Lorient serenaded by a military band playing the specially composed *Kretschmer March*.

It was to be their last voyage. From the outset, periods of fog and heavy seas made the submariners' lives difficult. Also, the British anti-submarine forces were ever increasing in strength and vigilance. On 7 March *U-99* once more narrowly survived a depth-charge attack; Prien's *U-47* had no such luck, being sunk by the escorts of the same convoy. As days went by without Prien making radio contact, Kretschmer became inescapably aware of his fellow ace's fate.

By 15 March, *U-99* was drawing towards the end of a relatively fruitless patrol when it received a message that a convoy had been sighted south of Iceland. By the following morning, Kretschmer and Schepke were both with the pack of U-boats moving around the convoy, harassed by Sunderlands and the des-

troyer escorts. Because of uncharacteristically careless work by a look-out, *U-99* lost contact with the convoy in the afternoon, but shortly after dark the boat caught up with its quarry once more, and immediately attacked. Forging through a gap in the escort screen, Kretschmer torpedoed a tanker which exploded in a sheet of flame. Afraid he might have been spotted in the glare of the burning vessel, Kretschmer momentarily dropped back into the darkness behind the convoy, but then he began a devastating run forwards through the formation, leaving another two tankers and two freighters sunk or sinking. *U-99* now had one torpedo left. Kretschmer picked out a tanker at the rear of the convoy and broke it in two with a hit amidships. There was nothing left for *U-99* to do but turn away from the wrecked and burning ships and head for Lorient.

Unknowingly, however, as Kretschmer moved away from the convoy, he drew close to the position of Schepke's *U-100* which was in difficulties. Schepke had surfaced to inspect the damage after being depth-charged by the destroyer HMS *Walker*. Despite its being a moonlit night, he had not expected to be spotted. But, for once, the British escorts' primitive radar equipment, normally useless for locating a U-boat, picked up a target. Guided by its radar operator, the destroyer HMS *Vanoc* bore down on *U-100* at full speed. The U-boat had no time to take evasive action and was struck by the destroyer's bows directly alongside the conning tower. The impact crushed Schepke behind his periscope and tore his legs from his body. *U-100* quickly sank, as *Walker* steamed up to join *Vanoc* on the scene.

At this point, unaware of the drama being enacted, Second Lieutenant Petersen, in the conning tower of *U-99*, sighted the two destroyers a mere half-a-mile away and immediately ordered a crash-dive. Instantly *Walker's* Asdic revealed the

Kretschmer's remarkable career was cut short by HMS *Walker* (bottom left), a destroyer commanded by Captain D. MacIntyre (below left). Brought to the surface by depth-charges (below), *U-99* was then blasted at close range and Kretschmer ordered his crew to surrender. Below right and far right: Kretschmer and his crew dock at Liverpool to a less than friendly reception. However, after the war old animosities were forgotten. Right: MacIntyre (right) returns Kretschmer's binoculars at a reunion in London in 1955.

U-boat's presence, and the destroyer raced in to depth-charge. The first pattern of explosions threw *U-99* about wildly. The second attack was still more accurate. Water and oil poured into the U-boat as tanks and pipes split. The shuddering blast-waves shattered gauges and instruments, and the engineer reported that the propellers had stopped. Without power, Kretschmer faced a stark choice: either to fill the ballast tanks with air and rise to the surface, or to sink inexorably to the bottom of the ocean. He chose the surface and inevitable surrender.

Fortunately for the crew, when *U-99* bobbed to the surface it was listing heavily away from the *Walker*, giving the men shelter from the destroyer's machine-gun and tracer fire during the time it took to signal their surrender. Kretschmer would not allow *U-99* to fall into British hands, however. As *Walker* drew near, he scuttled the U-boat; the surge of water as the vessel sank swept him clear of the conning tower. He was hauled up on to the destroyer, along with all but three of the crew.

Three days later, *Walker* docked in Liverpool. *U-99*'s crew were forced to march through the streets of the city, reviled by an angry crowd who regarded them as murderers. Kretschmer was driven off separately for interrogation. None of them would play any further part in the war. However, Kretschmer and the crew of *U-99* had, by their dedication to duty and combat skills, wrought havoc on the convoys plying between America and Britain.

THE AUTHOR R.G. Grant graduated in Modern History from Trinity College, Oxford. He has written extensively on military campaigns.

NON GRATUM ANUS RODENTUM

THE TUNNEL RATS

When the mighty US 25th 'Tropic Lightning' Infantry Division arrived in South Vietnam in 1966, it pitched its tents on top of a Viet Cong tunnel system in the strategic Cu Chi district, and was then attacked from within its own perimeter.

Further north, the 1st Infantry Division, the 'Big Red One', was also taking casualties from tunnel-based guerrillas. Both formations decided to establish specialist counter-force teams, and the Tunnel Rats were born.

Only about 100 men, all volunteers, were privileged to wear the Rats' distinctive badge (shown above) in the unit's four-year history. Recruits, chosen for their small stature and iron nerve, operated in small teams and were flown to the scene of an incident by helicopter. Underground, they worked in groups of two or three; each man armed with a torch, combat knife or bayonet, and handgun.

Initially, the Tunnel Rats acted on an ad hoc basis with little support. However, in March 1966 Captain Herb Thornton, the Big Red One's chemical officer and a man with tunnel experience, was transferred to the Tropic Lightning Division as an instructor and in 1967, after Operation Cedar Falls, tunnel-rat duties in the Big Red One were taken over by members of its 1st Engineer Battalion. Although both Rat outfits made limited use of up-to-the-minute technology in their underground campaign, most men relied on their own and their comrades' skills, born out of action. However, they faced a resolute foe with lengthy experience of fighting underground.

TUNNEL RATS

In the warren of tunnels beneath the Iron Triangle there was only one way of making sure you got your enemy – you went in after him

SERGEANT ROBERT Batten was the most fearsome member of an elite but little-known American unit in Vietnam – the Tunnel Rats. The name was unglamorous and brutal, but so too was the war that Batten and the other Rats fought. Their mission was to chase the Viet Cong (VC) out of the subterranean labyrinths that they had dug beneath the countryside surrounding Saigon.

'Batman', as Batten was universally known, was more famous among the enemy than his own side. Communist prisoners spoke in awe of him; he was the only NCO on the VC's '10 most-wanted' list. Four times wounded, he volunteered to stay in Vietnam for two extra tours of duty. His combat record was legendary. One tunnel operation he led netted 150 Viet Cong prisoners. A burly, red-haired man from New Jersey, he would explain: 'I love getting those gooks out of there. They think they have it made down in them holes. Well, they have it made like a rat's ass when old Batman comes after 'em.' 'Not worth a rat's ass' was the motto of the Tunnel Rats, America's unsung heroes of the Vietnam War.

Lieutenant Jack Flowers was a college drop-out from Indiana. Short and spiky, he had an aggressive crewcut and prominent lower jaw. He had been anti-war when he was drafted, and sought out the safest jobs when he arrived at the 1st Engineer Battalion at Lai Khe, the Tunnel Rats' base. Then one day, a helicopter pilot sneeringly called him a 'REMF' – a rear-echelon motherfucker – the fate, or good fortune, of most Americans who served in Vietnam. It stung, and soon afterwards Flowers surprisingly accepted the job of Rat Six (commander); he had witnessed the pride, esprit and professionalism of the Tunnel Rats. Now no-one would ever call him a REMF again.

Flowers heard shots and grenade explosions underground and then Batman appeared

Flowers was determined to lead the squad himself. For 30 days he would learn, and Batman could lead. Thereafter, Flowers would not ask any enlisted man to do what he would not do himself. He trained hard. There was hand-to-hand combat in a specially constructed culvert, going for the eyes or the jugular. There were rules to tunnel warfare; a Rat must never fire off more than three rounds from his handgun. Fire six and the enemy would know you were out of ammunition and finish you with his AK47.

Then came actual missions. When infantry companies in the field came upon tunnel entrances, they would radio for the Rats, who would rappel down from helicopters with their specialist gear. Some tunnels were 'cold', with no enemy inside. Others were 'hot', resulting in firefights underground or the setting of demolition charges to entomb, it was hoped, the guerrillas inside.

On 26 March 1969, the squad was summoned to a tunnel complex near the Saigon river, in the notorious VC-dominated 'Iron Triangle'. Colonel George Patton of the 11th Armored Cavalry, the son of the World War II general, had seen a North Vietnamese soldier vanish into a tunnel. The officer who pursued him had immediately been killed by a booby trap. When the Rats arrived, Batman took one man with him into the tunnel. Flowers heard shots and grenade explosions underground, then Batman appeared, saying that the other man was wounded. Bleeding from shrapnel wounds, the man was dragged to the surface. 'The pricks have got us cold,' announced

Left: Into the unknown. A lone Tunnel Rat abseils into a Viet Cong tunnel network. The descent often proved the most dangerous part of an operation; team members could face sudden death from a grenade or a burst of smallarms fire. Other surprises could include crude punji-stick traps or poisonous animals.
Above: Lieutenant Jack 'Rat Six' Flowers (centre) receives the Bronze Star from General Orwin Talbott, the CO of the 'Big Red One'; Sergeant Robert 'Batman' Batten (right) looks on impassively.
Below: Tunnel clearance during Operation Cedar Falls in January 1967. Platoon Sergeant James Lindsey (right) was killed two days after this picture was taken.

Batman, 'They're sitting on top of a trapdoor.' Flowers insisted on going down to investigate. He thought Batman had won enough medals already, and one of his men had been wounded.

As they entered the tunnel, Batman went point – led the way. When they reached the trapdoor in the tunnel roof, Batman pushed it upwards and then quickly fired three shots into the darkness. But the enemy had moved further into the tunnel system; the pursuit might be a long one. The two Tunnel Rats exchanged pistols for reloading, then Batman went ahead to another trapdoor leading downwards. Flowers followed the regulation five yards behind, the distance beyond which a grenade explosion would not be lethal. Batman lifted the new trapdoor and started firing. Suddenly, an automatic weapon was loosed off underneath. Dirt flew everywhere. Batman fell back, seemingly hit. When Flowers

reached him he was unhurt but temporarily blinded by the dust. 'Shoot in there,' ordered the sergeant, and Flowers fired into the hole as Batman sat rubbing his eyes, talking to himself and psyching himself up for the continued pursuit. Then he tried to move past Flowers. 'You've had your two trapdoors,' said the lieutenant. The rule was that the point man was changed after two trapdoors, so great was the stress and tension. Batman looked at Flowers groggily, six inches from his face, and conceded. Flowers lowered himself down to the next tunnel level.

One well-liked Tunnel Rat was stabbed through the eye by a retreating Viet Cong

The tunnel reached a corner, round which Flowers fired a few shots, then continued 10yds to an apparent dead end. A little earth fell from the ceiling at the end, revealing the existence of a rectangular trapdoor leading to the next level up. Flowers held his torch steadily on the door. The NVA soldier was evidently lying just over the trapdoor. Batman moved up beside Flowers and made to push up on it, but Flowers prevented him. He was Rat Six and the point man, and insisted upon dealing with the situation by himself. Batman crawled back a few yards. Flowers tensed sweat ran into his eyes.

The trapdoor was 12in above his head. He placed his torch between his legs, shining upward. Then he put his hand under the door and exerted a small amount of pressure. It yielded. Flowers took a deep breath of the dank air and twisted the trapdoor, setting it down crosswise on its bevelled frame. Then he paused, planning to slide it away and start firing into the void.

A foot above Flowers' glistening and grimy face, the trapdoor was quietly turned round and slotted back into its frame. Flowers froze – the gook was right there. Suddenly the door moved again. Something dropped into Flowers' lap, right in front of his eyes. He watched it fall, momentarily transfixed. Then, the danger to his life overwhelmed him as he screamed 'Grenade!'

He did not know how far he had crawled when the explosion ripped through the tunnel, peppering his legs with shrapnel, and rupturing both his and Batman's eardrums. Batman was urging him to keep moving when another explosion rocked the tunnel. This time the enemy was in pursuit. Flowers collapsed as his men on the surface reached out to extricate him. When he came round, Colonel Patton was standing over him. The tunnel exit was under one of Patton's tanks; the enemy was trapped. The wounded Flowers decided against further pursuit. Instead, every tunnel entrance was dynamited, caving in the whole structure. Colonel Patton ordered the bodies of the entombed enemy to be dug up for a body count.

Both Flowers and Batman were decorated for that incident. But more important for Flowers was having been blooded underground and thereby becoming Batman's equal. Grudgingly, Batman accepted Flowers' authority. There were more tunnel missions, each relying for its success on close teamwork and ice-cool nerves. There was contact, and there were casualties. One well-liked Tunnel Rat was stabbed through the eye by a retreating Viet Cong.

In May 1969 Sergeant Batten was finally sent home

after three years in Vietnam killing gooks. Flowers drank with him on his last night. Batman delivered a verdict on the lieutenant. Flowers had been determined to emulate his sergeant's toughness and courage, but Batman was not deceived.

'You're not a killer Six, and that's your problem. You're pretty good, the best Six I ever had, but you'll fuck up somewhere. Charlie [the Viet Cong] hasn't killed a Rat for some time. Either he'll get you or, what's worse, you'll get yourself.'

Batten quit the army when his final request to return to Vietnam was turned down. His replacement in the

During years of waging guerrilla warfare the Viet Cong and their predecessors in the Viet Minh built up extensive tunnel systems in South Vietnam using primitive tools (below right). Right: As part of the movement's political and cultural programmes, actors were able to perform in specially constructed subterranean theatres.

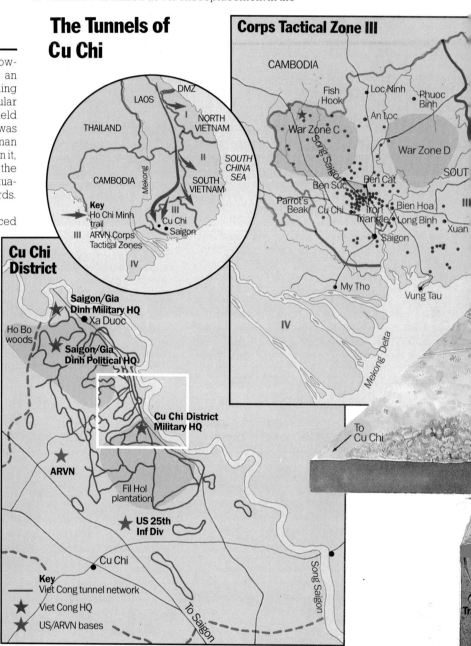

The Tunnels of Cu Chi

At the height of the Vietnam war in the late-1960s, a 200-mile complex of Viet Cong tunnels stretched from the South Vietnamese capital of Saigon to the border with Cambodia where the Ho Chi Minh trail ended. The tunnel system contained the Viet Cong's sinews of war: ordnance factories, hospitals, storage dumps of weapons, ammunition and rice, headquarters and conference rooms, dormitories, kitchens and firing posts. By day the Viet Cong insurgents hid beneath the ground, but by night the South Vietnamese countryside reverted to their control. And in 1968, when the Viet Cong launched their Tet Offensive on Saigon, it was from the tunnels of Cu Chi and Ben Cat that they emerged.

The Tunnel Rats' main enemy during the Vietnam War were the VC (Viet Cong – Vietnamese communists), rural, village-based guerrillas who could draw on nearly three decades of experience in unconventional warfare. What they lacked in modern and heavy weapons, air support and technical sophistication, the VC more than made up for with their cunning, ruthlessness and battle skills.

The VC and their predecessors in the Viet Minh, who had ousted the French from Indochina in the mid-1950s, knew that conventional battle would result in excessive casualties, but a protracted hit-and-run campaign coupled with political education of the masses could pave the way to final victory. Working on these two principles, they hoped to inflict high casualties on the American forces and undermine the South Vietnamese government. Given the enemy's massive superiority in firepower, the VC recognised that their military infrastructure in the south could only survive underground. The VC's tunnel system, begun in the war against the French, was gradually expanded during the 1960s until it covered a large part of South Vietnam. Operationally, the VC were organised along regular lines: although raids were carried out by small bands of guerrillas, larger formations were deployed against larger military targets.

Key
ARVN Corps Tactical Zones
Viet Cong tunnels
Viet Cong HQ
Viet Cong area

NAM

UTH CHINA SEA

o Bo oods

To Xa Duoc

Song Saigon

Cu Chi District Military HQ ★

To Saigon

Ventilation shaft

Concealed trapdoor entrance

Remote smoke outlets

Punji stake trap

Firing post

Kitchen

Air raid shelter

Conference room

Dorm room or

Water, gas and blast-proof trapdoor

Tunnel drop (absorbs blast)

Concealed river entrance

ecting el

First aid station

Well

Water table

Schematic diagram of a typical Viet Cong tunnel network

Rat squad was Peter Schultz. He was a good sergeant and demolitions man, but solidly built and over six-feet tall – the wrong physique for a Rat. Without Batten, Flowers was exposed, and the increased work and responsibility weighed upon him. He led mission after mission, but fatigue began to drain him, and with it fear. In one tunnel the enemy set off a large mine that completely buried him. It took Sergeant Schultz five minutes to dig him out, unconscious.

The end came in late July 1969. Flowers and the Rats were on a mission in the Iron Triangle where a VC base camp was discovered under construction, complete with woven baskets and poles to hoist the earth up the access shafts. The Rats explored a succession of holes in which some VC had taken refuge when US troops entered the area. All proved to be cold. At length only one hole remained, at least one enemy was sure to be down there. Flowers realised that every member of the squad had been down a tunnel that day except him. Schultz offered to go, but as the officer in charge, Flowers knew that he would have to take the most dangerous job himself. A grenade was dropped down the shaft first, but the Rats knew this was little more than a noisy warning gesture – the tunnel-dwelling Viet Cong had years of experience ducking round corners.

Flowers pictured the enemy down there on his knees, with his AK47 set on full automatic

The hole was about 15ft deep and curved away to one side at the bottom. Flowers knew that it was not connected to any other tunnel, so, if his theory was correct, the Viet Cong had to be down there waiting for him. The lieutenant sent for a 'Swiss seat', a cradle of straps for lowering him into the hole. Two Rats would pay out the ropes to lower him to a point three feet from the bottom then, at a signal, suddenly drop him to surprise the waiting enemy. It would take about 30 seconds to get down. Flowers assessed the situation coolly: this would be the one-on-one confrontation he had long anticipated. His squad looked at him grimly. Schultz offered him a second pistol, but he declined it, ordering that it be ready loaded to drop down to him. If they heard anything other than his pistol firing, they were to pull him up.

Flowers began his descent. Fear gripped him, the fear that possesses every young soldier who knows that his life might be over in a few, fleeting seconds. As he thought back over his life, the image of Batman kept reappearing to him saying, 'You'll fuck up, you'll fuck up.' His feet and elbows rubbed against the sides of the shaft, dislodging clods of earth that would tell the Viet Cong below that he was coming down. Flowers pictured the enemy down there on his knees, leaning against the side of the tunnel with his AK47 set on full automatic fire. In an aperture about four feet in diameter, it would be hard to miss.

The lieutenant knew that his one chance to survive would be to kill his enemy with the first shot from his pistol. He would aim straight at the face – a shot to the body would not disable his adversary enough to prevent him from firing his AK47. Flowers swung sideways, with his left arm over his chest and his right shoulder hunched to protect his temple and mini-mise the wounds he was bound to take. Three feet from the tunnel floor, he signalled to Schultz to release the rope.

Flowers hit the floor with his pistol firing. The first

Above: The 'welcoming' sign that hung over the 1st Engineering Battalion Tunnel Rats' 'hootch' (shelter) at Lai Khe. Bottom: His flashlight casting an eerie glow on the walls and floor of a Viet Cong passage, a Tunnel Rat looses off a special tracer round from his handgun. A high level of marksmanship and quick reactions were essential to the Rat's art. Below: The authors, Tom Mangold (left) and John Penycate (right) explore a preserved Viet Cong tunnel in Cu Chi district, the guerrillas' heartland near Saigon.

shot went through the VC's forehead, the second his cheek, the third his throat, the fourth, fifth and sixth pounded into his body. Blood racing to his brain, Flowers kept pulling the trigger, clicking on the empty chambers of his revolver. Schultz heard the firing and instantly hurled the loaded pistol down to his Rat Six. The gun clattered down the shaft. Cordite smoke lingered in the dark tunnel air.

Flowers stared dumbly in front of him, disbeliev-ing what his mind had created. There was no enemy soldier there, no adversary with a rifle, just a blank wall with six holes neatly grouped in the earth. Six. And the time-honoured law of the Tunnel Rats said no more than three. Sergeant Schultz and the others peered down the shaft. The Rat Six had faced his enemy. Inside Flowers' head, Batman laughed.

Nothing was said when his men pulled Flowers from the hole, but they all knew what would happen. Flowers' own rules would have to be applied to him as strictly as to any other Tunnel Rat. Schultz went to the battalion's executive officer and told him of the incident. The men's confidence in their leader was shaken, he might be a danger to them. Two days later at Lai Khe, the executive officer relieved Flowers of his Tunnel Rat command. He was blunt:

'Don't make me tell you what you already know. 'You're finished. You've fought your war. Stay out of sight for three weeks, then forget all about Vietnam and the Tunnel Rats.'

When the Rats were sent on their next mission, Flowers was not told about it until they had gone. For the sake of their morale, he was quickly shipped out of Lai Khe to divisional headquarters, where he was drunk for a week, then home. He just vanished. There were no farewells, no handovers. Fifteen years later, in the restaurant of the Philadelphia skyscraper where he worked as a stockbroker, Jack Flowers ruminated on the end of his war, 'Rat Six was dead. He died in some tunnel in the Iron Triangle. Batman was right. Charlie didn't get me, I got myself.'

THE AUTHORS Tom Mangold and John Penycate revealed the story of the Tunnel Rats in their best-selling book *The Tunnels of Cu Chi*, to be republished in paperback by Pan Books in the spring. Both men are journalists with BBC1's *Panorama*.

In April 1982, several weeks before the main landings at San Carlos, the men of M Company, 42 Commando, RM were tasked with the retaking of the island of South Georgia

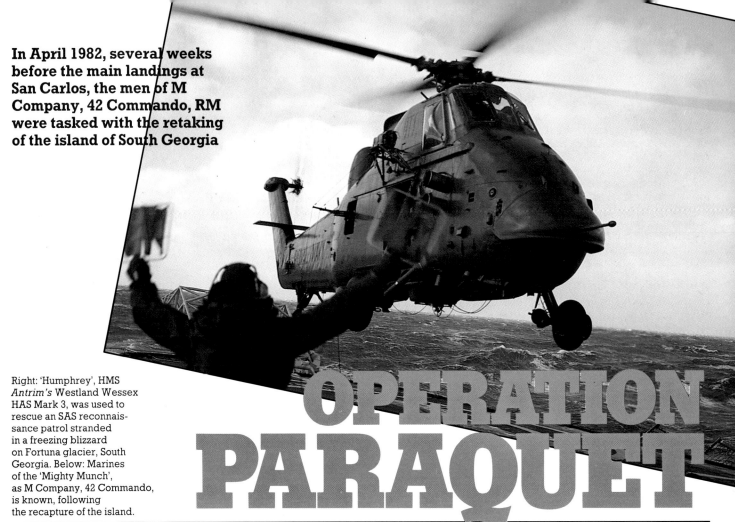

Right: 'Humphrey', HMS *Antrim's* Westland Wessex HAS Mark 3, was used to rescue an SAS reconnaissance patrol stranded in a freezing blizzard on Fortuna glacier, South Georgia. Below: Marines of the 'Mighty Munch', as M Company, 42 Commando, is known, following the recapture of the island.

OPERATION PARAQUET

SOUTH GEORGIA

On 3 April 1982, after doing its utmost to defend the island, the small but gallant garrison of Royal Marines stationed on South Georgia surrendered to an Argentinian invasion force. The British soldiers were supplanted by two detachments of Argentinian marines who based themselves in the settlements of Leith and Grytviken: the rest of the island was extremely inhospitable and no further outposts were considered feasible.

Situated over 800 nautical miles east of East Falkland, South Georgia was recognised by the British as a suitable target for a retaliatory measure against the Argentinians. Its recapture would satisfy the growing demand in Britain for action, and it was beyond the range of Argentinian aircraft. Should hostilities continue, it would make a useful refuelling and rallying point for eastbound vessels. In addition, it would provide shelter for ships caught in the frequent South Atlantic storms, and it was proposed as a base and last-minute training ground. On 7 April, Admiral John Fieldhouse received orders to organise the recapture of the island. The task of re-possessing South Georgia was given the codename Paraquet, an obscure spelling of 'parakeet'. However, the Task Group formed by Major-General Moore, Fieldhouse's land commander, immediately renamed their action Paraquat, after the powerful weedkiller. The men selected for the duty were M Company of 42 Commando, Royal Marines (whose badge is shown above), D Squadron of the 22nd Special Air Service Regiment, and 2 Section, Special Boat Squadron.

ON SATURDAY, 3 April 1982, I was recalled urgently from leave. The crisis in the Falkland Islands had broken and, as second-in-command of 42 Commando, Royal Marines, I had much to do to ready the Commando for operations. Then, on 6 April, my commanding officer, Lieutenant-Colonel Nick Vaux, told me that I was to prepare a force for a separate operation in South Georgia.

The force of Royal Marines was to comprise M Company under Captain Chris Nunn, a section of 81mm mortars under Sergeant Day, two sections of Recce Troop under Sergeant Napier, and a section of assault engineers under Corporal Bath. I was also taking two Naval Gunfire Support Forward Observation (NGSFO) officers, an NGSFO adviser from 148 Commando Forward Observation Battery, RA, and a small medical team under Surgeon Lieutenant Crispin Swinhoe.

On 9 April, the force embarked on two VC10s to join the ships of the Task Group anchored off Ascension Island. The flagship was HMS *Antrim*, commanding the frigate HMS *Plymouth* and the tanker RFA *Tidespring*, and these were later joined by the ice patrol ship HMS *Endurance*. Aboard *Tidespring*

there were two Wessex Mark 5 helicopters, earmarked for the insertion of my main force into South Georgia. The group was to set out and rendezvous at sea with 2 SBS and D Squadron, 22 SAS, who had sailed ahead of us on RFA *Fort Austin*.

My orders were to capture the towns of Grytviken and Leith, to neutralise Argentinian communications in the area, to capture or kill Argentinian armed forces personnel, and to arrest and remove Argentinian civilians. All this had to be achieved specifically with the minimum loss of life or damage to property. To achieve these objectives I knew that it would be essential to carry out covert reconnaissances in the critical areas of the island in order to learn the strength and dispositions of the enemy. I therefore allocated the reconnaissance of Grytviken and King Edward Point to 2 SBS, and that of Hurvik, Stromness and Leith to D Squadron.

On 15 April, we received the formal order to put our planned operations for the retaking of South Georgia into effect. All units worked up to full readiness as we steamed towards the island, and I tasked Chris Nunn to prepare a quick-reaction force from M Company, now sailing in *Tidespring*, to be

ready to assist the SAS and SBS reconnaissance teams in case of difficulty.

The weather as we approached the island was fast deteriorating, and eventually the wind increased to a southwesterly Force 9 gale. The first reconnaissance was to be carried out by D Squadron's Mountain Troop, commanded by Captain John Hamilton, but it was not until 0900 hours on 21 April that a helicopter lift became feasible. The two Wessex Mark 5s and the Wessex Mark 3 on *Antrim* took off at 1000 to make the 50km journey, but were forced to return after being unable to land. They tried again at 1300 and this time the troop was successfully landed on the Fortuna glacier. The helicopters returned safely through a wind which had now increased to Force 10, and were battened down in their hangars aboard the wildly pitching ships. At last light, with the wind gusting at 70 knots, 2 SBS launched their Wasp helicopters from *Endurance* into the Sörling Valley.

The silence in the ops room was electrifying as we waited for the first indication from the on-watch signaller of contact with the two patrols.

Below: Captain Chris Nunn, commander of M Company, with Surgeon Lieutenant Crispin Swinhoe, the task group's medical officer.

Above: The sorry hulk of one of the Westland Wessex HU Mark 5 helicopters that crashed onto Fortuna glacier while airlifting an SAS patrol from the ice in atrocious weather.

Above: Marines of the Mighty Munch at Wideawake airfield on Ascension Island wait to move out. Left: Men and their equipment are loaded on lighters to be transferred to their ships.

GEARING UP FOR PARAQUET

Coming at the beginning of the hostilities with Argentina, the early preparations for Operation Paraquet were extremely sensitive. So much so that when the main body of 42 Commando departed on 7 April, in order to sail to the Falklands aboard SS *Canberra*, M Company was hidden in the gymnasium at the barracks in Bickleigh, just outside Plymouth, forbidden to show themselves or telephone out. Only then did Lieutenant-Colonel Nick Vaux inform them of their impending operation.

Before leaving Britain, Major Sheridan signalled Ascension Island to request a firing-range on which his men could rezero their

weapons. On the journey down, the zero (the accurate adjustment of a weapon's sights with the point of aim) was inevitably displaced, and the SBS constructed a 30yd range for their use.

Although Major Sheridan was informed unofficially that an element of D Squadron, 22 SAS, was to participate in the operation, it was not until all their mountain and Arctic stores were being transferred from Wideawake airfield to *Antrim* that he received a handwritten note, delivered by helicopter, to confirm that the entire squadron was to be under his command. Since the Royal Marines' Mountain & Arctic Warfare Cadre could not be made available for reconnaissance on the island, that task was shared by the SAS and SBS.

Nothing was heard until 1100 hours on Thursday, 22 April, when a weak signal was received from John Hamilton on Fortuna glacier. He requested immediate extraction of his patrol and reported that casualties as a result of the hurricane-force blizzard were imminent. The men had been unable to move with their huge loads from the point at which they were dropped the day before, and their tents had been blown to shreds by the gale. The wind eased to Force 7 but the cloud base was low and snow showers remained frequent. At 1115 the Wessex Mark 3, piloted by Lieutenant Commander Ian Stanley, took off and led the two Wessex Mark 5 helicopters to Fortuna glacier. In the atrocious weather they could not locate the patrol and returned to *Antrim* to refuel. They returned to the search, and saw the patrol through a gap in the clouds; quickly descending to the glacier they snatched the patrol from their position on the ice. But then disaster struck. As the two Wessex 5s took off to follow the Mark 3 through the cloud, one crashed into the glacier. The accident was seen by the other Mark 5 which turned, landed and picked up the crew and passengers who had all miraculously survived the crash. Fairly heavily laden, the Mark 5 took off but then it too lost its horizon in the cloud and crashed. Meanwhile the Mark 3 arrived back on *Antrim* with no knowledge of what had happened to the other two aircraft. The extent of the casualties was unknown, but it was certain that if there were any survivors they wouldn't last long in the freezing blizzards.

In a remarkable and brilliant piece of flying Ian Stanley brought his helicopter back to *Antrim*

It was not until about 1500 that Ian Stanley was able to take off in his Mark 3 to look for the 13 missing men, and about half-an-hour later he radioed to say that he had found them and they were all alive. There was relief and jubilation on board. What we did not know at that moment was that he had decided to load all 13 and make one journey. To take only half would almost certainly condemn those waiting for the second flight to severe injury from the cold, or even death if he failed to relocate them in the atrocious weather. So all 13 men were bundled into the ageing Wessex, and in a remarkable and brilliant piece of flying Ian Stanley brought his helicopter and his frozen, exhausted passengers back to *Antrim*.

Anxiety had passed momentarily and it was a great relief to all that there had been no loss of life, but with my only troop-lift helicopters now lying useless on the Fortuna glacier, and with no information yet on the disposition of Argentinian forces on the island, I seemed even further away from my objective than before. There was still no news from the SBS patrol when I sat down that evening with Major Cedric Delves, commander of D Squadron, to plan our next move.

We concluded that the atrocious weather, which was blowing a Force 7 gale, had given sufficient cover to enable all the operations of the day to remain covert. His Boat Troop was aboard *Antrim*, so together we made a hasty plan to deliver the Troop silently into Stromness Bay. From there they would continue in Gemini inflatable boats to Grass Island and carry out the same task that earlier had been given to the Mountain Troop.

At 0330 hours on Friday, 23 April, *Antrim* moved slowly and silently under a starlit sky into the outer reaches of Stromness Bay. Five Geminis and their

Operation Paraquet
South Georgia, April 1982

Operation Paraquet – the retaking of South Georgia – was launched on 21 April 1982 with the insertion of an SAS reconnaissance team on the Fortuna glacier. Further SAS and SBS teams were landed soon afterwards, and at 1445 on 25 April the main invasion was set in motion when a combined force of marines and SAS troops landed near Grytviken.

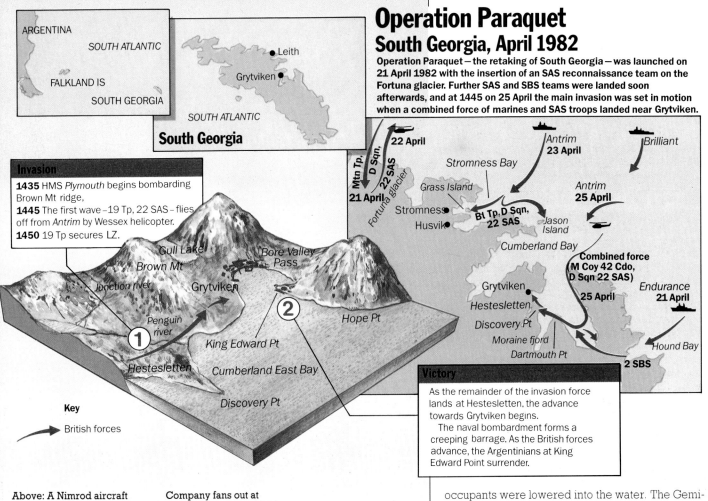

ARGENTINA
SOUTH ATLANTIC
FALKLAND IS
SOUTH GEORGIA

SOUTH ATLANTIC

Leith
Grytviken

South Georgia

Invasion
1435 HMS *Plymouth* begins bombarding Brown Mt ridge,
1445 The first wave –19 Tp, 22 SAS – flies off from *Antrim* by Wessex helicopter.
1450 19 Tp secures LZ.

Gull Lake
Bore Valley Pass
Brown Mt
Junction river
Grytviken
Penguin river
①
②
Hope Pt
King Edward Pt
Hestesletten
Cumberland East Bay
Discovery Pt

Key
→ British forces

Mtn Tp, D Sqn, 22 SAS
21 April
22 April
Fortuna glacier
Antrim **23 April**
Brilliant
Stromness Bay
Grass Island
Antrim **25 April**
Stromness
Husvik
Bt Tp, D Sqn, 22 SAS
Jason Island
Cumberland Bay
Combined force (M Coy 42 Cdo, D Sqn 22 SAS)
Grytviken
25 April
Hestesletten
Discovery Pt
Moraine fjord
Dartmouth Pt
Endurance **21 April**
Hound Bay
2 SBS

Victory
As the remainder of the invasion force lands at Hestesletten, the advance towards Grytviken begins.
The naval bombardment forms a creeping barrage. As the British forces advance, the Argentinians at King Edward Point surrender.

Above: A Nimrod aircraft drops the order to begin Operation Paraquet into the sea near *Antrim.* **Left:** M

Company fans out at Hestesletten. **Below:** Major Sheridan on the island.

occupants were lowered into the water. The Geminis then circled the ship before heading off in two groups on a compass bearing to Grass Island. As they disappeared into the inky blackness, I was able to view Leith harbour through a nightscope. Lights were visible in the old whaling station, but they soon disappeared as *Antrim* slipped back to sea.

A message was transmitted at 0700 that morning by the officer commanding the Boat Troop to say that two of his five boats were missing, together with their occupants. The other three were established ashore and on Grass Island and were observing Leith and Stromness. I had to assume now that the secrecy of the whole South Georgia operation had been jeopardised, as it was quite possible that the boats and the six missing men had been captured by the Argentinians. For the second time in 24 hours we were faced with a major catastrophe.

The Navy was becoming increasingly concerned at the possible presence of a submarine, but at that moment Cedric Delves and I were mainly concerned with finding the missing SAS men. The Wessex Mark 3, piloted again by Ian Stanley, took off shortly after to sweep the area of sea off Jason Island in the hope of finding the two boats. At 1030 he returned with three troopers. Their boat had been blown out to sea, and despite the men's frantic paddling it had drifted some six miles eastwards. They had been winched aboard the helicopter, the last man up piercing the inflatable Gemini to sink it. With the weather worsening, no further search was possible for the other boat.

There was still more bad news to come. Early that afternoon we received a message from 2 SBS to say that during the night a strong northwesterly gale had blown large chunks of ice from the sea into Cumberland East Bay and their inflatables had been ripped open as they tried to reach Dartmouth Point. They had managed to return to the shore and now needed more boats in order to continue with their mission. If that was not possible, then they asked to be extracted and reinserted elsewhere.

At 0300 in the morning of 24 April, the commander of *Antrim*, Captain Young, ordered his group to clear the island and rendezvous 200 miles to the northeast, where they could refuel from *Tidespring*, now joined by RFA *Brambleleaf*. The tankers were heeding the submarine warning and were remaining well out of sight. While the Navy planned how to deal with the submarine, I was put under more pressure from London to act, but I repeatedly declined until I had some firm intelligence of enemy strengths and dispositions. That evening we set course at 22 knots to return to South Georgia to do battle with the submarine, being joined on our way by HMS *Brilliant*, one of the Navy's most modern anti-submarine frigates. To my great relief I saw two Lynx helicopters on her flightdeck, and I now knew that a helicopter assault was again possible. *Tidespring*, meanwhile, carrying M Company, was to steam in and join the main group later on.

It was vital that we moved immediately to land and exploit the demoralised state of the enemy

In the early morning of 25 April the helicopters of the Task Group engaged the Argentinian submarine, *Santa Fé*, and damaged it sufficiently to force it into the relative safety of Grytviken. This was a major success, and I realised that we needed to follow it up quickly if the momentum was to be maintained and if the initiative were to remain firmly ours. I surmised that if the sailors from the submarine got ashore they would almost certainly be deployed in defence of King Edward Point, so it was vital that we moved immediately to land and exploit the demoralised state of the enemy.

I reviewed the locations of the combat units in the Task Group. *Tidespring* was 200 miles away with M

Company. I had 2 SBS and a troop of SAS on *Endurance*, and another SAS troop on *Plymouth*, but *Endurance* was to the southeast hiding in Hound Bay, and *Plymouth* was unable to land either the Wessex or the Lynx helicopters on her flightdeck. This meant that my initial landing force must come from *Antrim* and subsequent deployment of troops would have to follow winching up from the other two ships. I had 65 men on *Antrim*, increased to 75 with the addition of her own Royal Marine detachment under Sergeant Kendall. This force had just over half of the estimated strength of the enemy, a ratio of two to one against. Not the most favourable situation, I thought, but I knew it was a gamble that we would have to take.

While Chris Nunn organised the 75 men into three small troops of 20 men each, and a small command element for me, I sat down in the ops room to prepare my orders. Our NGSFO adviser, Lieutenant-Colonel Keith Eve, worked out a fire-plan based on the use of the twin 4.5in guns on *Antrim* and *Plymouth*. My plan was to land the first wave, namely 19 Troop, 22 SAS, under command of Cedric Delves, by Wessex Mark 3 and two Lynx helicopters onto Hestesletten, an area of flat glacial moraine about four kilometres from Grytviken. Thereafter, the two small rifle troops under command of Chris Nunn and an SBS officer would stream ashore using the same helicopters. The Tac HQ, the medical party and I would go in the last aircraft after the 81mm mortars had deployed. My plan also included one NGSFO officer deploying with the first wave, and the other airborne in a helicopter to direct the pre-bombardment. I also wanted 2 SBS and the two SAS Troops from *Endurance* and *Plymouth* to land by helicopter in Bore Valley Pass once the slopes of Brown Mountain were secure. Their particular task would be to move to the high ground above Grytviken and King Edward Point and provide covering fire for the advance to contact from Brown Mountain through Grytviken to King Edward Point.

This plan was put before the commander of the Task Group at 1000, but he wished to debrief the captain of *Brilliant* and the helicopter pilots after the submarine action before deciding on a time for

Above: Marines of 42 Commando inspect captured Argentinian weapons following the garrison's surrender. Above right: South Georgia's Neumayer glacier, seen from a helicopter cockpit. Right: Marines wait on the jetty at Grytviken as divers discuss the extent of the damage below the waterline to the Argentinian submarine *Santa Fé*. Bottom: Argentinian prisoners marshalled at King Edward Point on Cumberland East Bay.

MAJOR GUY SHERIDAN

Guy Sheridan joined the Royal Marines in 1960, and after completing the officers' course at the Commando Training Centre at Lympstone, he was posted to serve with 45 Commando in Aden. Returning in 1962, he underwent specialised training in mountain and Arctic warfare.

Sheridan then joined 40 Commando for service in Malaya and Borneo. Apart from serving with the Royal Marines he was seconded to the Sultan of Oman's Army from 1968 to 1970, where he commanded an Arab/Beluch company on active service for a year in Dhofar province with the Muscat Regiment.

In 1972 he was given command of the Mountain & Arctic Warfare Cadre, a position he held until 1974. After staff training at Camberley and Bracknell, he served for two and a half years in Iran with a British Military Training mission. During the Falklands crisis in 1982, Guy Sheridan was second-in-command of 42 Commando, and he commanded the landing forces that repossessed South Georgia. He subsequently rejoined his Commando for the remainder of the conflict, and he was awarded the OBE for distinguished service in the campaign. He is now a lieutenant-colonel.

Sheridan represented Britain in the World Biathlon Championships in Finland in 1971, and was a member of the squad which trained for the 1972 Winter Olympics. He has completed long ski traverses of the Zagros mountains in Iran, the western Himalayas, and the Mackenzie mountains in Yukon, Canada.

H-Hour. A period of three hours followed while this went on and I became more and more anxious that the enemy, now boosted in numbers by the crew of the submarine, might be using the time to organise proper defences at Grytviken and King Edward Point. It was not until 1330 that H-Hour was finally agreed as 1445. I gave my orders, which included a fire-plan at 1345, and radioed the orders to 2 SBS and the two SAS Troops for their Bore Valley Pass landing.

It was to be approximately a five-minute flight from *Antrim* to the planned landing site (LS) as Hestesletten, flying close to the southern shore of Cumberland East Bay and passing over Dartmouth Point and Moraine Fjord. The three helicopters were loaded one by one on *Antrim's* flightdeck, and at H−10 the first salvo of 4.5in shells was fired from *Plymouth*. Directed by one of my NGSFOs, now airborne in a Wasp helicopter from *Endurance*, this bombardment was set up to neutralise the slopes of Brown Mountain which dominated the whole of Hestesletten. At H-Hour, 1445, the three helicopters, doors off and loaded to bursting point with 19 Troop, took off in wave formation. Simultaneously, *Antrim's* 4.5in guns launched their devastating fire onto the landing site to neutralise the area, switching at H+5 onto the slopes of Brown Mountain.

The SAS Troop's mission was to secure the landing site for the first of the small Royal Marine Troops to arrive. They were then to advance and secure the steep ridge that descended to the sea from the summit of Brown Mountain. This ridge dominated Hestesletten and as 19 Troop arrived on the landing site, the naval shells were raining down upon it.

At last we were ashore, and when Ian Stanley reported an unopposed landing I knew I was halfway to achieving my task of repossessing the island. Looking northwest, a kilometre of level, stony ground, covered in places with large clumps of tussock grass, stretched away to the steep slopes leading up to the Brown Mountain ridge. I assumed that all this was in dead ground to the enemy, whom I believed were grouped in and around Grytviken and the British Antarctic Survey (BAS) base at King Edward Point. A shallow river, known as Penguin River, wound round the foot of those steep slopes to the sea, and it was about 15m wide. It was clear that there was no enemy on those slopes and, if there had been, the 4.5in bombardment had done its job. But when I arrived in the last helicopter stream, I was surprised to find the SAS Troop still on the LS. I angrily told them to get on with their task, which they did after firing two Milan missiles onto the top of the mountain and engaging a herd of elephant seals blocking the way on the banks of Penguin River.

This was the third phase of my fire-plan, and it was designed to demoralise the Argentinians

Not a shot had been fired at us and it was not long before the Troop was clambering up the very steep shale to the crest of the Brown Mountain ridge. I was hard on their heels with Corporal Stannett, my signallers and the medical team. Meanwhile, the other two Troops had fanned out and were advancing on my right and to the rear. One of my NGSFOs, Captain Chris Browne, was now positioned on Dartmouth Point and was directing naval gunfire onto the exposed and rocky ground between the ridge and King Edward Point. This was the third phase of my fire-plan, and it was designed to demoralise the

Above: The commander of the Argentinian garrison on South Georgia, Captain Alfredo Astiz, signs the formal surrender document in front of Captain David Pentreath of *Plymouth* and Captain Nicholas Barker of *Endurance*. Although Astiz had gained a dubious reputation while serving his government on the mainland, he was eventually repatriated without interrogation. Background: The Union Jack and the White Ensign of the Royal Navy are raised over South Georgia.

Argentinians, the gun line passing over the BAS base to explode the shells on the other side of the cove to the enemy. Once on the crest we observed Grytviken and King Edward Point through binoculars.

On the Point, at the end of a jetty was the submarine, and there were numerous sailors moving about on the casing and on the jetty, I swung my binoculars further along the settlement and saw a large, orderly group of personnel in blue and green uniform lined up on the foreshore by the main flag-pole of the BAS base. From the flag-pole fluttered the blue and white Argentinian flag, and then I saw a large white flag hanging from a building beyond. A glance up to Shackleton House, the large building at the end of the base, revealed another, and there was one more near the radio shack. Then across the water came the distant sound of patriotic singing, and the reality of the moment manifested itself. 'They've surrendered,' said Cedric Delves.

'Good,' I replied and, turning to my signaller, gave the order, 'Cancel the Bore Valley Pass landing.' Cedric and his small command team walked round through Grytviken and I asked for a Wasp helicopter to take me over the cove to the BAS base. I asked *Antrim* to sail into the bay and be prepared to give us support if necessary. As Chris Nunn's Troop came over the crest, he formed his men into an arrowhead formation for the final three kilometres to Grytviken. The next day the small enemy detachment in Leith, under Captain Astiz, surrendered to *Plymouth* without a shot being fired.

South Georgia was back in British hands without a casualty to us. There were 137 enemy prisoners, joined the next day by another 15 marines and 47 scrapmen from Leith. The only casualty that day, 25 April, was an enemy sailor who lost a leg in the initial attack on the submarine. We had achieved the task with the minimum loss of life and damage to property. I noted in my diary that evening, 'A satisfying day'.

THE AUTHOR Lieutenant-Colonel Guy Sheridan, while a major and second-in-command of 42 Commando, RM, commanded the land forces that repossessed South Georgia. He was awarded the OBE for distinguished service during the South Atlantic campaign.